Praise for *Learning Blen*

"Villar has captured the excitement of Blender as a 3D modeling, animation, and motion graphics tool in one straightforward, easy-to-follow textbook. The Blender software is growing in popularity and now more than ever is considered one of the must-have tools in the tool shed for 3D."

—*Dr. Tim J. Harrington, Solution Manager, Academic IT*

"*Learning Blender* is a great introduction for anyone wanting to learn how to create and edit in 3D using Blender, the free open-source application. Learning to work in 3D can be tough, and Villar uses characters to teach many different techniques, including modeling, lighting, shading, rigging, and animation. The book is filled with great tips and tricks, and can help anyone learn how to work in 3D."

—*Mike Kaltschnee, Danbury Hackerspace Inc.*

"*Learning Blender: A Hands-On Guide to Creating 3D Animated Characters* by Oliver Villar is definitely a valuable addition to your library of golden resources! It doesn't simply show you the hows and whats, but the whys.

The emphasis on fundamentals is something this book is very strong at. I highly recommend this to anyone wanting to know more about the modernized Blender and character creation in general.

Simple, intuitive, and very refreshing!"

—*Reynante M. Martinez, Blender Guru*

Learning
Blender

Addison-Wesley Learning Series

Visit **informit.com/learningseries** for a complete list of available publications.

The **Addison-Wesley Learning Series** is a collection of hands-on programming guides that help you quickly learn a new technology or language so you can apply what you've learned right away.

Each title comes with sample code for the application or applications built in the text. This code is fully annotated and can be reused in your own projects with no strings attached. Many chapters end with a series of exercises to encourage you to reexamine what you have just learned, and to tweak or adjust the code as a way of learning.

Titles in this series take a simple approach: they get you going right away and leave you with the ability to walk off and build your own application and apply the language or technology to whatever you are working on.

✦Addison-Wesley   **inform**IT | Safari

Learning Blender

A Hands-On Guide to Creating 3D Animated Characters

Oliver Villar

Addison-Wesley

ocn 884140132

Upper Saddle River, NJ • Boston • Indianapolis • San Francisco
New York • Toronto • Montreal • London • Munich • Paris • Madrid
Capetown • Sydney • Tokyo • Singapore • Mexico City

For information about buying this title in bulk quantities, or for special sales opportunities (which may include electronic versions; custom cover designs; and content particular to your business, training goals, marketing focus, or branding interests), please contact our corporate sales department at corpsales@pearsoned.com or (800) 382-3419.

For government sales inquiries, please contact governmentsales@pearsoned.com.

For questions about sales outside the U.S., please contact international@pearsoned.com.

Visit us on the Web: informit.com/aw

Library of Congress Cataloging-in-Publication Data
Villar, Oliver.
  Learning Blender : a hands-on guide to creating 3D animated characters / Oliver Villar.
     pages   cm
  Includes index.
  ISBN 978-0-13-388617-7 (pbk. : alk. paper)
  1. Computer animation. 2. Blender (Computer file) 3. Computer graphics. 4. Three-dimensional display systems. I. Title.
  TR897.72.B55.V55 2015
  006.6'96—dc23   2014028384

ISBN-13: 978-0-13-388617-7
ISBN-10: 0-13-388617-4

Text printed in the United States on recycled paper at RR Donnelley in Crawfordsville, Indiana. Second printing, November 2015

Editor-in-Chief
Mark L. Taub

Executive Editor
Laura Lewin

Development Editor
Michael Thurston

Managing Editor
John Fuller

Project Editor
Elizabeth Ryan

Copy Editor
Deborah Thompson

Indexer
Infodex Indexing
Services, Inc.

Proofreader
Linda Begley

Technical Reviewers
Tim Harrington
Daniel Kreuter
Mike Pan

Editorial Assistant
Olivia Basegio

Cover Designer
Chuti Prasertsith

Compositor
Kim Arney

To my parents and family, for their support in my journey.
To my friends, for their patience, happy moments, and encouragement.
To everyone who crossed paths with me at some point of my life:
I've been able to learn a lot from all of you.

❖

Contents at a Glance

Contents

Preface

Creating animated characters is a skill that requires a lot of practice and dedication. It involves a wide variety of very different skills and that's what you're going to learn as you progress through this book's chapters. Let's quickly find out what this book is about and what you can expect from it. Also, if you already have experience creating 3D characters with other software, you've came to the right place, as you'll find some instructions on how to switch between two different programs, which can be frustrating and occasionally even more difficult than learning how to create 3D characters.

Welcome!

Welcome to *Learning Blender: A Hands-On Guide to Creating 3D Animated Characters*. In this book, you'll learn how to use Blender to complete a complex project. The book covers every part of the process so you will understand what is involved in the creation of a 3D character and can decide which part of that process you most enjoy and might want to explore further. In other words, this is not a specialized book that will make you a modeling genius or an expert animator; instead, it will help you understand every part of the animation process. The idea is that once you finish reading this book, you will have the knowledge to take any project from preproduction to the final result.

If you're a freelancer (or want to be), this book is tailored for you because freelancers often get small jobs requiring a great variety of skills. Thus, having basic or medium skills in diverse tasks can be more useful than being very good at just a single specific skill.

If you want to work for a big company and prefer to be specialized, it is also helpful to understand the complete animation process; for example, if you're a modeler but you understand how rigging works, when you create your models you'll be able to identify any possible issues your rigger colleagues may encounter and that will help you make their work easier. When you work on a team, you'll only work on a portion of the project, but if you have some understanding of what the rest of the team's job is, your work will be more valuable to them, and everyone will be happier!

You may already be familiar with Blender and want to learn about 3D character creation. In that case, you can probably skip the first three chapters and go straight to the parts of the book that describe character creation. (Do this only if you're completely sure you understand the basics of Blender.)

Finally, if you just want to get started in this amazing world of 3D animation and jump into a fantastic journey, this book will provide you with detailed insights on how to handle 3D projects. If you've never used 3D software before, don't worry if it initially looks a bit overwhelming—that's normal; the software provides lots of options and unique features that may be unfamiliar to you. While we often tend to be intimidated by what we don't know, if you keep exploring and practicing, you'll soon begin to enjoy the learning process and your results will reflect the effort you've invested. Good luck!

Switching from Other 3D Software

Years ago, I decided to switch to Blender, so I understand what you will encounter. That's why, throughout the book, I share tips about the differences between Blender and other 3D software. I changed to Blender after using commercial software (3ds Max, Maya, and XSI) for years. Back then, when I jumped into Blender (version 2.47), it was not as user friendly as it is now. It's still very unique software and when you open it for the first time, it may look a little alien to you.

Don't worry, it's completely understandable if it doesn't make sense right away—just don't give up! It won't be easy at first. It took me three or four times checking different versions of Blender until I finally decided to go for it and start learning it for good. You'll see "weird" things, like right-click selections (we'll go through this one in the first chapters) or the omnipresent 3D cursor, with apparently no function at all, that you'll always see in a scene.

Also, you'll have to learn a lot of shortcuts. This is what makes the learning curve for Blender very difficult at the beginning, but once you get used to shortcuts, you'll love them because they will allow you to work a lot faster in the long run. For example, before I used Blender, it was difficult for me to work with fewer than three different 3D views on the screen at the same time. Now I work in full screen with only one view, in a much more relaxed way. It's like using the *Expert Mode* in other software all the time!

I've taught a lot of people how to use Blender and have talked with many others who came to Blender from another animation software; what usually happens is that they struggle at first (that's why most people give up and stick to commercial software), but once they understand the basics, they start to love it and are soon devoted to it. They find that a lot of tasks are just easier or faster to do in Blender than they are in other software.

I really encourage you to keep exploring Blender and find out what it has to offer. I've learned to use a lot of different kinds of software and tools, and after repeating the learning process and switching between software several times, I've come to know the methods that work best for me, which I'll share with you. The key to adjusting successfully to change (not only in software, but in any aspect of work or life) is to learn how to *adapt yourself and be flexible*. To some extent, you have to open your mind to allow the new software or work situation to get in. For example, some people might complain that Blender doesn't have a particular tool or that a certain task was easier to accomplish in another type of animation software. Avoid this negative attitude at all costs and *try to understand the new software*, as each type of software has a different philosophy behind its development and work flow. Complaining is a waste of time and energy you could otherwise invest in something much more useful, like learning how to use the software. *Force yourself to adapt!*

Decide what you're going to do and *set a deadline* for its completion: Begin with an easy project and do the best you can to complete it. That way, whether you have a good result or a bad result, at least you will have finished something. Having a deadline keeps you from drifting around for days and going crazy with small details that make the process too long. Usually, people start playing around with the software without a definite purpose in mind. This will give you a random output rather than a specific result. It won't motivate you and will give you the impression that you can't use this software.

Instead, if you *propose a simple project*, you have a goal to work toward and this will allow you to find and master the tools you need to achieve that goal. Once you finish your project, even if it's not perfect, you will have learned to use some tools and will have a completed project to show for your efforts. This will ultimately motivate you to improve your skills next time with a more complex project that will require you to explore and learn about additional Blender tools.

Keep in mind that the key here is to start learning little by little, taking small steps to keep you motivated. If you start with a large, complex project that involves a lot of different steps, you may encounter problems at some point that will frustrate you. When you work on something small, even if you run into difficulties and the final result isn't perfect, you don't have that much time invested in it, so a less-than-perfect result won't be a big issue. Over time, as you complete a few of these little projects in Blender, you'll have acquired a knowledge base and will understand how the new software works; at that point, you can judge if you're interested in learning more or if you are more comfortable with other software you've used.

There are many types of animation software available and each one is different, so depending on your work, your style, your taste, and your personality, you may prefer one over the other. What is intuitive and comfortable for some people may not be for others. However, if you give this new software a good test drive, maybe you'll encounter some challenges, but you'll also find features you didn't know about that are really cool. In my case, I was very comfortable with 3ds Max, but after trying Blender extensively for a few days (Yes, only a few days—it was very intense, though!), I honestly couldn't go back. Of course, I missed a few tools but, on the other hand, I found Blender's advantages clearly worth it (in my case, anyway), so I've been using it ever since.

I hope this motivates you and encourages you to actually try Blender and give it a chance instead of just opening it and deciding you don't like it because you can't master it in 5 minutes. (I'll bet you didn't master any other software in the first 5 minutes either!) The keys to success with learning a new software are to *develop a project with a feasible goal, set a deadline, and try your best to make it happen!* No excuses, no complaints! Discipline and perseverance are critical elements to your success. While these tips are just guidelines and describe the method I use every time I need to learn new software, it may not be that useful for you or you may find a better approach. But if you don't know where to start and feel discouraged, just try it!

How to Use This Book

This book is divided into five parts to help you to keep track of your progress:

- **Part I, The Basics of Blender (Chapters 1, 2, and 3):** These first chapters will help you understand Blender's features and tools so you can create your first basic scene with it.
- **Part II, Beginning a Project (Chapters 4 and 5):** Before you start any project, you'll need to do some preparation work and start with a design.
- **Part III, Modeling in Blender (Chapters 6 and 7):** You'll learn how to use Blender modeling tools to create a 3D character.
- **Part IV, Unwrapping, Painting, and Shading (Chapters 8, 9, and 10):** In these chapters, you'll learn all the steps to add color and create textures that will improve and define your character's looks.
- **Part V, Bringing Your Character to Life (Chapters 11 and 12):** Creating a skeleton that deforms your 3D character can be tricky. In these chapters, you'll see how to make a skeleton work properly and you'll finally make your character move.
- **Part VI, Getting the Final Result (Chapters 13, 14, and 15):** Once your character can walk, you'll composite it into a real video. For that, you'll need to use Blender's camera tracking tools and compositing nodes. Also, in the last chapter, we'll discuss some additional Blender features and tools.

Of course, you can skip to the parts of the book you're most interested in, but if you're new to Blender, it's recommended that you start from the beginning so you can understand the software before you start with something as complex as the creation of a 3D character. However, if you're already familiar with Blender, you can go ahead and skip the first three chapters and start learning about character creation.

In each chapter, if some basic knowledge is required, I explain it before diving into the real step-by-step process. You'll also find tips and useful shortcuts along the way to help you work faster and more efficiently!

Chapter 1, What You Need to Know about Blender, describes this open-source 3D animation software, the history of its development process, and how it is funded. You don't really need to know this information in order to use Blender, but it's quite interesting and it will give you an overview of some of Blender's strong points and how the software evolved.

Chapter 2, Blender Basics: The User Interface, takes you through the user interface, basic navigation, selection tools, and Blender's innovative nonoverlapping windows system.

In Chapter 3, Your First Scene in Blender, you'll learn how to create a very basic scene that lets you play with the main tools, simple modeling, materials, and lighting. You'll also learn the differences between rendering with Blender Render and Cycles.

After this introduction, you'll start the main project: creating a 3D character. Chapter 4 explains everything you'll need and discusses preproduction and how to get ready for any project. You'll learn that preparation is essential! The reason why I chose to create a character as a project for this book is because this process requires you to use almost every feature of the software to complete the project: modeling, texturing, rigging, animation, rendering, and compositing.

In Chapter 5, you'll learn the character design process. Making some sketches before you start working in 3D is very useful, so when you jump into Blender, you'll have a clear idea of what you want to create.

Chapters 6 and 7 cover Blender 3D modeling tools and the step-by-step process of modeling a character.

In Chapters 8, 9, and 10, you'll unwrap the character, create textures to add some color to your 3D model, and then apply materials to control how the light affects the model's surfaces.

In Chapter 11, I describe rigging, the process of creating a skeleton that deforms the character model and provides you with the controls to pose and move the character intuitively.

Chapter 12 covers animation. You'll learn about the basic animation tools in Blender and make your character walk.

In Chapters 13 and 14, you'll see how to track the camera of a real video and composite your character into a scene, so that you end up with something cool to show your friends, rather than just a character inside Blender.

Chapter 15 concludes the book and describes some additional features of Blender, such as dynamic simulations, particles, and smoke and fire, so that you get an idea of some additional features that Blender provides.

Supplemental Material

Of course, I encourage you to develop your own creations from scratch and to use your own video to track the camera, but if you prefer to follow the book step by step (with the same materials that are used in the book), or if you may want to skip some parts of the book, you'll find all the material you'll need to start from any point in the book in the ancillary materials on the companion website: informit.com/title /9780133886177.

- Blend files with different character-creation levels of progress
- Texture images for the character
- Real video for camera tracking
- Final results files
- Video tutorials for some parts of the book
- PDF of a Blender keyboard shortcut reference

With no more hesitation . . . let's start learning!

Acknowledgments

While the author of a book usually takes most of the credit, a lot of people are needed to make the book a reality. Thanks to Laura Lewin, Olivia Basegio, and Elizabeth Ryan, who have patiently been with me during the whole process and have helped me with everything I needed. Thanks to Michael Thurston and Deborah Thompson, who did a great job of cleaning up my nonnative English and making sure that everything I wrote was consistent and made sense. Thanks to Daniel Kreuter, Mike Pan, and Tim Harrington, who did an amazing job reviewing the manuscript and providing very valuable feedback that definitely made the final result a lot better. Thanks to everyone else at Addison-Wesley who worked to make it possible for you to have this book in your hands.

Of course, this wouldn't be possible without the work of the Blender Foundation, Ton Roosendaal, all the Blender developers, and the amazing Blender community. Thanks, everyone.

Special thanks to the *Luke's Escape* team, which I'm honored to be a part of, as the image featured in this book's cover is the result of their work for the short film that they allowed me to use here. Thank you!

About the Author

Oliver Villar, born in Galicia, Spain, in 1987, has been drawing since he was a kid. His interest in art brought him into 3D, which he's been studying since 2004. He used different commercial 3D software before discovering Blender in 2008. Since then, he has used Blender professionally as a 3D designer and tutor. In 2010, he funded blendtuts.com, a website devoted to offering quality Blender training videos to the community. Currently, he's working as the co-director of *Luke's Escape*, a 3D animated short film made with Blender.

Learning Blender Ancillaries

Here is a list of the bonus resources available to you. You can download the files from the companion website: informit.com/title/9780133886177. Click the Register Your Product link to gain access to the content.

These videos show the result of the project you will create (making an animated 3D character and integrating it with a real video) in two different resolutions (HD and Full HD).

Project Result 720p.mp4 (HD)
Project Result 1080p.mp4 (Full HD)

Video tutorials (Blender Video tutorials help you get started with Blender and cover in a more visual way some of the topics explained in the book. Total Running Time: 5+ Hours):

01_Blender's Interface.mp4
02_3D Navigation.mp4
03_User Preferences.mp4
04_Selections.mp4
05_Object Manipulation.mp4
06_Your First Scene.mp4
07_Your First Render (Blender Render).mp4
08_Your First Render (Cycles).mp4
09_Modeling Basics I.mp4
10_Modeling Basics II.mp4
11_Modeling a Face.mp4
12_Rigging a Leg.mp4
13_Skinning.mp4
14_Facial Rig.mp4
15_Camera Tracking.mp4
16_Compositing.mp4

Blender Files (character-creation Blender files at different stages of the process so readers can analyze them or start to work at any point of the book, without having to start from scratch):

01_eyeball.blend
02_eyeballs.blend

03_face_model.blend
04_torso_model.blend
05_legs_model.blend
06_boots_model.blend
07_hands_model.blend
08_cap_model.blend
09_hair_model.blend
10_details_model.blend
11_unwrapping.blend
12_texturing.blend
13_shading_bi.blend
13_shading_cycles.blend
14_skeleton_bi.blend
14_skeleton_cycles.blend
15_skinning_bi.blend
15_skinning_cycles.blend
16_jim_final_rig_bi.blend
16_jim_final_rig_cycles.blend
17_walk_animation_bi.blend
17_walk_animation_cycles.blend
18_camera_tracking_bi.blend
18_camera_tracking_cycles.blend
19_compositing_bi.blend
19_compositing_cycles.blend
jim_cool_animation_example.blend

Resources (designs, reference images, textures, and real video):

01_Character Designs:
    01_Sketches:
        Body Sketches.jpg
        Color Tests.jpg
        Final Silhouettes.jpg
        Head Sketches.jpg
        Refined Design.jpg
        Rough Design.jpg
        Silhouettes.jpg
    02_References:
        Body Back Reference.jpg
        Body Front Reference.jpg
        Body Size Reference.jpg
        Head Back Reference.jpg

Head Front Reference.jpg
Head Side Reference.jpg
Body Views.jpg
Face Views.jpg
02_Character Textures:
base_texture.png
jim_diffuse.png
jim_hardness.png
jim_roughness.png
jim_specular.png
jim_textures.psd
uvs.png
03_Footage:
Real Footage.mp4

Extras:
Jim Illustration Time-Lapse.mp4
Jim Illustration.jpeg
Blender Keyboard Shortcuts Reference.pdf
Blender Keyboard Shortcuts Reference.jpg

The Basics of Blender

What You Need to Know about Blender

Blender has quite a remarkable story, as open-source software works in a very different way than typical commercial software. It is helpful to know this if you intend to use Blender professionally, as it may give you an insight into how powerful its concept is. In this chapter, you'll learn about how Blender was created, how the development process works, how it is funded, and what type of community surrounds the Blender world.

What Is Blender?

Blender is open-source software that provides one of the most complete 3D-graphics creation suites. It includes tools for modeling, texturing, shading, animation, compositing, rendering, video editing, and more. Since the development of version 2.50, which introduced a completely new user interface (UI), Blender's user base has grown significantly. It has reached animation studios and is now being used in top movie productions (*Life of Pi* and *Red Riding Hood*, for example, shown at the Blender Conference 2013 in Amsterdam, the Netherlands).

Its principal target audience is professional, freelance 3D artists and small studios, and Blender works very well for their needs. It still isn't widely used by big studios for several reasons. Larger studios typically have long-established software, and the commercial software they use often has impressive third-party plug-ins developed over several years for specific uses in production. Blender is still growing and lacks a lot of third-party support, but despite being relatively new to the professional landscape (initially, it was used mainly by hobbyists), it is overcoming those problems and big productions have begun to use it for processes such as modeling and UV unwrapping—two areas in which Blender is very efficient.

Blender is known for being very different from other software and that's why some people are hesitant to use it. It doesn't follow a lot of the same standards that other 3D software has been using for decades, and this is usually an issue for new users. That's also the charm of Blender—once you experience it, it is very possible that you'll love it because it is so different! Initially, you may find that a lot of features and techniques are difficult to understand, but once you learn the basics, everything then begins to seem very intuitive and sensible.

Blender, because it is open source, doesn't need to sell licenses so it can bypass the way other software use to work and go for something new and quite unique. In the words of Ton Roosendaal (Blender Foundation's chairman and creator of Blender), *"I would never look up to average—I want to lift up the average. It's not following conventions, it's following a vision."*

Blender's development is funded primarily through voluntary donations from users. This should give you an idea of how a lot of people find it so useful that they donate to its continued development even when they can use it for free. This can be difficult to understand for people who use only commercial software, but it's something you often find with open-source software: people are more willing to contribute because it's free.

Popular, open-source software such as Blender has a lot of contributors and grows quite fast. This is very good for users because you get new features and tools periodically. It has a downside, though: It's difficult to stay abreast of everything new and be aware of updates to the latest versions. Also, instructional material has a short lifespan, even when it can be used for years, because even though the basics are the same, certain options, icons, and other features can experience subtle modifications in a newer version.

Commercial Software versus Open-Source Software

You can't understand open source from the point of view of the "usual" copyright and privacy system in which you can't use something if you didn't pay for it. The business model is completely different as well.

Commercial Software

Usually, the business model for companies that develop commercial software is to sell the software license itself. If you want to use commercial software, you have to pay for a license, but you don't really own the software. Some software companies may not allow you to use the software for particular purposes (such as getting into its code to study or change it) and you may only be able to use it for a fixed amount of time before having to pay for an upgrade or a new license. In certain cases, you can use the software for free, but only for learning purposes; you need to purchase a license for it if you want to use it professionally to generate income. In other cases, what you get for free is only a limited version of the software, and you need to purchase the full version in order to access all its features. Here's where piracy comes in: some people can't afford the software and others just don't want to pay for it, so they use illegal copies, which results in a negative economic impact on the commercial software developers.

You can't develop new features in commercial software if you're not employed by the company that owns the software, and even if you are, you have to follow that company's guidelines, of course (and you're not allowed to copy your code or show it to the general public). Anyone may develop plug-ins, but you are not allowed to change the software core or its basic features.

Open-Source Software

Open-source software is usually misunderstood as free-of-charge software. However, free has a double meaning here: not only does it not cost money to use the software, but its source code is also freely available to everyone. Some software can be free of charge (freeware), but not free in terms of liberty of use; that is, you can't access the core, the source code, and modify it to fit your needs.

What open source means is that the user has the power to access the source code of the software and modify it at will. Developers also encourage you to check the code, use the software for commercial purposes, and even redistribute it. Basically, open-source software is the exact opposite of commercial software. You can download this software and immediately use it commercially. The business model of a company that creates OSS is not to sell the software itself, but to sell related services such as instructional material, training, and technical support. This type of company often relies on donations from the public as well.

The good thing about open source is that anyone in the world can download the source code and develop a feature he or she likes, and other people can use that new feature later. You are free to modify the source code, copy it as many times as you want, learn from it, and give it to your friends or classmates. Sometimes, open-source software (OSS) is developed by an individual or a small team. Some OSS is, of course, quite complex and highly organized, and may even have additional companies contributing to its development.

Another fact worth noting is that there are several types of open-source licenses, such as General Public License (GPL), Eclipse Public License (EPL), and Massachusetts Institute of Technology license (MIT). Before using open-source software, you should get some information about the terms of those licenses to make sure you understand what you are allowed do with that software.

The History of Blender

Lots of people think that Blender is relatively new, but that's not accurate. Blender was born in the early 1990s, making it more than 20 years old. Recently, an "ancient" file—Blender's first bit of code—was found by the Blender Foundation's chairman Ton Roosendaal and it dated back to December 1992. However, it is true that the software became much more relevant to the public within the last few years with the release of version 2.50, which included a completely revamped, written-from-scratch interface and core that make it more user friendly and powerful than its previous versions.

In 1988, a new Dutch animation studio, NeoGeo, was cofounded by Ton Roosendaal. Not long after, the new studio decided it had to write new software to create its animations; as a result, in 1995 it started to build what is now known as Blender. In 1998, Ton founded a new company called Not a Number (*NaN*) to further develop and market Blender. Due to difficult economic conditions at the time, NaN wasn't a success and investors stopped funding the company, shutting down Blender's development in 2002.

Later in 2002, Ton managed to build the nonprofit organization, Blender Foundation. The users community donated 100,000 euros (an amazing sum, and it only took them 7 weeks) to get the previous development investors to allow the open sourcing of the software and make it available for free. Finally, Blender was released under the terms of the GNU General Public License on October 13th, 2002. Since that day, Ton has led a team of enthusiastic developers who want to contribute to the project.

The first Open Movie project (*Elephants Dream*) was born in 2005, with the goal of gathering a team of artists who could use Blender in a real production and also provide developers with feedback that would ultimately improve the software significantly. The goal was not only to create the movie with open-source tools, but also to release the end result and production files to the public under a Creative Commons open license.

The project ended up being a great success and Ton created the Blender Institute in the summer of 2007, located in Amsterdam, the Netherlands. The institute is now the core of Blender's development and more Open Movies have been made there since: *Big Buck Bunny* (2008), the video game *Yo, Frankie!* (2008), *Sintel* (2010), and *Tears of Steel* (2012).

The development of Blender version 2.50 began in 2008. It offered a major improvement in the software's core, which was already becoming outdated. The final release of this version came in 2011. *Sintel* was made to put this new version to the test. It also helped improve the tools and bring back previous functionalities that were lost in the recent update. Since then, Blender has experimented with some other significant new features such as Cycles, a new render engine that supports GPU real-time, raytracing-based rendering.

The Blender Institute's latest Open Movie, *Tears of Steel*, was made to implement and improve visual-effects tools, such as camera tracking, compositing nodes improvements, and masks to name a few, making Blender one of the more flexible tools in the 3D software panorama (see Figure 1.1).

Blender's development process has been refined over time, and there are now new versions being released every 2 or 3 months. As this book is being developed (July, 2014), the current Blender version is 2.71 and, in the last couple of updates, some improvements to the UI were added (such as tabs in menus to prevent excessive scrolling), along with bug fixes and some new features (volumetric rendering, smoke, fire, and deformable meshes, motion blur support for Cycles, and new modeling tools). But the Blender 2.7X series is not aimed at adding amazing new features; the goal in these versions is to improve current features, improve Blender internally, and set it up for version 2.80. When version 2.80 comes around, it will be easier to implement new features and maintain the forward and backward compatibility of tools, add-ons, and numerous

Figure 1.1   *Tears of Steel* (2012) was an Open Movie
project that had a goal of improving Blender VFX tools.

other features. Also, internal improvement will enhance performance, which is critically important for professional users.

The Blender Foundation and the Blender Institute

The Blender Foundation is the corporation that organizes Blender's development and any projects related to the software, such as Open Movies, conferences, and training. The foundation operates from the Blender Institute, where the main infrastructure for blender.org is located.

The head of the Blender Foundation is Ton Roosendaal. He organizes and sets the goals for the software and anything else related to Blender. Everyone can make proposals about features they'd like to see added to Blender, and after the main development team analyzes them to see which of them are feasible, the team begins development. This is very different from the development of commercial software, where the company decides what needs to be done and developers have no say in what is added to the software.

In fact, Blender's users don't even need to request new features; they can just go ahead and develop a feature themselves and send it to the foundation afterward. If it is found useful and interesting, and it fits the Blender guidelines (it has to be consistent with the rest of the software), the main development team will work on adding it to the official Blender version.

The Blender Foundation hires some developers to complete specific tasks, but most developers are volunteers who lend their time in order to learn and practice using the software, or just because they want to participate in its ongoing development. Some developers even raise their own funds to create and perfect the features they want to see in Blender.

Because it is open-source software, Blender has *trunk* versions and *branches*. The trunk version is the official version released at blender.org and it contains the stable features of Blender. Branches are development versions for testing new features, or alternative features that may or may not make it into the official trunk version at some point. (Commercial software also uses this method, but it's all internal: you can't go and create your own branch or test development versions unless the company that owns the software releases a beta version to generate feedback before the software's actual release.)

Of course, it would be chaotic if everyone could just step in and add their own ideas to the software, so the Blender Foundation's main tasks have become organizing all of the developers in one place, defining priorities, and deciding what features make it to the final official version. The foundation determines which features need branches and which branches should be removed. It also provides and maintains the platform for Blender, and operates the bug-tracker system in which users can report bugs that are then assigned to specific developers for correction (and they're usually really fast).

> **Note**
>
> If you're interested in testing development versions of Blender, you can visit www.graphi-call.org and www.developer.blender.org, where you can find the version for your system. This is not recommended if you aren't an experienced user as these versions are experimental and unstable, so you must use them at your own discretion.

The foundation also decides how donations are spent. Above all, the Blender Foundation is the nerve center of Blender development, and the Blender Institute is its physical location on the planet.

The Blender Foundation also organizes Open Movies with several goals:

- **Raising money:** People pay for the movies in advance, so the movie and its tutorials fund their own development.

- **Testing Blender in production:** Making a movie is the best way to test how Blender responds in a production environment. It provides developers with an opportunity to fix issues and discover what features can be improved.

- **Improving Blender:** Usually, each Open Movie has a goal. The goal of *Sintel* was to test the new version of the software and make it stable and production ready. *Tears of Steel* was made to improve Blender's visual-effects capabilities. Thus, each Open Movie has a list of features to add that ultimately improve

Blender and many users help raise money for the movie so they can also enjoy using these features in the future.

- **Generating content for the Blender Cloud:** Blender Cloud is a service that people can subscribe to (it's also meant to help raise money for Blender's development), where the Blender Foundation publishes video tutorials and content created for Open Movies with educational purposes.
- **Demonstration:** With these kinds of projects, the foundation demonstrates Blender's capabilities and shows the world that Blender is absolutely usable in a professional production environment.

The Blender Community

For every type of software, it's very important to have a community surrounding it that will provide feedback and engage others in using the software. But in open-source software, this is even more important: not only does the community provide feedback, but it also proposes new features, discusses development, creates new features, organizes events, supports the projects, and donates money.

Open-source software communities are also very open-minded. They are usually treated as "fanboys" or "fanatics" by other software users, but once you are a part of one of these communities, you understand why: they're not only talking about a particular type of software, but they are also usually adhering to a set of ethics as well, and they're willing to contribute their help for free to improve the software, or even donate funds to have some features developed.

The Blender community includes everyone who uses Blender and shares their experience in forums, websites, blogs, podcasts, and videos. The community helps new users, provides tutorials, writes articles, and raises and donates money to the Blender Foundation. Although learning Blender is not easy, with such a great community behind it to help you and to produce great content for free that you can learn from, it can make the process considerably less difficult!

Summary

As you can see, Blender has been around for years. It's free to download and use, even for commercial purposes. The Blender Foundation organizes the software's development and anyone can contribute to it by programming, reporting bugs, donating money, and purchasing the foundation's products. Two of the most attractive features with open-source software are the ability to play with the core code of the software to make it fit your needs and the opportunity to interact with its developers and its diverse, open-minded community.

Exercises

1. What is open source?
2. When did Blender's development start?
3. Do you need to buy a license to use Blender commercially?
4. What are the main functions of the Blender Foundation?
5. Can I sell the work I make with Blender?

Blender Basics: The User Interface

This chapter helps you begin to understand how Blender's user interface and main navigation features work. Blender has a distinct way of using windows and menus. You might have to rethink how you work with interfaces while you catch up, but don't worry, it'll be fun!

Downloading and Installing Blender

Before you start using Blender, you need to install it, of course! This is really easy: You only need an Internet connection and a visit to **www.blender.org** (Blender's official website). Once you're there, simply find the Download link on the home page or go to the Download tab.

This will display a panel with the current official version; here, you have to select your operating system and whether you want an installer (for Windows only) or a portable version (yes, you can just copy a portable Blender onto your pen drive and use it everywhere you go). You'll also select whether your OS is 32 bit or 64 bit (if you don't know, use 32 bit).

If you use Windows and download an installer, execute it and follow the instructions. If you download a .zip (Windows and Mac) or .tarball (Linux) portable file, extract it, and from the folder, select the executable file called blender.exe and launch it.

> **Caution**
>
> Before you download, make sure to read the information on the Blender website, as it provides instructions on packages or libraries you have to install in case Blender doesn't work. Currently, they are:
>
> - **Windows:** Visual C++ 2008 Redistributable Package
> - **Linux:** glibc 2.11 and SDL-1.2

Blender User Interface

As mentioned before, Blender's UI is different from the UI in other software. The main thing you'll notice once you start using Blender's interface is that it is made up of what are called areas (also known as frames). You can split and join areas to create your own workspace, depending on what you feel more comfortable with or what task you need to accomplish. If you need further help with the interface, you can find a video tutorial included on the book's companion website (www.informit.com/title/9780133886177) with downloadable files that explain the basics of this chapter.

Each area can show different tool sets and views, called editors. Each part of Blender, or each task you can perform with it, is developed in a specific editor; for example, 3D View, Outliner, Timeline, Node Editor, and UV/Image Editor are some of the various types of editors you will encounter.

At any time, you can split an area and decide which editor you want to use in it, a feature that provides you with great flexibility as you work. You can also save different workspaces so that you can load the one you need very quickly without the need to set it up again.

The following list describes what you will encounter the first time you use Blender (see Figure 2.1):

Info Bar (A): This is the main menu where you will find typical options like Save, Load, and Help. Also, there are two drop-down menus (Workspace is covered later in this chapter, and Scene lets you switch between different 3D scenes you can store in the same file), the Render Engine selector, and information about the current scene with which you're working.

3D View (B): Here is where the magic happens, where you can create your objects, model and animate them, and add lights, for example. By default, you can see a grid that shows the colored axes (X is red, Y is green), a light, a cube, and a camera (all you need to launch a render to turn your 3D scene into an image).

Tools Region (C): Some editors, such as the 3D View shown in Figure 2.1, have their own regions where you can see certain options relevant to that specific editor. There are usually two types of regions: Tools and Properties. The one you see by default on the 3D View's left side is the Tools Region, where you have access to common tools and actions.

Splash Screen (D): This screen appears as you launch Blender and it shows the version you're using, interesting links about Blender, and options such as Help and Recent Files. If you just want to start using Blender, close the Splash Screen by clicking somewhere in the interface away from the Splash Screen.

Timeline (E): This section represents the time dimension in your scene (by default, in frames) and allows you to watch the animation, see where you have set animation keys or time markers, and locate the start and end of the animation.

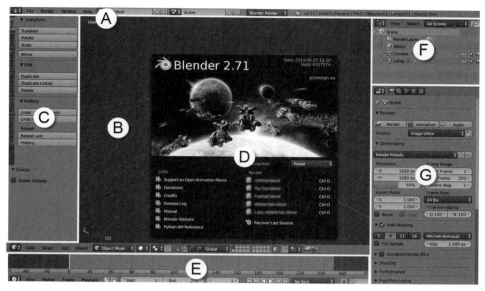

Figure 2.1   Blender's user interface and Splash Screen

Outliner (F): This area contains a schematic representation of the current scene, similar to a tree that you can collapse and expand. Here, you can check a list of every object in the scene and its relationships with other objects, or you can quickly select and find the particular object you're looking for.

Properties Editor (G): This editor is probably one of the most important features of Blender. Here, you'll find all the options you need for rendering. You'll create materials, change the parameters of the selection, add modifiers, and much more.

Understanding the 3D View

Let's now examine the elements of the 3D View, which is the main editor in Blender (see Figure 2.2). Some of these elements are present in other editors and this section will help you understand what these elements do.

View name (A): In the top-left corner (by default), you'll see the name of the current view (for example, User Perspective, Front Ortho, Right Ortho). So in case you're unsure about where the camera is located, a quick look at the view name will give you a clue.

Tools Region (B): Most of the editors have regions to the left and right of the view. You can show or hide the Tools Region by pressing **T** on your keyboard.

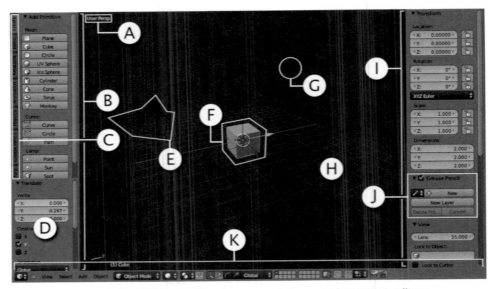

Figure 2.2   3D View in Blender—one of the most important editors

You can also adjust the region's width by hovering the cursor over its border and then clicking and dragging. If the Tools Region is hidden, on the left border of the 3DView, you'll find a little **+** button; click it and it will reappear.

Tabs (C): The Tools Region has context-sensitive tabs that you can click to show different types of tools. In Figure 2.2, for example, the Create Tab is selected, and it shows buttons you can click to create different geometric shapes, curves, lights, and other objects.

Operator panel (D): At the bottom of the Tools region is the Operator panel, which will show you the parameters of the last action you performed. For example, if you create a circle, the Operator panel will display options such as the number of vertices, the circle's radius, or if the circle should be filled—you can experiment with those options and see their effects in real time. As an alternative (useful if you like to work in full screen with no menus), you can press **F6** and the Operator panel will appear over the 3D View.

Camera (E): You can't take a render (the resulting 2D image generated from your 3D scene) without a camera in the scene. The camera defines the point of view, the field of view, zooming and depth of field, as well as other extra options that help you see in the viewport what will be rendered in the final image.

Default cube (F): The first time you start Blender, you have a cube in the center of the scene, so you already have a geometric shape to start working with. You can delete it by pressing **X** or **Del** on your keyboard and confirming if you prefer to start with another shape.

Lamp (G): If you want your render to look nice, you need lights that illuminate your scene and generate shadows. By default, Blender has a Point lamp in the scene to provide a basic illumination.

Grid (H): The grid represents the floor of your scene, with the X (red) and Y (green) axes as references to the scene's orientation and size. By default, each square in the grid represents 1 Blender Unit (it's possible to customize the grid if you need to).

Units

For a lot of users, it's very important to work with realistic units of measure. Blender, by default, works with "Blender Units." In the Properties Editor, on the Scene tab, you can find options to choose a measuring system under the Units panel. Selecting "None" will leave Blender Units as the default, but you can also choose Metric or Imperial systems. You'll be able to work at scale as well; just define the scale in its field once you select a measuring system.

Properties Region (I): Don't confuse this area with the Properties Editor; this region only contains properties and parameters that affect your interaction with the 3D View. It's hidden by default, but you can show it by pressing **N**. You will find options to transform objects, move the 3D cursor, view options, display options (such as the grid's size), and open background images to use as references. It's also context sensitive, so some options will change depending on your selection or the mode in which you're working. You can adjust its width in exactly the same way as you did with the Tools Region.

Tip

In other 3D software, you usually work with four 3D views at once. In Blender, there is an option to make a Quad View in a unique 3D View Editor. In the Properties Region of the 3D View, look for the Display panel and click "Toggle Quad View." You can also do this by pressing **Ctrl + Alt + Q**. In the same menu, you'll find additional options for using Quad View.

Panels (J): Blender menus, such as those in the Tools and Properties Regions or in the Properties Editor, are divided into panels. Each menu has different options and buttons for you to use. You can expand them or collapse them by left clicking the small, dark triangle to the left of the panel's title.

In Figure 2.3, you can see that downward-pointing triangle to the left of the title (3D cursor). When you click it, the triangle will point to the right and the panel will collapse to save space in your interface. Also, if you click the diagonal lines in the top-right corner, you can reorder the panels inside a menu by dragging and dropping.

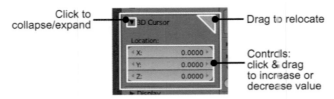

Figure 2.3   A panel from the Properties Region that controls the location of the 3D cursor

Header (K): Every area has a header, a horizontal bar at the top or bottom of the current view with menus and options for that view (see Figure 2.4). Hover the cursor over the header and press **F5** to switch its position from bottom to top or top to bottom.

Depending on your selection or the mode you're using, in the 3D View's header, from left to right, you can see:

- **Editor Selector:** Selects the type of editor in the current area.
- **Collapse Menu button:** Hides or expands the Editor's Menu in the header.
- **Editor's Menu:** Provides options you can use within a specific editor. In this case, for the 3D View, you have the options View, Select, Add, and Object.
- **Interaction Mode:** Selects the mode in which you're working (Edit Mode, Object Mode, etc.).
- **Drawing Method selector:** Toggles between the different display methods in the 3DView (for example, Wireframe, Solid, Textured, and Rendered).
- **Pivot Selector:** Provides a reference point in space for transforming an object.
- **Transform Manipulators:** Selects between the different manipulators to transform objects (Move, Rotate, and Scale).
- **Scene Layers:** The small blocks represent different layers in which you can store objects from the scene to keep everything organized.

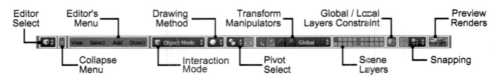

Figure 2.4   3D View Header and its contents

- **Global/Local Layers Constraint button:** Links the visibility of layers between the 3D View and the Scene Layers that you will render. If you want a layer to be rendered but you don't want it to be visible in the 3D View, you can turn that layer on from the Render Layers tab (see Chapter 14) and turn the Global/Local Layers Constraint off so the visibility of layers in the 3D View and in the final render is not linked.

- **Snapping selector:** Offers several options to snap the selection to other elements when you perform a transform operation.

- **Preview Renders:** These two buttons are for rendering real-time previews. The first button renders a still snapshot, while the second one renders the whole animation. These renders are captures of what you see in the 3D View.

Tip

If an area is too small and you can't see all the options in the header, you can hold and drag middle mouse button (**MMB**) over the header to the left and right to scroll it sideways and see the rest of the options.

Navigating the 3D View

Now that you know what's going on in the 3D View, let's see how to navigate through it to check your scene and get in touch with the world you're creating. When your cursor is hovering in the 3D View, you can perform a variety of actions to change your point of view.

Tip

To use Blender's default navigation configuration efficiently, it is highly recommended that you use a keyboard with a NumPad and a mouse with a scroll wheel and middle button (see Figure 2.5). If you don't, you can still navigate with other buttons by setting them up in the User Preferences, or with the conventional number keys on a keyboard, but you will have limited functionalities and navigation won't be as smooth.

- **Pan (Shift + MMB):** Moves the camera parallel to the current view.
- **Orbit (MMB or NumPad 4, 8, 6, and 2):** Rotates the camera around the scene.
- **Zoom (scroll wheel or Ctrl + MMB drag or Numpad + (plus sign) and NumPad − (minus sign)):** Moves closer or farther away from a point.
- **View Selected (NumPad .):** Zooms and centers the camera in the selection.
- **Predefined (Front, Right, and Top) Views (NumPad 1, 3, 7):** Changes the point of view aligned to one axis. Press **Ctrl** at the same time to get the opposite view (Back, Left, and Bottom).

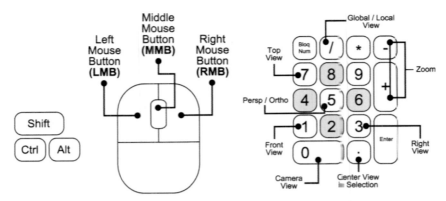

Figure 2.5   Most of the buttons you can use to navigate in the 3D scene are on the mouse and NumPad. Buttons highlighted in gray let you orbit the camera.

- **Perspective/Orthographic Switch (NumPad 5):** Switches between Perspective and Orthographic.

- **Camera View (NumPad 0):** Jumps to the point of view of the active camera. Select a camera and press **Ctrl + NumPad 0** to make that camera the active one. Press **Ctrl + Alt + NumPad 0** to place the active camera in the current view. Keep in mind that with **Ctrl + NumPad 0,** you can turn any object into a camera, so don't worry if you accidentally had an object selected when you pressed that shortcut and suddenly you see the scene from a strange point of view: it's meant to help you orient objects in a different manner. For example, you can use this feature to see the scene from the point of view of a directional light, which will give you a better sense of what the light will illuminate.

- **Global View/Local View (NumPad /):** Local View hides everything except the selection so you don't have other objects blocking your view while you work. Press **NumPad /** again to switch back to the Global View.

- **Walk Mode (Shift + F):** Moves slowly around the screen. Use the **arrow keys** or **A, S, D,** or **F** to navigate through the scene as if you were moving in a video game. Use **Q** and **E** to move up and down. Use the mouse to rotate the camera. You can increase or decrease the moving speed with the scroll wheel. Press **G** to enable a gravity effect (it will look like a game, as the camera will fall down to stay on top of the scene's geometry. Use an **LMB** click to accept the movement and an **RMB** click to cancel it.

- **Fly Mode (Shift + F):** This is an alternative for Walk Mode: you'll fly through the scene instead of walking. To activate this instead of Walk Mode, you need to set it as default on the Input tab of the User Preferences. You can rotate the camera with the mouse, pan with **MMB** and dragging, and fly forward and backward using the scroll wheel. Use a **LMB** click to accept the movement and a **RMB** click to cancel it.

> **Tip**
>
> If you are familiar with another piece of software such as 3ds Max or Maya, you may find the main Blender controls for panning and orbiting the camera uncomfortable. You can customize these keyboard shortcuts on the Input Tab of the User Preferences. I use these shortcuts myself:
>
> - **Pan: MMB**
> - **Orbit: Shift + MMB**

Managing Areas

As you've seen already, Blender's UI is made of areas or frames. Let's master them! First, you'll learn how to split and join them: the key to performing these operations is in the bottom-left and top-right corners. Each area will have little diagonal lines in those corners that you can click and drag. When you hover the mouse over them, your cursor will turn into a cross.

You can work with those corners in the following ways:

- **Split:** Click **LMB** and drag inside an area to split it. Dragging vertically will create a horizontal split, while dragging horizontally will create a vertical split. Right click before releasing **LMB** to cancel splitting (see Figure 2.6).

- **Join:** Click and drag an area's corner toward a contiguous area and that area will darken and show an arrow that displays the direction in which the areas will be joined. The area from which you've dragged will now take the space of the area into which you dragged. Keep in mind you'll only be able to join areas with contiguous borders of a similar size. Right click before releasing **LMB** to cancel joining (see Figure 2.6).

- **Swap:** Press **Ctrl + LMB** in one of these corners and drag over a different area. The editors inside those areas will be swapped.

- **Duplicate:** Press **Shift + LMB** and drag in the corner. The area will be duplicated in a new window, which is useful if you are using a second monitor.

- **Full Screen:** Hover the cursor over an area and press **Shift + Space** or **Ctrl + UpArrow**. That area will appear in full screen to give you more space to work. Press one of those shortcuts again to return to the original workspace.

- **Resize:** Hover the cursor over the borders of an area. The cursor will become a two-headed arrow. Click and drag to resize that area.

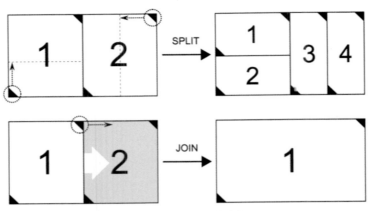

Figure 2.6   Splitting and joining areas

Workspaces

In the Info bar, there is a drop-down menu with stored workspaces. You can create your own workspace by pressing the + button near the selector. Customize these areas and editors as you prefer, then put a name to that workspace. Go to the menu or press **Ctrl + LeftArrow** or **Ctrl + RightArrow** to navigate through the different saved workspaces.

Editor Types

Now that you know how to use areas to shape your workspace, you need to see what types of editors you can show in those areas. You can select the Editor Type for an area by clicking the icon to the left of the editor's name (see Figure 2.7).

- **Python Console** is a built-in console that allows you to interact with Blender using its Python API; this editor is mainly for developers.

- **File Browser** allows you to navigate through your system's folders where, for example, you can look for images. Keep in mind you can drag images to other editors, such as dragging an image to the 3D View to use it as a background reference. File Browser is also useful when you're editing video and frequently need to access the video files and load them into the timeline.

- **Info** is the main menu found by default at the top-left corner of the interface. Also, if you drag down this area, you'll be able to see a Python Console that shows you logs and error messages.

- **User Preferences** is a window with different tabs that allow you to customize Blender keyboard shortcuts, change the interface's colors and theme, adjust performance settings, and manage add-ons.

Figure 2.7   Selecting the
Editor Type of an area

- **Outliner** is a tree graph of every element in the scene and is very useful when you're looking for objects or navigating through all of the elements of a scene. You can select specific objects or groups in complex scenes.

- **Properties** is one of the most important editors in Blender. It has different tabs for different groups of options you can access (depending on your selection, tabs may vary as they are context sensitive). This is where you set up your render size and performance, add modifiers, set the object parameters, add materials, control particle systems, and indicate which measuring units you want for your scene (see Figure 2.8). Another interesting fact to mention here is that these tabs are organized from most general to most specific: Render > Render Layers > Scene > World > Object > Object Constraints > Modifiers > Object Data > Materials.

- **Logic Editor** provides an interface to define behaviors and functions that control the objects in a scene; it is used to create interactive games inside Blender.

- **Node Editor** lets you create node trees for final image compositing, textures, and materials.

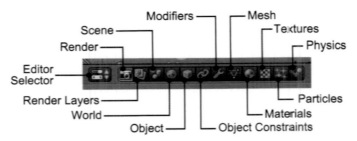

Figure 2.8   Properties Editor tabs

- **Text Editor** is used for scripting (you can even run Python scripts from it) or for adding some text notes to the scene (especially useful if you work with a team and want to add information about how to use the scene).
- **Movie Clip Editor** is used to load video footage, analyze it, and use it for camera or motion tracking. You can also create and animate masks that you can then use in the compositor, and you can stabilize shaky footage.
- **Video Sequence Editor** is used for editing video inside Blender.
- **UV/Image Editor** is used for loading images as a reference or to paint over them. It's also where you manipulate UVs and unwrap objects. You can use it to see the compositing result preview. Renders are also displayed in this editor.
- **NLA Editor** is similar to the Video Sequence Editor, but it works with animations. In it, you can load different animations for an object or armature and mix them together using strips, and you can even add transitions.
- **Dope Sheet** is a place to display objects in the scene and their keyframes (a keyframe is the state of an element in a given frame of the animation; see Chapter 12 for more information about using keyframes), making it very easy to adjust the timing of your animations. It can be used as an "advanced" timeline.

  > **Tip**
  >
  > In other animation software, you can access the basic timing control of keyframes from the timeline. In Blender, you can replace the basic timeline for a Dope Sheet to customize areas and activate the **Summary** and **Selected Only** options to display the keyframes Summary at the top of all the keyframes of the selected objects. This way, you'll have a timeline that allows you to control an animation's timing.

- **Graph Editor** is similar to the Dope Sheet, but it also shows animation curves, which you can use to control how interpolations between keyframes work and to fine tune your animations.
- **Timeline** is a window that shows the time in the scene and lets you play the animation and select the frame in which you want to work. You can also add

markers to easily designate important parts of the sequence and to set the start and end frames of the animation.

- **3D View** is where you control the 3D world by modeling, animating, and adding objects to a scene.

> **Tip**
>
> In Blender, you can even zoom in and out inside menus. Hover your cursor over a menu, press **Ctrl + MMB,** and drag up and down to make menu items bigger or smaller.

Selecting Objects

In order to do anything in Blender, you need to select objects. What you'll notice first is that you select objects with the mouse's right click! Users often go crazy when they learn this because most programs use a left click. There are at least a couple of reasons (probably more) for the **RMB** selections:

- **It's ergonomic:** Research over several years has shown that about 90 percent of the time, you use only left clicks in most programs. Blender's right-click selections share the workload between two fingers, so in the long run your hand is healthier.

- **Blender is different:** Blender doesn't follow conventional software standards and that's why it does things in a new way. The Blender UI changes the paradigm other software uses: for some actions, such as selecting an object, you use a right click, while for confirming an action or clicking various buttons you still use a left click. Also, you're supposed to work with shortcuts in Blender, so there is no need for a right-click menu. As a plus, left clicking alone has another use in Blender: it sets the 3D cursor location (you'll learn about that soon).

Selected objects will be highlighted with an outline. While you select, you can press **Shift + RMB** to add or subtract objects from the selection. There are also various tools you can use to select a group of objects, including Box Selection, Lasso Selection, and Paint Selection (see Figure 2.9).

Box Selection (A): Press **B** and **LMB** drag to determine the size and position of a box. By default, any objects inside the box will be added to the current selection, but you can subtract them by dragging the box with **MMB** instead of **LMB**.

Lasso Selection (B): Press **Ctrl + LMB** and drag to draw the lasso shape over the objects you want to select. The objects inside the lasso will be added to the current selection.

Paint Selection (C): Press **C** and a circle will appear around the cursor. Drag the scroll wheel to pick the size of the "brush," and then click and drag with **LMB** to add to the selection or with **MMB** to subtract.

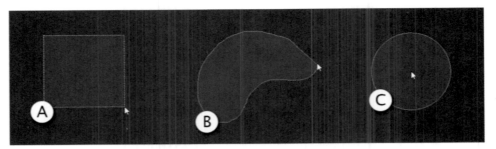

Figure 2.9   Selection methods to select groups of objects

If you want to select or deselect all the objects in the scene, just press **A**.

> **Tip**
>
> In Blender, as in almost all software nowadays, you can Undo and Redo your actions.
>
> - **Undo:** Press **Ctrl + Z** to go back to the previous scene state if you made a mistake, or if you were just experimenting with something but didn't like the result.
> - **Redo:** Press **Shift + Ctrl + Z** to reverse the effect of the Undo command.

When you select multiple objects at once, the last one selected (and only the last one) will become the active object and it will have a brighter highlight. The active object has several different uses, such as providing a pivot point or for copying its attributes to the rest of the objects in the selection. However, if you have multiple objects selected and you apply a modifier, for example, it will be applied to the active object, not to the whole selection.

> **Tip**
>
> When you start using Blender, you might find it difficult to use the right-click selection. In fact, you have an option in the User Preferences to switch selections to the left click. However, I don't recommend that you do so; Blender has been designed to work with right-click selections and switching to the left click will make you lose some functionality. Also, you'll get used to the right click very soon and then you'll see how comfortable it is!

Using the 3D Cursor

Something you might not understand when you first open Blender is why there is always a circle in the middle of the view. What is its function? It's the 3D cursor and it's a special feature in Blender. While it can initially be a little disturbing, it becomes really useful once you've learned about it.

Here are the main functions of the 3D cursor:

- You can use it to set the location where new objects will be created.
- You can use it to align objects.
- You can also use it as a pivot point to rotate or scale objects.

Press **Shift + S** to reveal the Snap menu (see Figure 2.10). It includes various options that are primarily used with the 3D cursor. It's also divided into two sections: the first one transforms the selection and the second one places the 3D cursor. (At this point, you may not understand some of these Blender terms, such as transforms, vertices, or skeletons, or how to access them, but don't worry; you'll learn about them in the next chapters!)

For example, if you want to align an object to a specific place on the surface of another object, you can select a vertex of that object, then press **Shift + S,** and select Cursor to Selected. Select the other object, press **Shift + S**, and select Selection to Cursor.

By pressing **,** (comma) or **.** (period) on your keyboard, you can switch between using the Box Center Pivot and using the 3D Cursor Pivot. Sometimes, placing the 3D cursor and using it as a pivot to rotate or scale objects comes in very handy! For example, let's say you want to pose a character. Thanks to the 3D cursor, you don't need a skeleton for simple posing: you can select the vertices of the leg, place the 3D cursor in the articulation, and rotate those vertices using the cursor as a pivot point.

> **Tip**
>
> In the Blender User Preferences (**Ctrl + Alt + U** or in the File menu), on the Interface tab, you can find the *Cursor Depth* option. If you turn it on, when you click **LMB** over a surface, the 3D cursor will be placed on that surface, making it easier to align objects to the surface.

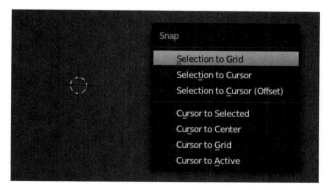

Figure 2.10   3D Cursor and its Snap menu (**Shift + S**)

Blender User Preferences

In the File menu, or if you press **Ctrl + Alt + U,** you will find the Blender User Preferences, which will appear in a new window you can close once you're done selecting your preferences (see Figure 2.11).

This window has different tabs across the top that you can use to customize your preferences in Blender. Let's check out what you can do on each one of them:

- **Interface:** Here, you'll find a lot of options to set the Blender Interface to your desired parameters so you feel more comfortable working with it.
- **Editing:** On this tab, you'll find some options for editing things like materials, animation curves, and grease pencil, and you'll be able to adjust how objects are aligned when you create them or how duplicate objects should behave.
- **Input:** You can edit keyboard shortcuts in this tab, as well as some other options that determine how you work with Blender using your mouse and keyboard.
- **Addons:** On this tab, you can manage extensions that come with Blender, or download and install others to add some new functionality to Blender. A lot of these extensions are deactivated by default, but you can look for the ones you're interested in and turn them on to use them while you work.

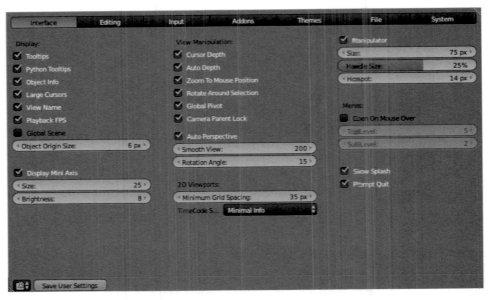

Figure 2.11   Blender User Preferences

- **Themes:** Here, you can create your own color schemes to make Blender more appealing to you or to fit your corporate color scheme if you want!
- **File:** This tab defines general file paths, what external software to link with Blender (like a default player for rendered animations), and how Blender saves files. You can also set up the Auto Save feature on this tab.
- **System:** On this tab, you can set up performance options to improve how Blender works, depending on your computer, such as selecting your graphics card (useful when you want to work with GPU rendering with Cycles). Or, you can change your own preferences for things like the default lighting applied to objects in the solid view, as well as text size and font, or the method Blender will use when drawing 3D objects.

Tip

I highly recommend that you check out all these options. If you don't know what they do, hover the cursor over them to get a brief pop-up description. Some of these preferences may make your life easier when using Blender, especially if you're coming to it from other animation software.

Click Save User Preference at the bottom-left corner of the User Preferences window to confirm your selections and make your new preferences appear the next time you open Blender. Alternatively, keep in mind you can even save how your scene, workspace, and menus look when you open Blender: Just set everything up as you prefer (even replace that default cube with another interesting shape if you want), and press **Ctrl + U** to save your selections as the "startup" .blend file.

.blend Files

The Blender file format is **.blend**. However, if you have the *Save Versions* feature turned on (you can find this option in the Blender User Preferences on the File tab), Blender will automatically generate backup files *.blend1, *.blend2, *.blend3 (the asterisk represents the original filename) when you save. By default, Blender will save one backup file, but you can increase the amount of versions saved from the User Preferences. These backup files can be opened from within Blender just like the original file; they just have a different extension so you can easily distinguish between the original files and those automatically saved by Blender. Another option you can turn on in the same menu is the *Auto Save Temporary Files*: you can set a timer in intervals of minutes and Blender will save the file in the temporary folder when that interval passes. Usually, you only access Auto Save files when something goes wrong or you need to recover a file you've lost or didn't save.

Also, keep in mind that if you use images as textures or use any kind of external files inside Blender, they won't be inside the .blend file by default. However, you can pack them inside the .blend file; you'll learn how to do this procedure in Chapter 9, Painting Textures.

Summary

At this point, you understand how Blender's interface works. Now, it's a matter of learning how to manipulate objects and actually "get the job done." You saw how areas divide the interface and what types of editors you can display on them, and you've learned the shortcuts for navigating through the 3D scene. You've also learned that there is the possibility of easy and quick customization if you don't like the default interface.

Exercises

1. Create a new workspace, splitting and joining areas to get a single area and then delete the workspace afterward.

2. What is the NumPad used for in Blender?

3. Select all objects in the scene and deselect them again.

4. Why does Blender use a right click to select objects?

5. What are the main functions of the 3D cursor and how is it used?

6. Is it possible to change keyboard shortcuts in Blender? If so, how?

7. What is the format Blender uses for saving files?

3

Your First Scene in Blender

If this is your first time using Blender, you'll find this chapter especially useful. You've now been introduced to the basics of Blender and, with practice, you'll have the interface under control. It's time to create objects, interact with them, add modifiers, materials, and lights, and then render your creation! This chapter presents a very simple exercise to help you better understand how to create your first scene. You'll also learn about Blender Render and Cycles, the two render engines included in Blender. In the ancillary materials on this book's website, you'll find a video tutorial that explains the steps followed in this chapter to help you create your first scene in Blender.

Creating Objects

As you open Blender, you'll find the familiar "default cube" sitting in the middle of the scene. You can use that cube to build your model or you can delete it. To delete objects in Blender, just select them and press **X** or **Del** and click **Delete** in the dialog box that will appear to confirm the deletion.

First, you want to create an object and there are different ways to do it.

- In the 3D View, in the Tools Region (press **T** if the Tools Region is hidden), on the Create tab, click the object type you want to create.
- In the 3D View header, choose the Add Menu and from it select the object you want to create from the different object categories.
- With the cursor in the 3D View, press **Shift + A** and the same Add Menu from the header will appear.

In any of the options above, the object will be created in the position of the 3D cursor inside the 3D scene.

Once you create an object, in the Operator panel (at the bottom of the Tools Region) you'll be able to find parameters to modify it, such as adjusting the depth and radius of a cylinder. Make sure you have made any adjustments you want to the object before moving it or performing any other action on it because after you create the object it is converted to a mesh and you'll no longer have access to those parameters. The parameters of the last performed action will appear in the Operator panel, so pay attention to this area as you'll find really cool options there! As an alternative, you can press **F6** with the cursor over the 3D View to see those options in a pop-up.

Animation software often has a "test" object; in Blender, it's the monkey head (called *Suzanne*), and you'll use it for the test scene in this chapter. Create a monkey mesh using any of the three methods described above that you prefer. Then, create a plane, as this will later serve as the floor of your scene. Don't worry if the head and plane intersect in the middle of the scene and are not aligned; you'll correct that in a moment.

Moving, Rotating, and Scaling

After you create objects in your 3D scene, you need to be able to control where they are located, how they are oriented, and what size they are. In this section, you'll see how to do just that. Moving, rotating, and scaling are the three different transform operations you can perform on an object.

Using Manipulators (Basic Mode)

When you want to transform objects or elements in the 3D scene, Blender offers manipulators that help you control those transformations. Let's take a look at the different manipulators shown in Figure 3.1.

- **Move (A):** Changes the position of an object in space
- **Rotate (B):** Controls the orientation of an object
- **Scale (C):** Manipulates the size of an object
- **All transforms (D):** Provides the option to use more than one transform manipulator at once

In the 3D view header, you can select the type of transform you want to perform. If you press **Shift** while clicking on different transform icons, you can perform multiple transforms at once. (In Figure 3.1, the fourth example (D) shows all three transform manipulators being used at the same time.)

Using the different manipulators, you can move, rotate, and scale objects. These manipulators will appear at the pivot point of the object (marked as a little orange spot) and you perform an action with them using the following controls:

- **LMB** click one of the axes to make the object move, rotate, or resize on that specific axis (X is red, Y is green, and Z is blue). **LMB** click again to confirm the transform.
- To get to the precision mode, press and hold **Shift** *after* you click to transform; this will make the transform slower, allowing you to make precise adjustments to it.

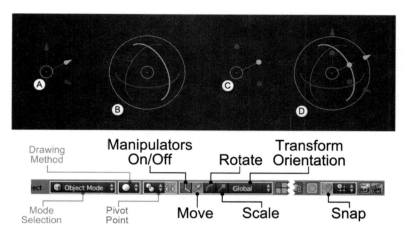

Figure 3.1   Manipulators in Blender, including the
3D View header and the transform controls

- To lock one axis and manipulate the other two, press and hold **Shift** before you click the axis you want to lock. For example, if you press **Shift** and then click the Z-axis to move it, the object will actually move on the X- and Y-axes. (This option only works when moving or scaling, and is not available with rotations.)

- Each manipulator has a small white circle in its center. Click it with the Move manipulator to move the object using the current point of view as a reference (dragging it parallel to the view). Click and drag the small white circle within the Rotation manipulator to get to the orbit mode, which allows you to rotate on all axes at once. Click and drag the small white circle of the Scale manipulator to scale the object on every axis. The Rotation manipulator also has an outer white circle; click and drag it to rotate the object using the current point of view as the rotation axis.

- Hold down **Ctrl** while using these manipulators to switch between normal transforms and Snap Mode. This feature will allow you to snap to several elements while you perform transforms. If snapping is activated, holding down **Ctrl** will "free" the object when transforming; if it's deactivated, holding down **Ctrl** will enable the snapping. This feature is very useful because you won't need to continuously turn the Snap tool on and off by clicking the Snap icon on the 3D View header.

- In the 3D view header, you can select *Pivot Point* and *Transform Orientation*. The pivot point defines the point around which objects rotate. By default, the Transform Orientation (access this menu by pressing **Alt + Space**) is Global, which means it's aligned to the 3D *World* axes (default scene axes). You can switch it to the *Local* axes of the selection to rotate objects using their own orientation.

> **Tip**
>
> If you don't like the default behavior of transforms in Blender, which has you click once to start transforming and then click a second time to confirm, you can activate the Release Confirms option in the User Preferences on the Edit tab. This option will make the transform behavior faster so that you click and drag, and the transform is confirmed as you release the button. This is the typical behavior in other software. This feature only affects right-click transforms (when you click and drag using **RMB**).

Using Keyboard Shortcuts (Advanced Mode)

While you can use manipulators easily, the "expert" and really fast method for transforming objects in Blender is to use keyboard shortcuts. Sometimes, the manipulators will prove useful, but most of the time and especially for simple transforms, using the keyboard is faster and more efficient.

- Press **Ctrl + Space** to show or hide the manipulators, (you can also do it by clicking the Manipulator On/Off icon on the 3D view header).
- Press **G** (Grab) to move, **R** to rotate, and **S** to scale. When you do this to move and rotate the objects, they will move and rotate according to the view. **LMB** click to confirm, or click **RMB** or **ESC** to cancel.
- After pressing **G**, **R**, or **S**, if you press **X**, **Y**, or **Z**, the selection will only transform on that global axis. Press **X**, **Y**, or **Z** twice to align to the selection's local axis.
- As an alternative to the previous option, when you're transforming with no attachment to a given axis, you can click **MMB** and drag the object to select a global axis on which you can align your object.
- Precise transforms, snapping, and axis locking using **Shift** and **Ctrl** while transforming with manipulators also apply when you use keyboard shortcuts.

> **Numerically Precise Transforms**
>
> When you're performing a transform, Blender allows you to input numerical values. For example, if you look at the 3D view header when you are rotating an object, you'll find that the header buttons disappear and are replaced with a display of the values of the transform in action. At this point, you can enter values directly from your keyboard and Blender will use them for the current transformation. Here are two examples:
>
> - **Move an object 35 units on the X-axis:** You can use manipulators and write the desired numerical value while dragging, but we'll use the keyboard shortcuts. Press **G** to move, then press **X** to snap the object's movement to the X-axis. Now you can drag the object through the X-axis. Enter **35** from the keyboard and the object will move 35 units on the X-axis. **LMB** click or press **Enter** to confirm the operation.
> - **Rotate an object -90 degrees on the Y-axis:** Press **R** to rotate, **Y** to snap to the Y-axis, and enter **-90** from your keyboard. **LMB** click or press **Enter** to confirm the operation.

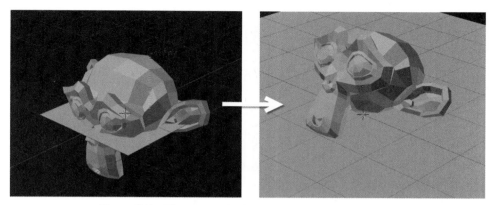

Figure 3.2   The scene, before and after the transforms

As you can see, using this method makes transformations really fast and easy to perform. The shortcuts are also intuitive and you can use them in almost any editor—**G**, **R**, and **S** will always move, rotate and scale.

Arranging the Objects in Your Scene

Now that you know how to transform objects, let's make our monkey head sit on the floor and then make the floor bigger (see Figure 3.2).

1. Right click to select the plane, press **S** to scale, and enter **5** from your keyboard to make the plane 5 times bigger. Press **Enter** to confirm. You can also use the manipulators if you feel more comfortable with them.

2. Select the monkey head, moving and rotating it until it looks like it's sitting on the floor. As a recommendation, you can switch the 3D View to a side view to see what's going on more clearly, and transform the head there using **G** and **R.** Keep in mind that if you're in a side view and rotate using **R,** the object will rotate on the X-axis.

Naming Objects and Datablocks

Before proceeding, you need to learn how to name objects. This will come in handy when you're working in really complex scenes and you'll want to be able to recognize objects by their names. Otherwise, you'll find yourself lost in a sea of objects called "Plane.001," "Sphere.028," and other generic names. If a Blender scene was a wall made of bricks, each brick would be a datablock.

Renaming Objects

There are several different ways of renaming an object:

- Locate the object in the Outliner. Right click its name and select the Rename option. Alternatively, you can double click the name. Type in the new name and press **Enter** to confirm.
- In the 3D View Properties Region, you can rename the object in the Item panel. Left click the text field, type in the name, and press **Enter** to confirm.
- In the Properties Editor, go to the Object tab (the one with a yellow cube) and, at the top left, click in the text field to type in the new name. Press **Enter** to confirm.

Managing Datablocks

Datablocks are the most basic Blender components. Every element you can build, such as objects, meshes, lamps, textures, materials, and armatures (skeletons), is made out of datablocks. Everything in the 3D scene is contained in an *object*.

Whether you're creating a mesh, a lamp, or a curve, you're creating an object. In Blender, any object has object data (*ObData*) inside it, so the object itself acts as a kind of container for the data. The ObData defines the type of element an object contains. As an example, let's look at a mesh and see the difference between the object and the object data in Figure 3.3.

You can see how to check for an object's name inside the Properties Editor. The image to the right shows how the "Mesh's Name" is inside the "Object's Name." In the image, the ObData is a mesh; if it were a lamp or a curve, the icon would change accordingly. The Properties Editor always shows information about the selected object, but if you click the *Pin* icon, the currently selected object's information will be pinned and, even if you select a different object, the Properties Editor will keep displaying the pinned object's information.

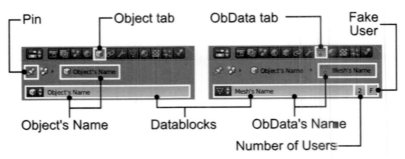

Figure 3.3   Properties Editor Object and Object Data tabs

Here are some key points about objects and ObData.

- **Objects** are containers for ObData. An object defines where an element (such as a lamp or mesh) is placed inside the 3D world and it carries location, rotation, and scale data. It also contains modifiers or constraints, as they affect the object as well.

- **ObData:** ObData defines what's inside an object. If the ObData is a mesh, for example, you'd see a mesh with its vertices and faces inside the object. When you access the ObData, you can adjust its parameters. If you click the drop-down list of the ObData datablock, you can load a different ObData into the object. For example, you could load a different mesh into the object's position. Several objects can use the same ObData (these objects are called instances or linked duplicates), which means that even if they are in different positions in the scene, all of them will synchronize their contents, so if you adjust the mesh vertices in one of them, the others will reflect those changes as well.

Duplicates and Instances (Linked Duplicates)

You need to understand the difference between a duplicate and an instance. A duplicate is a new object created from an existing one so it looks the same as the original, but it's independent and there is no link between the new one and the original. An instance is also a new object; it can be in a different position, but it's directly linked to the original object, so if you change the ObData in an object, it will affect its instances as well.

When you duplicate an object (**Shift + D**), some ObData will be duplicated with it while other ObData will be instanced. You can define the defaults for this in the User Preferences on the Editing tab. For example, if you duplicate an object, by default it will duplicate the mesh data contained in it, but it will use the same material data, so both objects will use the same material datablock.

On the other hand, instancing (**Alt + D**) will only duplicate the object, but the rest of ObData it carries inside will be linked and synchronized with the original. An alternative method to instance a mesh is to go to the Properties Editor, on the ObData tab, and select a different mesh from the drop-down list in its datablock.

To the right of some datablock names, you'll find an **F** button as well as a number. The number indicates the number of users that datablock has. For example, in Figure 3.3, the mesh ObData has 2 different users; this means that 2 different objects are using that mesh data (there is an instance in the scene). If you want to turn an instance into an independent and unique datablock, just click the number and it will indicate a single user.

If, at some point, a datablock (like a mesh or a material, for example) has 0 users and you close the file, Blender cleans out the unused datablocks in the file, so you'll lose that great material you created but weren't currently using. That's why the **F** button is there; it creates a "fake user" of that datablock, so even if you're not using it in the scene, it will have 1 user and that will prevent the datablock from being deleted when you exit the project.

Keep in mind that you will usually work with the names of objects. Most of the time, you don't need to access the name of ObData like meshes, so if you are running low on time, you can probably skip ObData naming.

Naming Your Scene's Objects

After you understand what datablocks are and how to rename objects, name the objects in your scene accordingly (for example, the plane should be called "Floor"). Sometimes, you'll have to select a datablock's name from a list, so naming datablocks intuitively will help you find the one you're looking for.

> **Tip**
> When you have lots of objects in a scene, it can be difficult to select a specific one, as others may be in the way. If you right click over the objects in the 3D View several times, the selection will jump between the objects under the cursor, and if you press **Alt + RMB**, Blender will display a list of objects under the cursor, so you can select the one you need. Of course, this is only useful when your objects are named intuitively.

Interaction Modes

Blender provides different ways to modify objects in your scene (such as modeling, texturing, sculpting, and posing) and they're called Interaction Modes. By default, you work in Object Mode and are able to move, rotate, and scale; basically, Object Mode allows you to place objects in a scene. But there are other modes. Probably one of the most useful ones is Edit Mode, which is used to edit the ObData. For example, you would use Edit Mode to model a mesh, access its vertices, edges, and faces, and change its shape.

You can find the Interaction Mode menu on the 3D View header (see Figure 3.4); the options it displays depend on the type of object you have selected. For now, you'll just focus on the Object and Edit modes. You'll learn about the other modes throughout the rest of the book.

You use Object Mode to create and place things in your scene (even animate them if you aren't using armatures, which are Blender skeletons used to animate characters and deform objects). In Edit Mode, you can perform modeling tasks on the mesh. You can quickly switch between these modes without having to access the selector by using the **Tab** key on your keyboard.

When you select an armature, you will use Edit Mode to access the bones inside it and manipulate them. Pose Mode will be available as well and it's the one you'll use when animating a skeleton (you'll learn more about this in Chapters 11 and 12). If you

Figure 3.4   The Interaction Mode selector; on the left are
the options available when a mesh object is selected; on the right are
the options available when an armature is selected.

select a mesh, you'll have access to modes such as Sculpt, Texture Paint, and Vertex
Paint, as shown in Figure 3.4.

As you can see, a lot of options are available and, depending on what you want to do
at any point in time, you just have to select the right Interaction Mode for the actions
you want to perform.

Applying Flat or Smooth Surfaces

The monkey head looks weird with the rough edges and polygons that currently comprise its shape. This look is useful for some things, but for objects that should look
more organic, you may prefer to have a smooth surface. This option only changes the
surface's appearance; it doesn't add any geometry. There are different ways to smooth a
surface in Blender:

- Select the object you want to smooth and, in the Tools Region on the Basic tab,
  you'll find a Shading option with two different buttons: Smooth and Flat. If you
  click one of them when you're in Object Mode, every face of the object will use
  that shading method.

- In Edit Mode, select the faces you want to shade and use the Smooth or Flat shading options on the Basic tab of the Tools Region.

- In Edit Mode, select the faces you want to shade with the smooth or flat method
  and press **W** (this will display the Specials menu). From the Specials menu, pick
  the option you want: Shade Smooth or Shade Flat.

Figure 3.5 shows where these options are in Blender's interface.

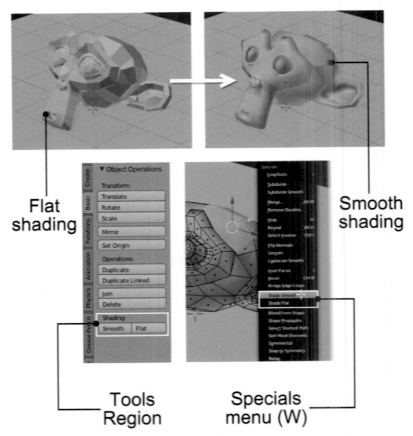

Figure 3.5   A comparison of flat and smooth surfaces
and the menus to access these options

Modifiers

Even though you used smooth shading in the mesh, the object still doesn't look just
right, as it has a very low resolution. You could use a Subdivision Surface modifier to
add more detail to the surface and smooth it out (at the cost of adding more polygons to
the object). A modifier is an element you can add to an object to alter it, such as a deformation, the generation of geometry, or the reduction of existing geometry. Modifiers won't affect the original mesh, which gives you a lot of flexibility, and you can turn
them on and off when you want.

Adding Modifiers

Clicking the wrench icon in the Properties Editor opens the Modifiers tab, where you can add modifiers (see Figure 3.6). When you click the *Add Modifier* button, a menu will display every modifier you can add to the active object (not all the modifiers are available for every type of object). Left click a modifier from the list to add it to the active object.

When you add a modifier, a node will be added to the modifier stack, which works similarly to layers: if you keep adding modifiers, they'll add their effects to the previous modifiers. Keep in mind that the modifier stack works in the opposite order of layers in other software such as Photoshop: in Blender, the last modifier you add will be at the bottom of the stack, and its effect will alter the effects of the modifiers above it in the list. The order of the modifiers is crucial to defining the resulting effect they'll have on the object.

For example, if you model one side of a mesh and apply a Mirror modifier to generate the other half, and then apply a Subdivision Surface modifier to smooth the result, the Subdivision Surface modifier should be at the bottom of the list; otherwise,

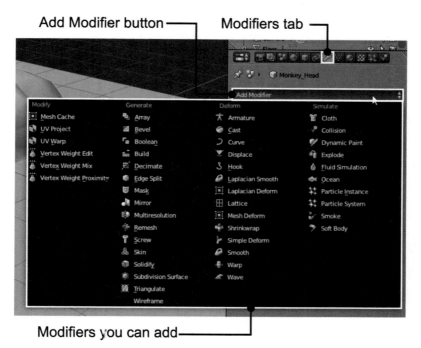

Figure 3.6   In the Properties Editor, on the Modifiers tab, you can add modifiers to the active object.

the object will be smoothed before being mirrored, and you will see the seam in the middle.

Adding a Subdivision Surface Modifier to Your Scene

The Subdivision Surface modifier is one of the most common modifiers used in models because it allows you to increase the details and smoothness of a low-resolution model interactively. You can change the number of subdivisions at any time to display a smoother surface. The modifier basically divides each polygon and smooths the result. As a rule of thumb, when you apply this modifier, the number of faces in your model is multiplied by 4 for each subdivision you apply; therefore, be mindful of the polygon count when setting high subdivision values. You can use this modifier to smooth out your monkey-head object, as shown in Figure 3.7.

When you add a modifier, you'll get a panel in the modifier stack with options that will be specific to the modifier you pick. These are the main options you'll find with a Subdivision Surface modifier:

- In the top row of the modifier's panel, you'll be able to expand/collapse the modifier (clicking the little triangle to the left), name it intuitively (useful when you have a lot of modifiers added to an object), and define in which contexts this modifier should be visible. There are two buttons with arrows pointing up and

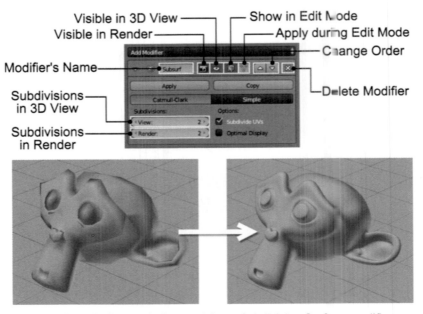

Figure 3.7   Before and after applying a Subdivision Surface modifier

down that you can use to change the order of the modifiers when you have more than one in the stack. Clicking the X button will delete the modifier.

- Next, you'll find two buttons: Apply and Copy. Apply will transfer the effect of the modifier to the object itself. It deletes the modifier but its effect on the object is permanent. Copy just duplicates the modifier.

- Under the Subdivisions section, you'll have two sliders where you can define the number of subdivisions that the modifier will perform in the 3D View and in the render. This is very useful because when you're in the 3D View, you usually want to save resources to ensure that this view is responsive, but in a render you want a high-quality result. You can set a low number of subdivisions for the 3D View and a higher number for the render.

Copying Modifiers to Other Objects

When you apply a modifier, it only affects the active object, which is the last selected object (even if you have 20 selected objects). If you want that modifier to be applied to every object in the selection, there are two methods to do this:

1. Press **Ctrl + L** to access a menu of linking options. In this menu, you'll find an option that lets you copy modifiers or materials from the active object to the rest of the selection (so just make sure to select the one you want to copy from last).

2. Activate the *Copy Attributes* add-on and press **Ctrl + C** to access a special menu to copy attributes from the active object to the rest of the selected objects. Within those attributes, you'll find the modifiers as well.

Blender Render and Cycles

Blender has different built-in render engines: *Blender Render* and *Cycles*. In the middle of the Info Editor (the bar at the top of the interface), you'll find a button that lets you select the render engine you want to use. By default, Blender Render is selected, and if you click the button, you'll see two other options: Blender Game and Cycles. Blender Game allows you to play with real-time graphics as if Blender were a game engine. You can create games and interactive content that will run in the Blender Game engine.

Blender Render is the "old" engine; it allows you to setup materials that simulate reality, but it's just a simulation, so achieving realistic results can be difficult. Although it's not a realistic render engine, if you control its parameters, materials, and lighting correctly, you can achieve pretty realistic renders with good quality. By its nature and because it is not as realistically accurate, it's also a lot faster than Cycles and that makes it a nice alternative for nonrealistic rendering or when you're short on time.

Cycles, on the other hand, is slower, but it's a physically based render engine, so light and materials behave realistically using mathematical functions that simulate real light behavior. Light bounces off surfaces and generates indirect lighting, just as real light would. Getting a realistic result with Cycles is much easier. However, it requires different skills because Cycles is designed to use materials built with nodes, but when creating very basic materials you don't really need to use nodes at all. Cycles also lets you render using GPU, so if you have a good graphics card, you can speed up your render times considerably.

You need to decide which render engine you want to use before you start building the materials for your scene. For the most part, the different engines are not compatible and their lighting systems are also quite different, so switching between the engines once you have your materials set up is usually not a good idea. You would have to rearrange your materials or even build them again from scratch so they would work properly in the other engine.

Materials

Materials define how an object looks, such as what its color is, whether the object is dull or shiny, or if it is reflective or transparent. With materials, you can make an object look like glass, metal, plastic, or wood. In the end, both materials and lighting define how your objects look. In this section, you'll see how to use materials for both Blender Render and Cycles.

From the Materials tab (the shiny red sphere icon) in the Properties Editor, you can add new materials or select existing ones from the drop-down list shown in Figure 3.8. A single object can have more than one material and these materials appear in the list at the top of the material properties. You can add and remove new slots for materials with the + and – buttons to the right side of the list, and you can assign each one of them to a selection of faces when you're in Edit Mode.

Blender Render Materials

In Blender Render, all materials are built in the same way: you have a set of parameters and you can build any kind of material using them. For example, you can activate transparency and reflections (Mirror) to simulate materials such as glass or metal. Each

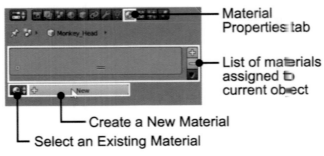

Figure 3.8   On the Material Properties tab, you'll use this menu to add new materials.

one of these attributes has different parameters, such as color, intensity, hardness, and glossiness. Here are brief descriptions of some of the main options available:

- **Diffuse:** The main color of the material.
- **Specular:** The color, intensity, and hardness of a material's shine.
- **Shading:** The different shadowing over a material. The Shadeless option makes the material completely unaffected by lights and shadows in the scene.
- **Transparency:** The transparency of the material. The basic attribute is Z Transparency and it is very fast to render because it just reduces the material's opacity. Raytrace is more accurate and offers some parameters for controlling the refraction to make it look more realistic.
- **Mirror:** The reflectivity of the material; this option allows you to define the glossiness (roughness) of the reflections.

Cycles Materials

In Cycles, the process of building materials is quite different. You can use the Node Editor with Blender Render to achieve complex materials, but Cycles only allows for the use of really basic materials if you're not willing to use nodes. Don't worry; for now, we'll keep it simple. Inside a Cycles material, you'll find the Surface panel, which includes various types of surface shaders.

- **Diffuse:** Creates a basic material with only color on it, but no shine, reflection, or other special properties
- **Glossy:** Makes the material reflective and shiny
- **Emission:** Makes the material emit light into the scene
- **Transparent:** Lets light pass through the material
- **Glass:** Simulates a glass surface
- **Mix:** Mixes two different shaders to achieve a more elaborate effect on the material

There are many surface shaders; these are just some of the main ones. Each one of the shaders has different parameters to control how light affects it, such as *color* and *roughness,* for example. Accessing nodes makes it easier to create complex and custom materials by combining the effects of some of the shaders above and using textures (you'll learn more about this in Chapter 10).

Adding Materials to Your Scene

To add some color to your scene, add two new materials. This is a very basic setup that you should be able to accomplish easily in both Cycles and Blender Render.

1. Select the monkey head.
2. Click the Materials tab in the Properties Editor.

3. Add a new basic material and set the diffuse color to red.

4. Repeat the process with the floor, but set the material to white.

Turning on the Lights

You already have materials set up, so now it's time to make the scene look more realistic with some light and shadows. Lights are compatible with Blender Render and Cycles, but given the different nature of both render engines, the lights have different effects, so if you switch from one render engine to another, you may need to adjust their parameters. Also, one of the benefits of Cycles is that because it is a realistic render engine, it allows you to use emissive materials, which can turn any mesh into a light emitter to illuminate the scene. This can simulate cool and very realistic effects that cannot be achieved with normal lights. In this first scene, we're only going to use a couple of point lights (Chapter 14 will provide more information about lighting).

Light Options in Blender Render

In Blender Render, if you go to the Lamp tab in the Properties Editor (the yellow star icon that appears when you have a lamp selected), you'll find options such as Color and Energy (Intensity). You can select the type of light as well. Also, in the Shadow panel, you can deactivate the shadows or control how they look: the Soft Size parameter makes the shadow softer, but you may need to increase the Samples to make it look better. Usually, around 7 is adequate, but go higher if you need more quality; fewer samples result in a noisy shadow. Keep in mind that adding more samples will increase render time.

Lights Options in Cycles

When you access the same Lamp tab in Cycles, the options for light properties are different. You may need to click the Use Nodes button to activate all the options. You can also control the type of light; the Size parameter adjusts the softness of the shadows and, under the Nodes panel, you can set the light's Color and Strength.

Light options in Cycles may look rather simplistic; this is because Cycles is a physically realistic render engine and there are no "artificial" settings such as shadow quality.

Adding Lights to Your Scene

Follow these steps to create a basic lighting scheme for your scene. Remember, you can access the menu for adding new objects to the scene with the **Shift + A** keyboard shortcut.

1. Select the light in your scene or create a new one if you don't have a light yet.

2. Duplicate the light and place it to the other side of the scene to fill the shadow areas.

3. Arrange the intensity and colors of your lights so that the one on the right is brighter, while the one on the left is dimmer and has a different color. We want the main light to come from the right, so that one should be brighter.

Moving the Camera in Your Scene

Of course, you need a camera in your scene so Blender knows from which point of view to look when it takes the final render.

1. Select the camera in your scene or create a new one (**Shift + A**) if you deleted it previously.

2. Place the camera so it's focused on the monkey head from a point of view that appeals to you. You can divide the interface into two different 3D Views; in one of them, you can look through the camera (**NumPad 0**), while in the other view, you can adjust the placement of the camera. Also, you can use the Walk or Fly mode (**Shift + F**) to position and orient the camera while in Camera View.

Figure 3.9 shows what your scene should look like.

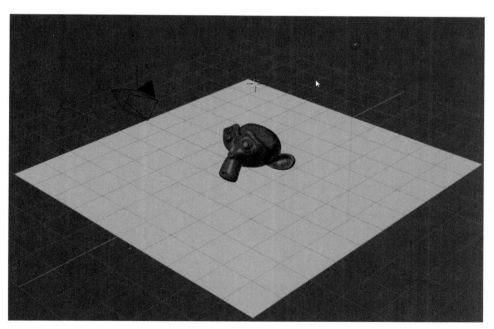

Figure 3.9   At this point, your scene should look something like this.
The monkey is on the floor, the camera is pointing at it, and two lights
are illuminating everything in the scene.

Real Time Rendering

In Blender, you have options to see a rendered preview in the 3D View, while you work and adjust parameters. It's very useful to be able to see what's going on in the scene and how the shadows and materials behave as you arrange them.

Real Time Rendering, in this case, is not actually "real time"; it just means that you are performing the render interactively, and you can change things in the scene as you render it. The speed of the render depends, of course, on your computer's processing speed. If you are using Cycles and you have a powerful GPU, you may want to use that GPU to increase the speed of the rendering.

To access Real Time Rendering Mode, just change the drawing method from the 3D View header to "Rendered." When you're done, you can go back to Solid Mode or any other 3D View display mode. Keep in mind that when you use the Real Time Rendering Mode, you won't see the selection highlights or manipulators, so you may want to keep a second 3D View open to manipulate objects.

Rendering

Rendering is the process that converts your 3D scene into a 2D image. During this process, Blender calculates the properties of materials and lights in the scene to apply shadows, reflections, refractions, and so forth—everything you need to build your cool final result and turn it into an image or a video.

To set the resolution and format for the image, you need to go to the Render Properties tab in the Properties Editor (the camera icon). You can set the resolution in the Dimensions panel and the format in the Output panel. (The output is not needed for still images, as you can save them after the render, but you should set it if you're rendering an animation.) After selecting a resolution and format, click Render to complete this simple process. Now, let's see the difference between rendering with Blender Render and Cycles.

Rendering in Blender Render

There are a lot of options you can adjust for the render, but in Blender Render there aren't many important options to configure. You can set up things like the anti-aliasing samples to get a smoother render or improve the performance depending on your computer's specs, but for this basic scene the render is adequate as it is.

Rendering in Cycles

However, if you render in Cycles, you'll need to increase the samples. Cycles uses samples to render, so if you don't use enough samples, you'll get a noisy image. Each sample refines the scene further, so with more samples, you get cleaner renders. This is handy for doing quick test renders and not spending lots of time because even if the render is noisy, you can get an idea of how everything is working, so you can change the number of samples based on how much time you have.

On the Render Properties tab, look for the Sampling panel and set the render samples to some higher number, such as 100. (Depending on your computer, this may result in a very slow render, so keep that in mind.)

Saving and Loading Your .blend File

Now you're at a good point to save your file. Rendering can take some time and something can go wrong in the meantime (power failures, software crashes, etc.) that could cause you to lose your work. That's why it's recommended that you save your file often.

You can save your file by pressing **Ctrl + S**. If you're saving it for the first time, Blender will display a menu where you can select the location where you want to store your file and how you want to name it. If you've saved the file previously, **Ctrl + S** will overwrite that previous version. If you press **Shift + Ctrl + S,** Blender will display the Save menu again so you can select Save As.... This allows you to create a new copy of the file with a different name.

To open a file, press **Ctrl + O** and Blender will show you the folder navigation menu where you can look for the .blend file you want to open. In the File menu, you can also access the Open Recent... option, which shows you a list of the latest files you've worked on so you can quickly open them. Of course, you don't need to use those shortcuts if you don't remember them; you can always access the Save and Load options from the File menu.

> **Tip**
>
> There's a little trick for saving different versions of a file really fast. Sometimes, you want to save your progress in a new file, so you can end up with different files from different parts of the process, allowing you to go back to a previous version if necessary.
>
> Go to the Save As... menu (or press **Shift + Ctrl + S**) and press the NumPad + key: Blender will automatically add a number to the filename. If the filename is already numbered, Blender will add 1 to it.

Launching and Saving the Render

You can start your render from the Render Properties tab in the Render panel. You'll find three options there Render (still frame), Animation (render an animation of several frames), and Audio (renders only audio). You can also use shortcuts: **F12** will render a still frame and **Ctrl + F12** will render an animation. (If you render an animation, make sure you configure the output file path and format on the Render tab, so the images are saved automatically where and how you want.)

When you start rendering, you'll see the process inside a UV/Image Editor, and once the render is complete, you can save the resulting image. Press **F3** to save or go to the *Image* menu on the header of the UV/Image Editor to access the *Save as Image* option. Press **Esc** to return to the 3D View.

Figure 3.10   The results of these very basic renders with
Blender Render (top) and Cycles (bottom).

Figure 3.10 shows the images that result from both engines' renders It's clear that even with a really basic scene, Cycles gives more realistic results (but it also takes more time to render).

Summary

You've learned how to create and move objects, add modifiers and materials, and launch a render. This chapter gives you a lot to process, but hopefully you've got the basics of how to interact with your scene, so now you can go deeper and you're ready for the more extensive information in the chapters to follow.

Exercises

1. Create and manipulate a few objects.
2. Add some other modifiers and play with them to see what their effects are.
3. Add more lights to the scene and play with materials to improve the results.

Beginning a Project

4

Project Overview

Every project has different steps you need to follow in order to be successful. The order in which you proceed through the steps to reach the final result can be called the "workflow" or "pipeline." In this chapter, you'll learn about the process you will follow throughout the rest of the book to create a character from scratch. You'll gain basic knowledge about how you can divide any project into stages and execute it. In the next section, you'll learn about the three main stages that a project goes through.

The Three Stages of a Project

Usually, any project in 3D, graphics, or video goes through three different stages: preproduction, production, and postproduction.

Preproduction

Preproduction is everything that happens before the actual production of a project, such as preliminary sketches, ideas, designs, and planning. It's probably the most crucial stage of any project, and a lot of amateur projects fail because of the lack of good preproduction. (Some projects don't have any preproduction at all!)

When you plan and organize what you will need to do to complete a project, chances are you're going to be better prepared for what's to come. If you skip preproduction and jump right into production because you can't wait to see the results, you'll likely encounter unexpected problems and issues you didn't anticipate. You'll have to redo a lot of work and lose lots of time or, in the worst-case scenario, you'll give up.

Good planning allows you to anticipate any possible problems before they actually happen and this way you can prevent them from occurring. If you run into something you don't know how to do, you can make some quick, basic tests to find a solution *before* you get far enough into the project to discover that it doesn't work.

As a result of this preparation, the actual work during production will be a lot faster, easier, and straight to the point, as you'll already know how to proceed. Keep in mind that even with a good preproduction stage, you will still run into issues. This is how it goes, but at least a lot of those issues will be handled before they become bigger problems, so the more preparation, the better.

There is another important advantage to preproduction: it can motivate you during the production stage. When you think about everything you'll have to do and then define the process step by step, it suddenly gets easier because you don't have a *big* project before you, but instead you have a list of small and manageable tasks. You'll go through this list, keeping track of your progress, and you'll always know what you have done so far, what you still need to do, and what may be missing.

There is a popular phrase that sums up preproduction pretty well: *"Think twice, work half."* A great result doesn't come from working harder, but from working more efficiently. You need to think of efficient ways to work. Usually, you'll discover them only after you've done something wrong, but that's when you learn and gain valuable experience!

Production

Once you have everything planned for a project, it's time to start with the actual job, which is production. In a movie, for example, production would be the stage of the project in which the sets are built and the scenes are filmed with the actors and props in place as planned during preproduction. Thorough preproduction will help you complete production more easily and in a more straightforward process.

Production is probably the hardest stage of a project because it's the point of no return. After production is completed, it's very difficult to change things. Let's say you're building a house; during preproduction, it's very easy to change the design of the house using a computer or an architectural drawing, but it's really difficult and time-consuming to make changes once the walls are in place!

That's why preproduction is crucial: it helps you make sure you're not going to make mistakes while you're developing the final product. Production is difficult enough; there are a lot of challenges and it's impossible to predict every possible problem that might arise until you're actually making the product, so any preparations you can make to smooth out the process helps a lot.

Postproduction

Postproduction is everything that happens between production and the final result. It's like putting the finishing touches on a new house with details such as painting the walls and adding interior decoration. In a movie, it would be the stage in the process in which you add the final visual effects and retouch what was filmed during production.

Depending on the project, postproduction can be easy or hard, simple or complex, and it can involve just minor details or something really important. Postproduction is when you actually decide how the finished project will look.

Suppose you film two actors having a conversation inside a room. During postproduction, you can color correct the scene, switch it from day to night, change what will be seen through a window, blur things out, zoom in, or even add a new character! The possibilities are endless and they will define what people will see when you release your image, video, film, or whatever your project may be.

Defining the Stages

Now you know the three main stages that a project goes through, but it's very important to know where each stage ends and the next one starts, as each project is different. Let's study some examples to understand these differences better.

A Film without Visual Effects

Today, almost every single film has some visual effects. However, let's consider a film that doesn't have any visual effects. This will help you understand the basic process of film production, and then we'll discuss some different production options.

> **Note**
>
> Remember that visual effects are not just explosions, spaceships, aliens, or monsters. There are a lot of visual effects (commonly referred to as invisible effects) that are much more subtle and you may not notice them while you're watching a film. Set-extensions, background replacements or set cleaning, for example, are present in almost every single movie you watch and they are also visual effects.

During preproduction, the filmmakers create the film's script and decide what will be the climax moments (and maybe even film them to test whether they really work). Every film goes through storyboarding, the process of making quick drawings to define where the cameras will be positioned and what will happen on each shot, so the production team can plan each shot, see what they'll need on set, know what type of lenses to use in the camera, and identify where the actors will be positioned. Then, the filmmakers search for the locations where they're going to film the scenes. They also have to create the costumes the actors will wear and all the props they'll have to interact with. Then the filmmakers cast the actors and all of the extras who will appear in the film. Finally, the filmmakers must assemble the technicians who will film the movie and manage all the equipment, build the sets, and so forth. Usually, composers begin to develop the music at this stage so that a rough edit of the film can be made using the storyboard and the timing of each shot can be defined.

Everything is now ready to start filming, so production begins. At this point, the actors already know the script and the team knows what they need to do on each shot and what has to appear on camera. Production is usually not a very long process; because all aspects of the project were organized during preproduction, the production stage (the most expensive stage) is as short as possible. When production is completed, the movie has been filmed according to the decisions made during preproduction about where, when, how, and with whom.

Once filming is completed, postproduction can begin. The film must be edited at this point, perhaps by using some color correction to make a scene look more vivid, warm, or cold, depending on the feeling the director wants each scene to convey to the audience. Perhaps the director decides that a shot would work better if the main actor's face were closer, so the video editor zooms in a little. Suppose the name of a business appears in the background and the director doesn't want it to be recognizable; some simple visual effects can remove it or replace it with the name of another business that will pay the filmmakers for advertising! This is the point at which the last retouches are added to the film, the complete soundtrack and all the sound effects are included, and the final result is achieved.

A Visual Effects Film

Let's now analyze the differences that a film with complex visual effects would have compared to the previous example.

During preproduction, the production team would need to think about what visual effects to use, how they're going to be filmed, and what will be required to create them. Generally, the visual effects team works very closely with the director during preproduction to see what's possible, what's not possible, and how the effects will be achieved. (Usually, almost anything is possible in visual effects; it just may be way too expensive for a particular film's budget.)

During production, the visual effects team may need to film some shots in special ways, using green screens or using markers or puppets the actors can interact with so that later the team can add an animated character to that scene. Lighting in the sets has to be measured and recorded, so the team can simulate it later in the 3D world to make it match the lighting on the real set. Some effects like explosions may need to be filmed separately so they can later be integrated with the footage of the actors.

After the movie has been filmed, it's time to begin the postproduction stage, but because this film involves visual effects, the line between production and postproduction tends to blur and sometimes these stages actually overlap. The visual effects artists probably work on some shots even before production begins so that during filming, all the different elements that comprise a scene will fit together seamlessly.

The visual effects team has its own preproduction, production, and postproduction stages. They plan the specific effects and determine how a shot will be accomplished; then they proceed to production and work to create the elements of the visual effects, and finally combine those elements, adjusting colors, shapes, textures, and so forth.

An Animated Film

The stages of an animated film are even more difficult to distinguish, as the entire film is computer-generated, the line between production and postproduction is not so clear.

During preproduction, all aspects of the film are planned and designed as usual, but then production and postproduction tend to overlap because every aspect of these stages happens in the 3D software. Usually, it's easier to divide the stages, with production creating the action (developing characters, sets, and animation), and post-production creating the effects such as water, splashes, particles, cloth, dust, smoke, fire, explosions and other simulations. Then, the final compositing will bring all these diverse elements together.

A Photograph

Yes, even something as simple as a photograph can be divided into the three production stages. Even if photographers are not conscious of it, they're performing the stages of production with their own photos.

First, photographers complete the preproduction stage by thinking about what they're going to shoot and where. During production, they must go to the location, pose the subject, and finally take the photo. Then, even using a smart phone, they can do some postproduction work such as adding an aging effect to the photo, or increasing its contrast, or maybe even changing it to black and white.

A Character-Creation Plan

Now that you have a better understanding about the three main stages of a project, let's define the process you'll follow throughout the remainder of this book to create a complete 3D-animated character.

Preproduction

A character-creation process starts, of course, with a character design.

- **Designing:** Make some drawings to define what the character will look like, what clothes it will wear, and what features might suggest its personality.

Production

This stage can be rather complex and extensive because it's the main part of the process in which you go from the design to the completed character.

- **Modeling:** Model the 3D character in Blender following the design you created in the preproduction stage.
- **Unwrapping:** Turn the 3D model into a two-dimensional mesh internally so you can project a 2D image texture on it.
- **Texturing:** Paint the textures for the various aspects of the 3D model's surface, such as clothing textures, skin, hair color, and so forth.
- **Shading:** Take texturing a step further by creating materials that will define the surface properties of your character, such as how reflective or shiny they will be, or whether they will be rough or smooth.

- **Rigging:** Add a skeleton to your character and define how it will work and how it will control the character.
- **Animating:** Pose the character using keyframes at different times of an animation to make the character perform an action such as walking or running.
- **Video recording:** Record a video into which you'll place your character later.

Postproduction

Once the character is finished, there is still some work to do to make it look pleasing or to put it into a scene.

- **Camera tracking:** Simulate a camera's movement in the actual footage you record so you end up with a camera in the 3D world that will move similarly to the real camera and allow you to insert 3D elements into your video.
- **Lighting:** Add lighting to your scene to make the lights and shadows fit the video you recorded during the production phase. The addition of lighting is usually part of the production stage, but because this project's main goal is the creation of a character, this time lighting will be part of postproduction.
- **Rendering:** Convert the 3D scene into a 2D image with shadows and lighting.
- **Compositing:** Take the video and the 3D objects, combine them, and make any necessary adjustments to them so they fit together and look realistic.

Summary

Now you have an idea of the process you're going to go through to create your own animated character and you understand the three main stages of every project. Preproduction is especially important and you have to keep that in mind for future projects. A lot of people fail even after significant planning and preparation, so imagine the probability of failing if you don't make thoughtful preparations and design choices in preproduction. Almost every professional 3D artist has gone through this process and understands the importance of preparing and organizing projects beforehand. Take advantage of learning from their experiences!

Now you're ready to start working on the actual project!

Exercises

1. Take any movie that you like and imagine how it would be divided into preproduction, production, and postproduction.
2. Have you ever had a project fail? Analyze where you failed and think about how you'd do the project differently using the three stages discussed in this chapter.

5

Character Design

The first part of your character-creation project will, of course, be preproduction. When building a character, preproduction is usually considered the design process. There are a lot of ways to design a character and each artist has a different method. In this chapter, you'll explore one of the most common approaches that you can later adapt according to your skills. Some other methods will be noted so you can try them if they sound interesting to you.

You can use any medium to design your character: paper or digital. In this chapter, the whole process is carried out in a digital medium using digital painting software and a pen tablet, but of course you can use any other painting medium.

Character Description

Before you start drawing or imagining what clothes a character will wear, how big its eyes will be, or what color to make its hair, you need to have at least a basic idea of who your character is. The design will ultimately represent the character's personality, so understanding how that character thinks and acts will help you represent it. For example, it's easier to know the type of clothes the character will wear if you know its profession; if it's a knight or a soldier, it will wear armor or battle gear, but if it's an accountant, wearing armor or carrying a weapon would make no sense at all, no matter how cool it looks!

Also, the attitude of a character can define its looks: a very dynamic character would be fast moving, while a sad character would probably tend to slouch and move very slowly. A happy character could have a big smile and large, expressive eyes, while a depressed character might have small, tearful eyes and a mouth that frowns.

Basically, developing a good description of your character will definitely help you understand how it would behave; as a result, you can get into its head and imagine what it would wear and how it would walk, talk, smile, laugh, and cry. Different people can react in completely different ways to the same situation and this also applies to the characters you create.

You don't need to develop the character's complete history or personality if you don't want to go that far. A simple description of its personality and how it looks would be enough. So let's take a look at a brief description of the character you'll build in this book. Let's call the character Jim. From now on, you need to have a personal relationship with Jim to be able to understand how he thinks and acts. Consider Jim a living being and not just a thing.

> **Note**
>
> Learning about body language helps a lot when determining how a character with a specific attitude would look, including the clothes it would wear. Reading a specialized book on the subject is highly recommended if you want to design great characters.

Personality

A description of Jim appears below. The various aspects of his personality are related and some of them are influenced by the others: for example, a lazy person would never want to be an adventurer, and if you don't tend to be happy and love challenges, there is no way you would go into the unknown to discover new things—you need lots of motivation for that. The lesson here is that the aspects of a character's personality must be coherent (unless for some reason the story requires it to be otherwise).

> Jim is a 15-year-old kid. He is very active and participates in a lot of sports with his friends. He always looks happy, he likes challenges, and his dream is to become an adventurer and discover new things. His ambitions are motivated by his never-ending curiosity and, as a result of his curiosity, he pays a lot of attention to details. He also likes to be different from the rest of the kids his age. And . . . he manages to get himself into trouble quite often.

Context

You now have a basic understanding of Jim's personality, but there is another very important thing that defines a character and that is the story's context, or the world in which the character dwells. Let's check it out:

> It's the year 2512 and humans have populated quite a few planets. Space exploration is the major topic in the news and astronauts are treated as heroes. Cars now fly and don't produce pollution. Robots are everywhere, making human life easier, and some even develop relationships with humans. A downside of this very futuristic setting is that it's difficult for an individual to stand out from the rest of the population: everyone wears the same kind of clothes, everyone owns similar cars, and everyone lives in buildings that look the same.

Can you see how this context could affect what Jim would look like? Also, humans living on several planets across the universe and space exploration is the focus of the news every day are good reasons to make a young boy dream about being an astronaut, right? If the context was in prehistory, a kid's dreams would be very different: maybe he'd want to be a mighty hunter or a fearsome shaman.

Context (where he lives, his culture, and his relationships) clearly defines your character's personality and ways of thinking and acting. In Jim's case, his context encourages him to be an adventurer, explore space, and find new planets ... or even aliens!

Style

Before you begin to imagine how your character would look, the style you'll aim for has to be defined. In this case, let's opt for a cartoony look. The reason for this is that while you'll learn the full animation process, we don't want to make Jim so complex that his animated character is hard to achieve. So for learning purposes, Jim will have smooth shapes without too many details.

We'll keep him simple, but we still want him to look cool. You can go for something more realistic, something dark, or even kind of abstract; just decide ahead of time and create some drawings, or find some photos or other materials to help you determine his style, as this will be essential to how the character ultimately looks.

Something else you want to keep on the table while you define the style (and every other thing that has to do with the appearance of a character) is technical limitations. For example, you might not want to have really long hair on a character, as it will make the animation or simulations much more complex.

Also, style depends on the medium in which the character will be used. In movies, you can use more detail and complexity, as there will be time to render each frame, but if you're working on a videogame character, the limitations are greater, as the character needs to work in real time, so you would need to use fewer polygons, less resolution in textures, or less complicated effects in order to increase the performance and allow a computer (or a console) to render the images in real time.

Appearance

Now that we have Jim's personality, the context of his world, and his style, we can start thinking about his appearance. For example, he lives in a futuristic environment; when we think of futuristic worlds, we often picture plain-colored clothes with clean lines, so white and blue clothes could look right.

Here, it's OK to use clichés because certain characteristics are embedded in people's minds and give them an idea about a character or theme; that's precisely why clichés work, so don't fear or avoid them.

Let's say that clothes in the future are tight and fitted to the body. Furthermore, Jim is healthy, active, and plays sports; he's in good shape, so it wouldn't be a problem for him to wear closefitting clothes as he wouldn't be ashamed of his body. Also, he's an adventurer, so maybe he worries less about appearance and more about clothes that are functional as well as comfortable.

In the character's description, it was mentioned that he liked to be different from everyone else, so if everyone wears similar clothes, he would surely add some unique details to his attire to represent that attitude: maybe a pin, perhaps a jaunty hat (this would also help represent him as adventurous), or even some kind of reference to space travel and exploration.

Designing the Character

In this section, you'll follow a typical process you can use to create a character. It usually progresses from more general concerns to more detailed considerations: you start creating the basic shapes and then, little by little, you refine them and add color to get to the final result.

Silhouettes

It's a good idea to start with quick sketches and basic shapes that will help you explore and find the right proportions for your character (see Figure 5.1). Then, you can pick the ones you like and keep developing and adding details to them. This is a technique a lot of artists use when designing a character. Silhouettes are very important and a great character design is recognizable by its silhouette. You can recognize *Super Mario, Mickey Mouse,* or *Sonic* just by seeing their silhouettes; this means they have an original and unique design.

In this case, you're just learning about 3D character creation, not designing the ultimate marketable character, so we don't need the whole world to recognize Jim by his shape. The goal is to design a character that looks cool and has personality.

Looking at the silhouettes in Figure 5.1, you can see how, from the same character description, you can imagine completely different shapes for a character. Now you have

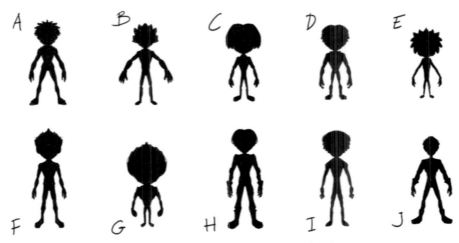

Figure 5.1   The silhouettes of Jim drawn for the purpose
of studying the desired proportions and shapes

to decide which one you like the most, or which one best fits the style you're looking for. In this case, let's say the silhouettes we like the most for their shapes and proportions are A and F. They're kind of realistic, but have big hands, big feet, and big heads. A big head (in comparison to the body size) will help to identify Jim as a kid; for example, look at J and you'll see that it looks more like an adult, as its head is smaller, and E, with a really big head compared to the body, resembles a little boy.

In Figure 5.2, you can see the final silhouette. It is a mix of the versions we liked the most but with a little more detail. The first silhouettes were just quick little thumbnails to get an idea for Jim's shape, while the final one is bigger and has more detail so it can be used as a reference in the next stage. It doesn't yet have the clothing details or the hat; they will be added later over the base design. For now, all you need is a quick glance at the character's main shape.

Note

The silhouettes in Figures 5.1 and 5.2 were done using **Krita**, a free open-source painting software that you should check out. You can look for more information at www.krita.org. There are more alternatives for painting, of course, and you can use any other software you feel comfortable with; some alternatives are MyPaint, Painter, Gimp, Photoshop, and Manga Studio, among others. A feature that was very useful for the silhouettes is mirror painting; it allows you to mirror in real time what you're painting on the opposite side of the canvas, which really speeds up the process—you see the full shape coming together while only painting one side of it.

Base Design

Next, you're going to create your base design by taking your final thumbnail and turning it into a drawing. Just sketch some strokes around the borders and define some of

Figure 5.2 The final silhouette is a mix of versions A and F.

the figure's interior shapes. At this stage, you want to end up with a basic version of the character, so don't worry too much about details; you'll add those in the next pass.

You'll also be adding clothing at this stage and you can place as many different variations as you want over the silhouette. It's OK to explore and create different versions of this base design, so that later on you can choose the designs you like, mix them together, and keep modifying them until you achieve the design you like best. However, keep in mind you don't want to add things that will make the design too complex later, so you should avoid complex design elements and aim for a more easily achievable design.

There is no need for a really refined drawing at this point; a quick rough sketch will do, such as the one in Figure 5.3. It will help you understand how the character may eventually look so that later you can dive into the specific design of each of its parts, and finally combine everything for a clean finished version. If something doesn't look great, don't worry, there's still a lot of time to change things and get them to work nicely.

As you can see, the hairstyle is not yet well defined; that's one of the parts of the character that will require some technical thinking, as hair is always a challenge. If you want to go for realistic hair particles (you can use 3D particles to grow hair on a surface, comb it, and cut it to create the hairstyle, and later add the effects of gravity or wind to it), you need to have a detailed understanding of how they look and move to make sure your hairstyle will work when designed using particles (otherwise it's easy to screw things up). If you prefer to go with a hand-modeled mesh, you'll have more options, but you'll also want to keep in mind the limitations of the mesh method. For this character, you will use a mesh, as it's easier, and for this type of character design it will work just fine.

For now, Jim's face is also just a placeholder that you will finish in the next section of this chapter.

Figure 5.3   Comparison between the final silhouette and the base design

Designing the Head

Now it's time to start the head, face, and hairstyle design. Maybe it's a good time to try hats, as well (as they'll affect the hairstyle). Figure 5.4 shows several sketches for Jim's face. Keep in mind that you probably won't come up with anything great during your first tries. (For this figure, I'm only showing you my best attempts.) You should keep drawing and designing until you're happy with the result; it might take hundreds of drawings or you may be lucky and find something you like on the first try. (Don't count on that, though!)

Looking at all the designs, let's opt for the one featuring a cap, as it will give Jim some personality and will look cool. It will also cover a big part of the head, making the hair creation a lot easier!

A typical baseball cap may not be very common in 2512 because people in that future society may wear crazy stuff on their heads, but remember how Jim wanted to be different? Here, you'll only be creating Jim, but if you also had to depict the city where he lives and more of its citizens, he would surely look different just by wearing a baseball cap in 2512.

Figure 5.4   Different sketches for Jim's head and some studies with a cap

Adding Details

You now have a base design for Jim's body and his head, so it's time to add the details. Maybe you don't know how to draw or paint, but don't worry! The goal with these designs is not to make them look perfect. Designs are mainly just sketches and quick drawings that help you to understand the shapes of your character. Understanding the character and how its details are constructed allows you to translate everything into the 3D model.

For example, let's say that you are modeling a watch. If you start modeling right away, maybe you'll end up encountering some issues and failing. Maybe it won't look right or realistic, and the reason is usually that you didn't study the shapes. It's always good to look for references and use them when you design something. You can even go ahead with only an idea in your head, but it's recommended that you put it on paper (or a screen) so you can actually see the design and explore it before diving into the 3D modeling process.

Figure 5.5 shows some of the sketches made to define Jim's clothing and the details selected for the definitive design. They were drawn from several points of view. The jacket, for example, has designs on its front and back. This is important because we probably wouldn't need the back side for a 2D model, but in a 3D model every side is equally important!

There are rectilinear lines along the whole suit, maintaining the style and making everything look more elaborate than just a plain surface. The shoulders, elbows, and

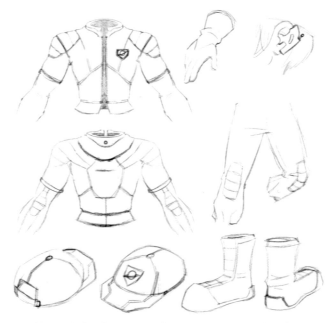

Figure 5.5   Sketches of character design details, including clothes, earpiece, boots, gloves, and cap

knees have padding, which gives the clothes the look of a uniform and is just what we want for Jim, since everyone in the future is wearing the same kind of suits.

Jim is also wearing an earpiece to listen to music or receive calls. The cap is also a personal detail to distinguish him from others and he's going to wear it turned around, like a rebel. His personality can probably be reflected in the colors of his clothes as well. Maybe some parts of the suit will be a different color to stand out from the clothes worn by the rest of the people in his world; that will be explored later in the coloring stage.

The back side of the jacket has a small backpack where the suit's electronic systems may be stored. The cut in the arms, above the elbows, seems to resemble what we see in today's astronaut suits.

There is also another detail added to the suit. Jim put space exploration symbols on the chest and on the front side of the cap; these symbols, along with the uniform-like style of the clothes, makes him look like an actual space explorer. For those symbols, I used Saturn, which is a very recognizable planet and a known icon of space exploration.

Refining the Design

At this point, you have a clear understanding of how everything looks: the face, hair, and clothes, as well as other details. Before you create the final artwork, let's get back to the base design and add some additional details. Also, it's a good time to sketch a view of the character from the back (see Figure 5.6).

Figure 5.6 Refined design over the base design, and a design for the back of the character

Everything is in place and looking good! Next, let's do some color testing.

Adding Color

Now that the base design is complete, it's time to add some colors to Jim and see how he looks with different color schemes (if you have been working on paper up to this point, this is a good time to scan your design and start using the computer, as it allows for testing more than one color scheme for the same design and for easy retouches). We need a version of Jim's front view with clean lines that allow us to use the color bucket in our editing program to quickly fill in areas with color (see Figure 5.7). Store each part of the character in a different layer, which will let you play with the skin-color values, for example, without affecting the rest of the colors. With this method, you can try several different options and pick the ones you like the most.

With your colors well organized by layers, testing a new color scheme may only take a couple of minutes or so. In Figure 5.7, different hair colors were tried so you could see how the process works, but in this case, let's say we already know the hair is going to be blue, just like the eyes, as it will complement the bluish grays of the suit. Pick the definitive color scheme for Jim. Let's continue with the version in the middle, the blue-haired one, as the light tones of the suit have less contrast than the other two.

Figure 5.7   Testing different color schemes over the design

Final Design

At this point, making a final illustration of the character is possible, as you know how it's built, how it looks, and its design details. In Figure 5.8, you can see a final version of Jim. This level of quality is unnecessary for a preliminary design, but it helps us become familiar with the character to learn about him and understand his proportions and features. Also, it will sometimes even identify any potential problems in the character's design when you try to pose it and watch it from a particular perspective; for example, some pieces of the suit might not work properly in certain positions. Usually, when creating a complex character, concept artists will do a lot of illustrations like this to make sure the character looks not only cool but also realistic.

In the downloadable files for this book, you can find a video showing the painting process for this illustration.

Figure 5.8   Using the final design to create an illustration of Jim

Character Reference Images

Ok, so you've designed your character. If you're experienced, you probably can start modeling right away. If not and regardless of your expertise, you'll want to create some references to use in the 3D modeling program, so that you have at least a general idea of the character's size or basic shapes, which will make the modeling process much faster. These images will stay in the background of the 3D View while you model, so you can model on top of them to make the shapes fit those references. The reference images should represent the character in a neutral pose, as that is what you'll need to model the character. Cool poses will come later.

For our example, you'll need six different reference images that you can place in the 3D Views. You'll put these in the background and place your model on top of them.

- Head, front view
- Head, back view
- Head, side view
- Body, front view
- Body, back view
- Body, side view

These reference images will help you make sure your 3D model fits your original design. Design elements tend to change during the 2D to 3D conversion, as 2D and 3D are completely different worlds, but by using references, you'll get something in 3D that's closer and more proportional to the 2D design you created.

For the head views, hair isn't needed for now; because you'll be modeling the head shape at this stage, the hair will be added on top of that shape later (see Figure 5.9).

For the body views shown in Figure 5.10, you can see the side view doesn't have arms; this is intentional, as you don't want the arms to be in the way just yet. Later, you can model them from the front and back images. In the side view, there would not be much relevant information about them, and they would be covering the body of the character, which is just what you want to have visible in the side view.

Notice the horizontal lines in the sketch. These must always be aligned so the character's features are in the same position in all of the views; then later on, you won't have

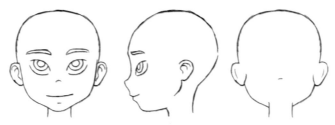

Figure 5.9   Face with front, side, and back views

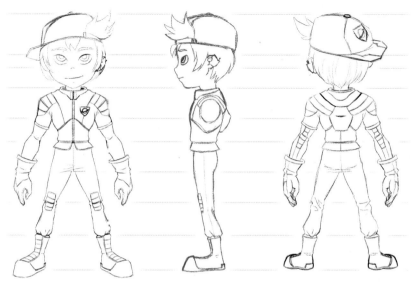

Figure 5.10   Body with front, side, and back views

trouble placing the characters in 3D. It's expected that your images won't be perfect; after all, they're hand drawings and there is always some level of error, but the better aligned they are, the easier it will be when you get to modeling. Otherwise, you'll have to do a lot of guess work when modeling your character because the reference images are not aligned and you may even have to reinvent some areas while you model.

> **Note**
>
> Feel free to play with these designs and change them to something that looks better to you or has a different style that you like more than this one. This may serve as a good starting point if you've never done character design and need some initial guidance. This should give you a base to start with and a method to follow, but you don't have to stick to it. Character design is a creative process, so be sure to try new things all the time!

Other Design Methods

As mentioned before, the method just described isn't the only one available for designing a character. A lot of artists, over time, create their own methods and techniques. The following list provides some other options you might try.

- Use a very simple 3D model made of spheres, cubes, or cylinders to quickly explore the silhouette's basic shape and proportions. This allows you to see how the character will look in 3D.

- Use random brushes in a painting program when exploring shapes. This will likely give you some unexpected results and let you discover cool things that you would otherwise have missed when working with pencil and paper.

- Use vector imaging software like Adobe Illustrator or Inkscape to test silhouettes. This is similar to the simple 3D-model method, but in 2D. What's cool about this method is that you can scale and rotate parts of the body very easily to try new things.

- Use the Skin modifier in Blender for character prototyping. You can look for information on how to use the Skin modifier: basically, you draw a character's skeleton with vertices and edges, and the Skin modifier gives it thickness and a solid mesh in which you can also control the thickness of each part. It's intended to be used to create base meshes for sculpting, but it is possible to use it to quickly test shapes for character creation.

- Use image compositing to pick parts of different photos or drawings and combine them to build your character's silhouette.

Summary

As you have seen, character design can be quite complex and you have to think about a lot of different elements. You can, of course, dive into the modeling with just an idea in mind, but that's probably going to be much more difficult, as you'll have to invent stuff on the fly. This design stage is crucial because it lets you define everything about your character: personality, attitude, looks, clothing, details, and so forth. Once you've done that, you'll know your character very well and you'll know it will look good once it's nicely modeled in 3D. Otherwise, you may find that after all your time and effort, the idea you had in mind was not clear enough and some things may not work as you expected they would.

Remember: preproduction is your friend!

Exercises

1. Check Jim's designs and see if you can add or replace certain elements to make the character look better.

2. If you're up for the challenge, design your own character!

Modeling in Blender

6

Blender Modeling Tools

Modeling is probably the most important stage in the character-creation process because it's the method you'll use to generate the polygons that will become the principal forms of your finished character. In this chapter, you'll learn the basics of modeling in Blender and how to use some of the main tools you'll have at your disposal. Then, in the next chapters, when one of these tools is mentioned, you'll be familiar with it. There are three primary technical considerations you need to address before you can properly model in 3D: identifying the elements that comprise a mesh, learning how to select them, and knowing what tools you can use to work with them. You'll learn about all of these subjects in this chapter.

Working with Vertices, Edges, and Faces

Every single 3D model is made out of the same three elements: vertices, edges, and faces. A vertex is a point in space. When you connect two vertices, you've created an edge and if you connect three or more vertices in a closed loop, then you've created a face. A face is basically a polygon. You can see these elements in Figure 6.1.

There are three types of faces: triangles, quads (four-sided faces), and n-gons (faces with more than four sides). In 3D, there is a "rule" that, if you can, you should use four-sided faces everywhere. The reason is that they deform better in animation, and if

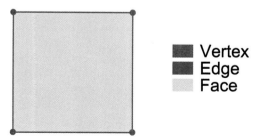

Figure 6.1   Vertices, edges, and faces—
the elements that make up every 3D mesh

you're going to use a Subdivision Surface modifier on the mesh, four-sided faces usually subdivide correctly. Triangles and n-gons can be problematic at times by creating "pinches" in the mesh.

There are some situations, though, in which using a triangle or an n-gon is more beneficial for the mesh; for example, in some complex formations, n-gons create better deformations and subdivisions than four-sided polygons. Experience in modeling is needed to discern those situations and there are a lot of articles by very experienced modelers on this subject that you're encouraged to look into, as it's not covered in the scope of this book.

Selecting Vertices, Edges, and Faces

The first thing you need to do to access these mesh elements is to enter Edit Mode through the Interaction Mode selector on the 3D View header, or press **Tab** on your keyboard. Once you're in Edit Mode, you'll be able to select vertices, edges, and faces. In Figure 6.2, you can see their icons on the header.

> **Tip**
>
> If you press Shift while you click on the element icons, you'll be able to select two types of elements at once. For example, in the Vertex selection mode, hold down **Shift** and left click the Edge icon and you'll be able to select vertices and edges at the same time.
>
> There is also a faster way to switch between the Vertex, Edge, and Face selection modes: just press **Ctrl + Tab** while in Edit Mode and a little pop-up menu will appear at your cursor's position with options to select these different elements.

Accessing Modeling Tools

There are different ways to access the modeling tools in Blender. You can access all the tools from menus, but most of the tools also have their own keyboard shortcuts to speed up the process. You can access the modeling tools as follows:

- **3D View header's Mesh menu:** In this menu, you'll find submenus for vertices, edges, and faces.
- **Tools Region (T):** Most of the main modeling tools are in the Tools Region when you're in Edit Mode.

Figure 6.2   The 3D View header and its icons
for selecting vertices, edges, and faces

- **Keyboard shortcuts to the 3DView will show these options:**
  - Vertices: **Ctrl + V**
  - Edges: **Ctrl + E**
  - Faces: **Ctrl + F**
  - Special tools: **W**

- **Search:** In Blender when you press the **spacebar,** a search menu will appear. You can type the name of the tool you want to use and then select it from the menu options to apply it.

Selections

In this section, you'll learn some tips about selections when you're in Edit Mode. For the most part, selections work exactly the same as they do in Object Mode (selecting objects was covered in Chapter 2), but in Edit Mode they will be applied to vertices, edges, or faces. For example, you can add to a selection by pressing **Shift** or you can do a box selection by pressing **B**. However, the following sections cover a few selection techniques that are available only in Edit Mode.

Shortest Path

If you right click to select a vertex and hold down **Ctrl** while you right click a second vertex, Blender will automatically select the shortest path between the two vertices (see Figure 6.3). This selection method also works with edges and faces.

If you keep pressing **Ctrl** and right clicking, the new paths will be added to the selection, making this a very fast way to select a series of vertices that follow a path. (It will prove very useful in Chapter 8, Unwrapping and UVs in Blender, to mark seams in a model.)

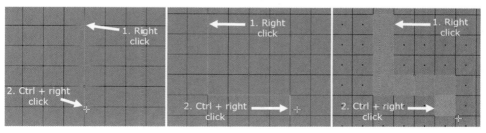

Figure 6.3   Some examples of how Shortest Path
selections work in vertices, edges, and faces

Proportional Editing

Proportional Editing is a very useful feature, especially when you're working on organic modeling. Basically, you select an element (either vertices, edges, faces, or objects), but when you move it around, the surrounding elements follow the selection, depending on the falloff type and radius of influence you apply (see Figure 6.4).

Using Proportional Editing is very easy: just find the icon on the 3D View header and select one of the methods to enable it. Alternatively, you can press **O** on your keyboard to turn it on and off. Once Proportional Editing is enabled, when you perform a transform, a circle will appear around the selection that indicates the radius of influence and you can roll the scroll wheel of your mouse up and down to increase or decrease that size.

When you enable Proportional Editing, another drop-down menu will appear next to the Proportional Editing icon, where you will be able to select different falloff types. Here are the Proportional Editing methods you can use (see Figure 6.4):

- **Connected:** This option affects only the vertices, edges, or faces that are directly connected to the selection (it won't affect parts of the same mesh that are separated).
- **Projected (2D):** Its effect won't depend on the mesh, but on the point of view from which you're looking at the mesh.
- **Enable:** This option will activate the effect of the Proportional Editing tool on the mesh surrounding the selection inside the radius of influence, even if it's disconnected.
- **Disable:** This option disables Proportional Editing.

> **Tip**
>
> In other software, this feature is called Falloff Selection, Soft Selection, Smooth Selection, or it can have other names with a similar meaning. It may work in a slightly different way, but it's basically the same as Blender's Proportional Editing.

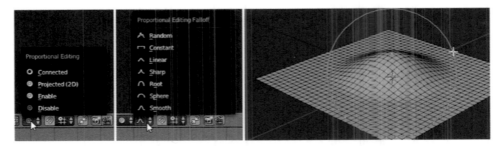

Figure 6.4   The Proportional Editing menu on the 3D View header (left),
the falloff types (middle), and the effect of the Proportional Editing
tool on a mesh when moving a single vertex (right)

Linked Selection

A mesh can be made of different linked parts that are not connected by edges and you may want to select one of them without selecting the others. There are two quick ways to select those linked parts:

- Select one of the mesh's vertices, edges, or faces, and press **Ctrl + L**. All the linked parts of the mesh will be selected.
- With nothing selected, place the cursor on top of a mesh and press **L** to select the linked parts of the mesh. Press **Shift + L** to add and subtract from the selection.

Loops and Rings

The shape that edges follow along a surface is usually called edge flow or mesh flow, and it's very important when modeling (you'll learn about this in the next chapter). In any mesh, you can find loops and rings. A loop is a series of connected edges that follow a path. A ring is a series of parallel edges along the surface of a mesh (see Figure 6.5).

You can quickly select loops or rings with two keyboard shortcuts:

- **Selecting loops:** Place your cursor on top of an edge, press **Alt,** and right click to select the whole loop.
- **Selecting rings:** Place your cursor on top of an edge, press **Ctrl + Alt,** and right click to select the whole ring.

Hold **Shift** and combine it with the shortcuts above to add to the selection.

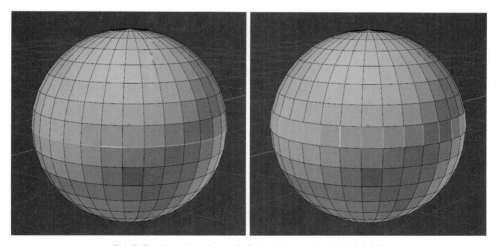

Fig 6.5   An edge loop (left) and an edge ring (right)

This technique works with vertices, edges, and faces, but in the case of faces, selecting a loop will perform the same selection as if selecting a ring.

Grow and Shrink Selection

When you have a selection of vertices, edges, or faces, you can press **Ctrl + NumPad + (plus sign)** or **Ctrl + NumPad – (minus sign)** to grow or shrink the scope of the selection through the connected elements.

Limit Selection to Visible

When you have the display mode in Wireframe (**Z**) you are able to select vertices, edges, or faces that are in front of the model, as well as those that are behind it. This is not possible with the Solid display, which only lets you interact with the parts of the model that are facing you.

In Edit Mode, when a mode other than the Wireframe display is active, right next to the icons on the 3D View header for selecting vertices, edges, or faces is an icon with a little cube that has marked vertices, with a back side that is not visible. If that option is turned on, you'll only see the parts of the model that are facing you, but if you disable it, you'll be able to see any of the elements behind the model and you'll also be able to select them. Sometimes, you want to select a large portion of an object and if the model has holes and cavities in it, is useful to be able to select all the vertices at once; however, most of the time you probably will only want to select elements that are visible and in front of the model, so that you don't accidentally select something behind it.

Other Selection Methods

On the 3D View header, in the *Select* menu, you'll find all the selection methods discussed above as well as several others. Those mentioned above are generally used most often, but you are encouraged to check out the rest of them as you may find others that are useful. Also, keep in mind that you can always go to the Select menu in case you don't remember the keyboard shortcut for any of the methods described above. (Proportional Editing is not in that menu; it's accessed from the 3D View header.)

Mesh Modeling Tools

This section provides a reference for the main modeling tools (alphabetically ordered) that are available in Blender. You'll learn how to use them, what options they have (which you will see on the Operator panel of the Tools Region in the 3D View right after invoking them), and what their effects are. Test them and learn them, as they will be used a lot in the following chapters. However, don't worry if you don't learn all their features right away; you can come back to this chapter whenever necessary.

> **Note**
> All of these tools can be found in the menus explained in the previous section.

Figure 6.6   Using the Bevel tool over a face

Bevel

Bevel is a very useful tool, especially for technical and inorganic models, and it basically creates bevels and chamfers. It can be used with vertices (the Bevel tool only works with vertices when you enable the Only Vertex option in the Operator panel after invoking the tool), edges, and faces. You can see how it's used in Figure 6.6.

To use the Bevel tool:

1. Select the element you want to bevel.
2. Press **Ctrl + B** and drag your mouse to increase or decrease the bevel size.
3. Roll the scroll wheel to increase or decrease the bevel divisions (segments).
4. **LMB** to apply / **RMB** to cancel.

In the Operator panel's Bevel tool options, you'll find the size calculation method, the size of the bevel, the amount of segments, the bevel's profile (in or out), and whether to apply the bevel to vertices only.

> **Tip**
>
> Blender's Bevel tool is similar to the Chamfer tool in 3ds Max.

Bisect

The Bisect tool lets you create a line across a selection and project it to generate an edge loop that will divide the mesh. After that, you're able to leave only one side of the mesh from that division visible, which is useful for creating cross sections of objects (see Figure 6.7).

To use the Bisect tool:

1. Select the part of the mesh you want to divide (sometimes it will be the whole mesh, which you can select by pressing **A** on your keyboard).
2. Select the Bisect tool from one of the menus discussed above (by default, there's no keyboard shortcut for this tool).
3. **LMB** the first point of the line you want to draw and drag to indicate the line's direction.
4. Release **LMB** to apply.

Figure 6.7   Using the Bisect tool with the default cube

In the Operator panel, you'll find options to redefine the cutting plane's position and direction. You can also erase the mesh on one side of the division, fill the inner part of the division, or leave it empty.

Bridge Edge Loops

The Bridge Edge Loops tool works well to join a series of adjacent edge loops. It's like an advanced Face tool (covered later in this chapter), but instead of creating one face at a time, it creates a group of them, joining two selected edge loops (see Figure 6.8).

To use the Bridge Edge Loops tool:

1. Select a string of edges (edge loop).
2. Select another edge loop in a separate part of the model (for optimal results, both edge loops should have the same number of edges).
3. Press **Ctrl + E** to access the Edge menu and select the Bridge Edge Loops tool.

The options for this tool let you control the type of connection that is made between the loops, twist the resulting geometry, and apply some merging options (only if the edge counts are the same in both edge loops that you're trying to connect). These options also include several features that allow you to control the number of segments (cuts) in the new geometry as well as its shape.

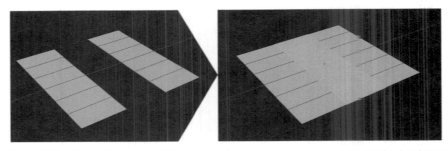

Figure 6.8   Using the Bridge Edge Loops tool to connect two separated edge loops

Figure 6.9   Using the Connect tool to join two vertices sharing a face with a new edge

Connect

The Connect tool joins two vertices with a new edge across a face (see Figure 6.9).
  To use the Connect tool:

1. Select two vertices (they have to share the same face).
2. Press **J** to connect them.

> **Tip**
>
> If you select a line of vertices, assuming that there is a face between one and the next, when you press **J**, Blender will connect them in order so you don't need to connect them one at a time.

Delete and Dissolve

In Blender, when you have some of a mesh's elements selected and you press **X**, a menu will appear that gives you several options. You can use Delete to remove vertices, edges, or faces, and that will have a variety of effects. If you select one of the other options such as "Only Faces," only the faces will be deleted, but the edges and vertices will remain.

  You'll also see an option for Dissolve, which is similar to Delete except that instead of making elements disappear, it replaces them with a single n-gon. This comes in handy when you're working on complex surfaces and you need to adjust the way in which the edges are placed: you dissolve the faces and then reconnect the remaining vertices manually (see Figure 6.10).

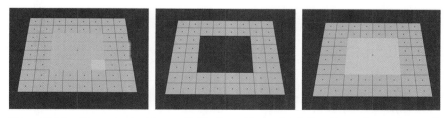

Figure 6.10   The selected faces (left), the effect of deleting those faces (center), and the result of dissolving those faces (right)

To use Delete or Dissolve:

1. Select a set of adjacent vertices, edges, or faces.
2. Press **X** and select Delete or Dissolve from the pop-up menu to delete or dissolve the selection.

When you use the Delete tool, depending on the option you select, you'll be presented with another set of options that let you control the degree of deletion for that particular tool or, in the case of the Limited Dissolve option, you'll have control over the angle at which the dissolved faces are joined together.

Duplicate

Duplicate is as simple as it seems. You can duplicate a piece of the mesh and place it somewhere else very quickly.

To use the Duplicate tool:

1. Select one or more vertices, edges, or faces.
2. Press **Shift + D.**
3. Drag your mouse to move the selection. You can use the **X, Y,** and **Z** constraints while moving, just as you would in a normal transform.
4. Left click to confirm.

Duplicate is quite a simple tool, but it gives you a lot of options. For example, from the Operator panel you can control the offset of the duplication, constrain it, and even access the Proportional Editing features.

Extrude

Another very useful modeling tool is Extrude. To understand how it works, imagine the floor of a house. You select the floor and, when you extrude it, you move it up as if it were a duplicate to create a ceiling, but then Blender will generate the walls to join the floor and ceiling (see Figure 6.11). You can use Extrude for vertices, edges, and faces. There are also different methods for extruding and more than one Extrude

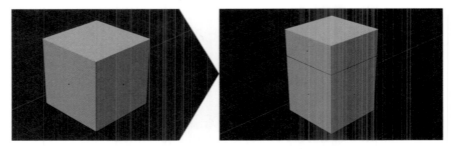

Figure 6.11   Extrude tool in action

option, such as Extrude Region and Extrude Individual: the first option will extrude the whole selection at once, while the second will extrude each face individually.

There are three methods for using the Extrude tool. Here is the first method:

1. Select one or more vertices, edges, or faces.
2. Press **E** to extrude.
3. Drag your mouse to move the new geometry. You can use **X, Y,** and **Z** to constrain it (if you extrude a face, by default, it will be constrained according to the orientation of the face).
4. Left click to confirm the extrusion.

This is the second method:

1. Select one or more vertices, edges, or faces.
2. Press **Ctrl** and left click where you want the extrusion to go and Blender will extrude automatically.

And here is the third method:

1. Select one or more vertices, edges, or faces.
2. Press **Alt + E**. This will bring up a menu with different extrude options. Select one.
3. Drag your mouse to adjust the height of the extrusion.
4. Left click to confirm.

Within the Operator panel for an extrusion, you'll find options to change the extrusion's direction and size or constrain to an axis and by what amount, as well as some Proportional Editing features.

Fill and Grid Fill

With the Fill and Grid Fill tools, you can select a part of the mesh where you have a hole and it will be filled. Generally, Grid Fill gives better results and cleaner geometry (see Chapter 7 for more information about clean geometry and topology) than Fill (see Figure 6.12).

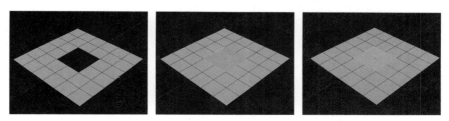

Figure 6.12   Mesh selection (left), Fill (middle), and Grid Fill (right)

To use the Fill tool:

1. Select the borders of the hole (sometimes you can select them as a loop with **Alt** and right clicking).
2. Press **Alt + F** to fill the hole with new geometry.

There are a few options with the Fill tool, such as the Beauty option, which will try to give you a better result when generating the new geometry.

To use the Grid Fill tool:

1. Select the borders of the hole.
2. Press **Ctrl + F** to access the Face menu (by default, Grid Fill doesn't have a keyboard shortcut) and select Grid Fill to fill the hole with new geometry.

Grid Fill tries to create a new geometry made of four-sided faces (a grid) and it gives you a couple of options to rotate the pattern and get a cleaner geometry. It also has a Simple Blending option that will relax some of the grid's surface tension.

Inset

The Inset tool is similar to the Extrude tool, but the new faces it creates are on the surface of the selection and will not change the surface's shape. This tool generates a copy of the geometry that is an inset of the original selection (it's possible to also add height to the new geometry). This tool only works with faces (see Figure 6.13).

To use the Inset tool:

1. Select a face or group of faces.
2. Press **I** to Inset.
3. Drag the mouse to increase or decrease the inset's thickness. Press **Ctrl** while dragging to change the height of the inset.
4. Left click to confirm the operation.

You'll find several interesting options for this tool. Boundary, for example, takes into account the boundaries of the mesh when applying the Inset (very useful when you're

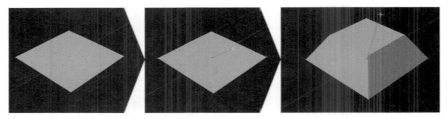

Figure 6.13   The Inset tool used with a face,
with the inset defined first and then the height

working on a mirrored mesh and don't want the faces in the mirror's plane to be affected by the Inset operation). Apart from that, you'll have other options to change how the thickness is calculated and define both the amount of the inset's thickness and its height. Finally, there are some options to "outset" instead of inset, or to apply the inset to each face of the selection individually. You can also select either the outer or inner part of the inset after applying this tool, depending on which part you prefer to work with.

> **Tip**
>
> In Blender, Inset works similarly to Bevel in 3ds Max. It may be confusing, but Inset in Blender is similar to Bevel in 3ds Max, while Bevel in Blender is similar to Chamfer in 3ds Max.

Join

The Join tool is not used when in Edit Mode, but in Object Mode instead. You can select two different objects and join them so they become a single object. This is the opposite of the Separate tool (discussed later in this chapter).

To use the Join tool:

1. In Object Mode, select two or more objects. Determine the object you want to keep as the primary one and select it last to keep it as the active object. Attributes such as the center of the resulting object or its modifiers will be taken from the active object before using the Join tool.
2. Press **Ctrl + J** to join them into a unique mesh.

> **Tip**
>
> Join and Separate are similar to the Attach and Detach options in 3ds Max.

Knife

Knife is a very useful tool that allows you to cut through the surface of a mesh to divide it into faces and edges, and generate new geometry (see Figure 6.14).

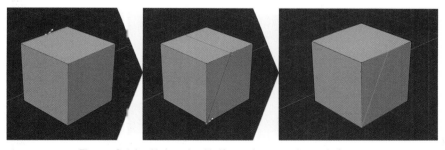

Figure 6.14   Using the Knife tool to cut through faces

To use the Knife tool:

1. Press **K**. Alternatively, you can press **Shift + K** to affect only the selected geometry.
2. Left click, move your mouse to define the cut plane, and left click again. Repeat this process until you're happy with the cut. The knife will show the points on-screen at which it's going to add a vertex to the cut and, by default, the Knife tool will snap to vertices and edges. Press **Shift** to avoid that snapping and do a free cut. Press **Ctrl** to snap to the center of the edges.
3. Once you're done with the cut, press **Enter** to confirm and apply the cut.

Loop Cut and Slide

The Loop Cut and Slide tool creates a cut through the whole loop you select, generating one or more new loops; then you can slide the new loop to where you want it between the next and previous loops (see Figure 6.15).

To use the Loop Cut and Slide tool:

1. Press **Ctrl + R**.
2. Move your cursor around the model to select where you want to add the new loop. A preview will be shown in pink. Then, place your cursor on top of an edge and it will detect the edge's ring and place the new loop across that ring.
3. Roll your scroll wheel up and down to increase and decrease the number of loops to add.
4. Left click to accept where you want the new loop.
5. Drag with your mouse to slide the new loop along the edges.
6. Left click again to confirm the action and apply the new loops. If you right click instead, you'll cancel the sliding and the new edge loop will be perfectly centered when applied.

Some cool options are available with this tool in the Operator panel. After you apply it, you can change the number of cuts and even their smoothness, as well as the falloff

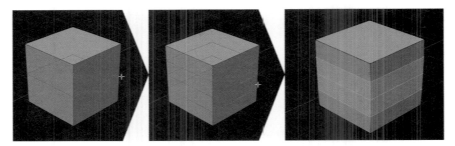

Figure 6.15   The Loop Cut and Slide tool used on the default cube

type of the smooth feature, to create curved shapes with the new geometry. Also, you can control the Edge Slide factor.

Make Edge/Face

The Make Edge/Face tool is very valuable because it lets you select two elements (only vertices or edges) and create an edge or face between them (see Figure 6.16). It has different effects depending on the elements you select. If you select two vertices, the tool will generate an edge between them. If you select three or more vertices (or two or more edges) it will create a triangle, a face, or an n-gon according to your selection.

To use the Face tool:

1. Select two or more vertices or two or more edges. (They need to be on the borders of the geometry; on the side where the face will be generated, there shouldn't be any geometry connected to those elements).

2. Press **F** to create the edge or face.

Merge

With the Merge tool, you can select two or more elements and merge them into a single element. This is similar to the welding tools in other software. There are several merging options with different results. This tool can be used with vertices, edges, and faces.

To use the Merge tool

1. Select two or more vertices, edges, or faces.

2. Press **Alt + M** and select one of the options. Depending on what you select, you'll be shown additional options. With vertices, you can usually decide where to merge them: in the position of the first selected one, the last selected one, at the center of the selection, or at the point of the 3D cursor.

   Collapse merges each one of the groups of connected elements individually, so if they're not connected, they won't be merged (useful if you want to get rid of a

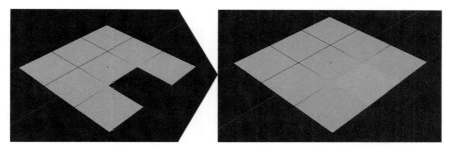

Figure 6.16   Using the Face tool to fill the hole between the four selected vertices

loop: you can select an edge ring and collapse it so each edge will be turned into a vertex). As an example, if you select two faces in different parts of a mesh and collapse them, each one of the faces will be converted into a single vertex at its center.

Once you merge elements, you can still change the merge type and where the elements are merged. This is useful for experimenting to see the different effects each one of the merge types has, or for just changing the type of merge if you selected the wrong one accidentally.

Remove Doubles

Sometimes, you may accidentally end up with duplicated vertices at some points of your mesh. Remove Doubles lets you automatically merge all the vertices that are very close to each other inside a range you can define.

To use the Remove Doubles tool:

1. Select the part of the mesh in which you want to remove double vertices. Usually, you want to remove them from the whole mesh, which you can select with **A**.
2. Press **W** to access the Specials menu and pick the Remove Doubles option (by default, it lacks a shortcut). In the Info area, usually at the top of the interface, you'll get a notification displaying the number of vertices that you removed.

After using this tool, you can go to the Operator panel and change the merge distance. At its minimum, it will only merge the vertices that are in the same exact position, but you can increase it to merge vertices that are close to each other. Remove Doubles is only applied to the selected vertices, but you can activate the Unselected option to include the unselected vertices that are very close to the selected ones.

Rip and Rip Fill

The Rip tool only works with vertices and lets you rip apart the selected vertex or vertices and create a hole in the mesh. Rip Fill does exactly the same, but it automatically fills the hole you created (see Figure 6.17).

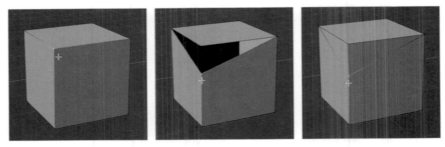

Figure 6.17   Selection (left), Rip (middle), and Rip Fill (right)

To use the Rip or Rip Fill tools:

1. Select one or more vertices.
2. Place your cursor on the side of the vertex you want to take apart. That will define the resulting vertex you'll displace after the rip.
3. Press **V** to Rip or press **Alt + V** to Rip Fill.
4. Drag your mouse to move the ripped vertex or vertices around.
5. Left click to confirm the operation.

Screw

The Screw tool lets you add a "screwing" or spiral effect around the 3D cursor, and you can select the amount of turns, segments, and height of the generated screw (see Figure 6.18).

To use the Screw tool:

1. Select a string of vertices or edges. (This tool doesn't work with faces.)
2. Place the 3D cursor where you want the center of the screwing effect to be.
3. Place your point of view in the direction in which you want to apply the effect. The center position will be defined by the 3D cursor, while the orientation will be determined by your point of view.
4. Access the Screw tool from the Tools Region.

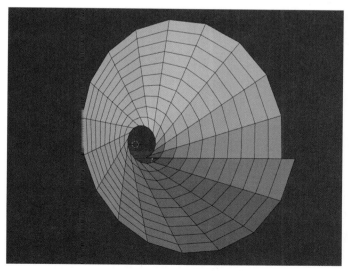

Figure 6.18   Result of using the Screw tool with an edge

After you perform the Screw operation, some options will be available to you, such as adjusting the center of the screw effect, its orientation, and the amount of turns and steps (segments) it has.

> **Tip**
>
> Keep in mind that when you modify the options in the Operator panel for an action, the next time you perform that action, those modifications will be its default values. For example, if you turn on the proportional size for an extrusion, next time you extrude, you'll be using that same proportional size.

Separate

You can select a part of the mesh and separate it into a different object with the Separate tool.

To use the Separate tool:

1. Select the parts of the mesh you want to separate.
2. Press **P** and you'll see a pop-up menu. You have to pick the Selected option to separate the selection. Use the By Material option to separate the mesh into parts that use different materials (only if you've applied different materials to parts of the mesh) or the Loose Parts option to separate the disconnected parts of the mesh (you don't need to make a selection to use the Loose Parts option).

Shrink/Flatten

Very simple but frequently very useful, the Shrink/Flatten tool scales the selected vertices, edges, or faces depending on their normal. (A "normal" is what the orientation vector of a face is called in 3D.)

To use the Shrink/Flatten tool:

1. Select the parts of the mesh you want to modify.
2. Press **Alt + S** (similar to scaling).
3. Drag your mouse to adjust the Shrinking value.
4. Left click to confirm the operation.

This tool also has some very simple options. It allows you to adjust the shrinking or flattening value and has some Proportional Editing options as well.

Slide

With the Slide tool, when you select a vertex, an edge, or a loop, you can slide the selection along the adjacent edges. While you can use this tool with faces, it's usually more intuitive when you use it with vertices and edges.

To use the Slide tool with vertices:

1. Select one or more vertices. (As a rule of thumb, it's recommended that you use this tool with only one vertex at a time, as having more vertices selected will make the sliding unpredictable.)
2. Place your mouse near the edge where you want to slide the vertex.
3. Press **Shift + V**.
4. Drag your mouse to slide the vertex. Blender will show a yellow line to let you see where you can move the vertex.
5. Left click to confirm the new vertex position.

To use the Slide tool with edges:

1. Select the edge or edge loop you want to slide.
2. Press **Ctrl + E** to access the Edge menu and choose the Edge Slide option.
3. Drag your mouse to slide the edge or edge loop.
4. Left click to confirm the operation.

The options in the Operator panel for the Slide tool are very simple. Basically, they allow you to adjust the distance and direction the selected elements will slide along their edges.

> **Tip**
>
> There is a quicker way to slide and it doesn't matter if you're working with vertices, edges, or faces. Just press **G** twice and you can slide your selection.

Solidify

The Solidify tool adds thickness to the selection. It only works with faces.
To use the Solidify tool:

1. Select the faces to which you want to add thickness.
2. Press **Ctrl + F** to access the Face menu and choose the Solidify option.

When you apply Solidify to a face or group of faces, you can use its options in the Operator panel to adjust the thickness you want them to have.

Spin

The Spin tool lets you pick a vertex, edge, or face (or a group of these elements) and extrude them around the 3D cursor (see Figure 6.19).

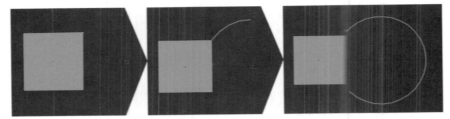

Figure 6.19   Using the Spin tool with a vertex around the 3D cursor

To use the Spin tool:

1. Select one or more vertices, edges, or faces.
2. Place the 3D cursor where you want the center of the resulting "circle" to be.
3. Position the point of view to define the orientation of the spin.
4. Press **Alt + R** to use the Spin tool.

Spin gives you options for defining the angle of the spin and the number of steps (extrusions during the spin), or for adjusting the center and axis from which the spin takes place. Also, you'll find the Dupli option, which makes duplicates of the resulting geometry instead of extrusions.

Split

The Split tool disconnects a selected part of the mesh from the rest of the mesh (see Figure 6.20). It works better with faces. (With vertices and edges, the effect will be similar to duplicating them if they are a part of a face.) Once the selected part is disconnected, you can move it freely to any other location. Split is different from the Separate tool in that Split keeps the mesh in the same object rather than creating a new object from it.

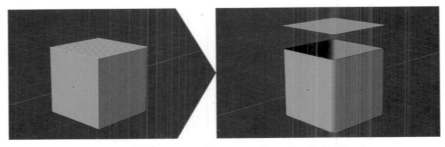

Figure 6.20   Splitting a face away from the default cube

To use the Split tool:

1. Select the faces you want to disconnect.
2. Press **Y** to Split.

Subdivide

As its name implies, this tool subdivides geometry. It works with edges and faces. An edge will be divided in half and will generate a new vertex right in the middle. A face will be divided into four new faces and, if you select an edge ring, Subdivide will generate a loop that divides all the edges of the ring right through the center of each edge. You can also increase the number of divisions (cuts) when using this tool (see Figure 6.21).

To use the Subdivide tool:

1. Select the geometry you want to subdivide. (The minimum is two connected vertices that are equal to one edge.)
2. Press **W** to access the Specials menu and choose the Subdivide option.

You can define the number of divisions (cuts) and their smoothness depending on the surrounding geometry. You can also generate triangles around the subdivisions to prevent the creation of n-gons and apply fractal noise patterns to the resulting geometry.

> **Tip**
>
> When you use many of these tools, you can drag your mouse to move things around. Remember that you can use the keyboard shortcuts to aid the transform: Press Shift to move things precisely, Ctrl to snap, or enter numerical values and use the X, Y, and Z keys to constrain the movement to their respective axes.

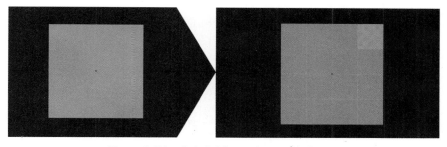

Figure 6.21   Subdividing a face with 3 cuts

LoopTools

LoopTools is an add-on that comes built in with Blender, but is not active by default. You can go to the User Preferences and activate it within the Add-ons tab. It will be accessible from the Tools Region in the 3D View and also from the top of the Specials (**W**) menu while you are in Edit Mode (see Figure 6.22).

This add-on provides some interesting and useful modeling tools that you're encouraged to check out. They're mainly tools that speed up the modeling process, so let's see what they do.

- **Bridge:** This tool was present in the LoopTools add-on before it was implemented in Blender. The version included with Blender (called Bridge Edge Loops) is not exactly the same, and its options are slightly different, though they provide similar results. Basically, this tool lets you select edges or faces and create new geometry that forms a bridge between them.

- **Circle:** This tool places your selected elements (vertices, for example) in a perfectly circular disposition.

- **Curve:** Select an edge or a face and use this tool to convert the straight edge loops into smooth curves. Use the Operator panel in the Tools Region to control the effects of this tool.

- **Flatten:** Select faces, edges, or vertices (a minimum of four), and this tool will move them to make them fit on the same plane. Imagine you created a surface mesh by hand and it's not completely planar; with this tool, you would select the whole surface and use the Flatten tool to make the surface absolutely flat.

- **Gstretch:** This tool requires that you use the Grease Pencil to draw a curve and it will then distribute your selection along that curve. Here are the basics of Grease Pencil, a tool mainly used for annotations in the 3D View: Press and hold **D** while you left click and drag to draw. Press and hold **D** while you right click

Figure 6.22   LoopTools add-on in the 3D View Tools Region

and drag to erase the strokes. In the 3D View Properties Region, you'll find the options to delete or change the parameters of the Grease Pencil layers. You can also access Grease Pencil tools from the Grease Pencil tab of the Tools Region in the 3D View.

- **Loft:** This tool is very similar to the Bridge Edge Loops tool, but it goes a little further. It allows you to "bridge" more than two edge loops together. Let's say you have three circles: with Loft, you can select all of them and it will create a bridge from the first to the last, passing through the middle circle and giving you the chance to control the shape in the middle of a bridge operation.

- **Relax:** This tool will smooth the selection and prevent sharp shapes.

- **Space:** This tool spaces your selection so the distance between all the selected elements is the same It's useful for technical modeling when you have several divisions made by hand, but you need them to be equally spaced from each other.

Tips and Tricks

In this section, you'll learn three tricks that will make your life simpler when you're dealing with models. They are tools and features that at first you might not realize are available, but Blender provides them for you to work faster and more comfortably.

AutoMerge

The AutoMerge feature is very helpful when modeling. When you activate it, if you place a vertex in another vertex's location, it will automatically merge them.

If you activate the Snapping tool as well (or just set it to Vertex Snap and press **Ctrl** when you want to merge), when you move one vertex near another one, the vertex you're moving will snap to the second vertex's location, making merging very fast and straightforward.

This technique is similar to welding tools in other 3D packages. You can activate AutoMerge from the Mesh menu on the 3D View header.

Hide and Reveal

Hide and Reveal is very useful! You can select a part of your mesh and press **H** to hide it so it's not in the way while you work on other parts of the model that may be hidden. When you're done, you can press **Alt + H** to reveal all the parts of the model that you've hidden.

Not only is this helpful to hide certain parts or make them visible, but it also allows for selective adjustments. For example, let's say you want to create a loop cut. Normally, doing so will affect the whole edge ring. But if you only want the loop cut to affect a part of the edge ring, you can hide some of the ring's parts and the tool will only affect the parts that remain visible. It also works this way with most of the modeling tools, so take advantage of it!

Snapping

Just as in Object Mode, you can activate the snapping tools on the 3D View header and also select the type of snapping you want: Vertex, Face, Increments, and so forth. If the Snap tool is active, when you move things around they'll snap. In addition, while pressing **Ctrl**, you can move them freely. Alternatively, if Snap is disabled when you press **Ctrl,** things will snap while you move them.

Summary

In this chapter, you learned about the main Blender modeling tools, what their effects are, how to use them, and how to adjust their options once they are applied to your mesh. This should give you a head start with modeling and you should be able to create simple models using these tools to modify and shape your meshes. You've also seen that you can perform almost all of these actions using keyboard shortcuts. (Of course, you can also access them through the menus and you can reference their keyboard shortcuts from those menus.) It may be difficult to remember all the shortcuts right away, but in the long run, you'll be thankful for knowing them because they will allow you to work a lot faster!

Exercises

1. Try every modeling tool in this chapter on some simple objects.
2. Model a very simple object that Jim can use in his adventures (a flashlight, for example). Figure out which tools to use, how to use them, and in which order.

7

Character Modeling

It's finally time to start modeling Jim! In this chapter, you'll learn about topology and some of the most popular modeling methods; then, you'll set up the reference images you created so that you can model over them; and finally, step by step, you'll model every part of Jim's body. This is one of the most crucial phases of the project because it will define the shapes and looks of the character with which you're going to work in the chapters to come.

What Is Mesh Topology?

Mesh topology is the method in which edges are distributed along the surface of a model. Two surfaces can have identical shapes but completely different topologies, so why is topology so important? Topology is especially critical when it comes to animated characters. When the character moves, the model is going to be deformed. A good topology ensures that deformations look realistic; otherwise, the mesh will pinch, stretch, or just deform incorrectly and look weird.

In Figure 7.1, you can see two different topology examples, one good and one bad. (These examples are very exaggerated and they are meant just to illustrate how a shape can be created with a badly distributed topology.) In the example on the left, the topology is poor: most of the edge loops run only vertically and horizontally, and they don't really adapt to the face's shape, which will certainly cause problems when, for example, you want to make the character open its mouth. In the example on the right, the topology is much better: edge loops flow with the face's shape and define it correctly.

Think of topology as the skin and the muscles of a face or other body part. Depending on how they will deform, they need to follow the shapes of the model; otherwise, the creation of the skin will have serious problems.

Here are some things you should keep in mind to make sure you have a good topology:

- **Use four-sided faces (quads) as often as you can:** Avoid the use of triangles or n-gons unless you really have a good reason to use them. Triangles and n-gons, when used carelessly, can generate pinches in the surface when the model is subdivided and deformed.

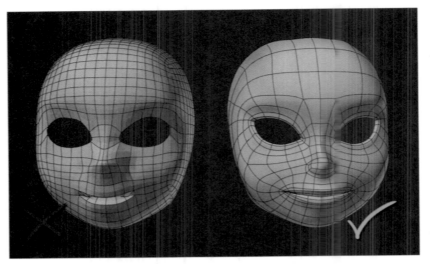

Figure 7.1   An example of a poor topology (left) and a good topology (right)

- **Use squares rather than rectangles:** Overall, if you're working with organic shapes, four-sided faces won't have the same length on all four sides, so try to avoid really long rectangles, as they'll be difficult to manage during deformations and other stages of the animation process that follow modeling.

- **Keep an eye on areas requiring complex deformations:** Some parts of a model will be more complex than others, not just because of their shape, but because when animated, you'll probably need a wide range of movement for them. The edge flow should be especially good in those areas to make sure the model will deform correctly later on. The eyelids, shoulders, knees, elbows, hips, and mouth are some examples of areas to which you should pay more attention to a good topology and perhaps even include more faces to provide additional geometry for more defined deformations.

- **Keep a low poly count:** Poly count refers to the number of polygons (usually measured in triangles, as any polygon can be divided into triangles) that form a model. More polygons mean more work in all the stages of modeling, which could result in difficulties if you have to change something. As a rule of thumb, you should keep the number of polygons to the minimum needed to achieve the shape and the level of detail you need for your model.

- **Follow the shapes:** Your edges should flow with the shapes. For example, around the mouth there should be circular loops that will create a realistic deformation when the character opens its mouth or talks. If those "lines" are vertical and horizontal, chances are your character will look cubical (the usual pitfall when you start modeling for the first time and don't yet have control over your edge flow) and quite strange when it opens its mouth.

> **Note**
>
> Topology is a complex subject and a whole book could be written about it, with techniques and ways to achieve a good edge flow or how to use n-gons or triangles correctly. If you're interested in learning more about mesh topology, look for resources on the Internet. A lot of great articles and websites are available to you!

Modeling Methods

Modeling can seem rather technical (and it really is), but modeling also offers a lot of freedom and creativity. Quite a few methods and techniques are available to explore and use as you need them. Working with some of them may be more comfortable for you than with others, or you may want to pick one or another, depending on the type of model you're working on. In this section, we'll present some of the most popular methods you can use.

Box Modeling

Box modeling is based on the premise that you can model anything from a simple primitive (for example, a cube, a sphere, or a cylinder). Don't be fooled by its name: the "box" in box modeling means only that the most essential shape can be the base for any kind of object. The idea behind this method is that if you start from a primitive, you can divide it, extrude it, and otherwise modify it to reach the shape you want.

With box modeling, you start from something very basic and, little by little, keep adding details to it. However, from the beginning, your model already has the basic shape it will need, so you only have to add as many details as you want. You can compare box modeling to sculpting with mud: for example, you would start with a sphere or other very basic shape, and then gradually add details, such as a Subdivision Surface modifier, to that shape to make it smooth.

Poly to Poly

Also called poly2poly, poly to poly is about "drawing" a shape one polygon at a time. You create vertices and edges, extrude them, and join them to make faces, basically constructing the model as if you were building a brick wall. Again, you'd add a Subdivision Surface modifier to smooth the geometry you created.

Sculpt and Retopologize

While box modeling and poly to poly are probably the most "traditional" modeling methods, sculpting came to the 3D scene just a few years ago and it's now widely used, especially for organic models. With sculpting, you create a very basic shape—topology doesn't matter much here. Then you sculpt it, adjust the shape, and add a lot of detail to it. After that, you can use the Retopo (short for retopology or retopologize) process, which is basically creating the final topology for the model with a poly-to-poly method, but the geometry you create snaps to the shape you sculpted initially.

This is by far the most creative modeling method and artists love it. It allows you to focus on the shapes of your model and not have to think about a lot of technical stuff like topology. Only when you're happy with your shapes do you worry about topology, which you create very easily because you don't have to think about whether the shapes will look right, as you already have that covered from your sculpture!

Modifiers

Using modifiers is not a method in itself, but modifiers play a big role when modeling in a lot of cases. Let's say you're modeling a character. You can model one side of it and use a mirror modifier so the opposite side simultaneously builds itself, mirroring the one on which you're working. You can speed up your work by using modifiers. Let's say you have to work on a complex curved model. Just make it in a plane and then you can deform it along a curve with a modifier. Modifiers help a lot and, in some cases, they'll be essential to the construction of your model, so they deserve a mention here.

The Best Method!

Well, if you had some idea that this section would tell you the best method to use when modeling, I'm sorry, but there is no *best* method. Each individual is more comfortable with one method over another, depending on the skills he or she has, the spatial vision, the particular project, and so forth. Some people switch between methods as needed: Modeling a car? Use box modeling. Creating a monster? Try Blender's Sculpt and Retopo features.

However, the most powerful modeling tool to keep in mind is that you can mix every possible method (only some of the most popular ones for character creation are mentioned here) in the same model as you may find it necessary! You can model one part with box modeling, another with poly to poly, and the most organic parts with sculpting. You can even adjust the shapes of your character using Sculpt Mode when you have the basic topology in place and then keep working with box modeling.

The possibilities are endless and that's why 3D modeling, even though it requires some technical knowledge, can be a very enjoyable and creative process.

Setting Up the Reference Planes

Before you start modeling, you need to load into your scene the character designs you created in Chapter 5 as "background images" to use as a reference while modeling. This will definitely help a lot to define the right proportions of our character, Jim.

Some people prefer to load references in planes that they can see when they rotate the camera around the scene. You can do this by adding planes in the views you need to show and then adding the images to those planes as a texture. This can be a little tricky (especially before you learn to use materials in later chapters) but Blender actually offers two easy ways to use reference images.

- Open the folder in which you have your images and drag them into the 3D View. Once they're loaded into the scene, you may need to adjust them a little. You can go to the Background Images menu in the 3D View Properties Region to make any necessary adjustments.

- Go to the 3D View Properties Region and scroll to the Background Images panel and turn that feature on to load your images (see Figure 7.2).

From the Background Images panel, you can load an image and decide in which view it will be visible. After you load your image, you'll be able to adjust its position, size, and opacity.

> **Note**
>
> These Background Images are only visible when you're using a predefined orthographic view (for example, Front, Right, Back, Top); they won't work if you're in a Perspective View or in a random orthographic point of view. If you have a NumPad, press **5** to switch between Perspective and Orthographic views; otherwise, you can switch views from the View menu on the 3D View header.

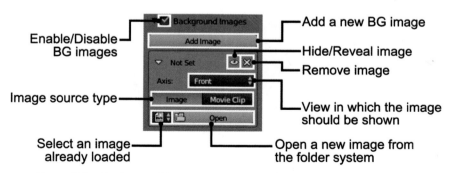

Figure 7.2   Background Images panel in the 3D View Properties Region

Load the reference images for the front, side, and back of the head into their corresponding views, so you can see them in the background while you're building Jim's head (see Figure 7.3).

> ### Caution
>
> It's very important that the reference images are properly aligned. In this case, they all have the same height and the front and back images are centered. In some cases, however, the images can have different sizes or margins, so you may need to adjust the scale and position from the Background Images menu in the 3D View Properties Region. To help you with those adjustments, you can use a very simple mesh that allows you to compare the size and position of the images with those of the 3D model. In Figure 7.3, you can see that a sphere was used to make sure that Jim's head references were properly aligned. Also, remember that the drawings are not physically accurate, so you'll have to leave some space for modifications to the images, as it's very difficult to make the 3D model fit the 2D images perfectly.

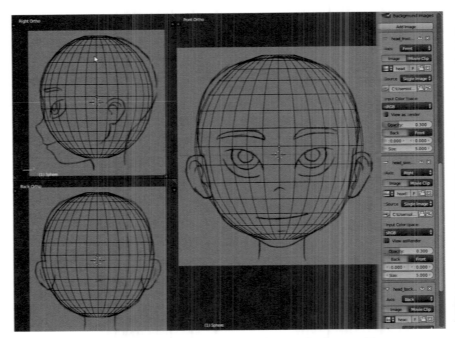

Figure 7.3   The three views with their reference background images

Modeling the Eyes

Of course, each person feels more comfortable by beginning to model a certain part of the body; some may prefer to start with the face, others with the body. For Jim, let's start with the eyes because that way you'll be able to use them as a reference when modeling the rest of the face, and especially the eyelids, because you'll be able to align those features to the eyes

Creating an Eyeball

Jim's eyes are drawn in kind of an animation/manga style (not completely round). The eyes are basically spherical, but to make them a little more realistic, you can create the cornea with the pupil beneath it. Figure 7.4 shows the process step by step and an explanation of what happens in each step follows.

1. In Object Mode, create a UV Sphere and, in the Operator panel, set it to have 16 segments and 16 rings.

2. Rotate the sphere 90 degrees on the X-axis so the poles are positioned at the front and back. This way, you'll be able to use the circular edge loops on the front pole to build the pupil.

3. Enter Edit Mode by pressing **Tab**. Select the two edge loops of the front pole and the pole vertex. A quick way to do this is to select the vertex in the pole and then press **Ctrl + NumPad +** to increase the selection twice.

4. Press **Shift + D** to duplicate the geometry you selected in the previous step and move the new geometry out a little or, for now, hide it by pressing **H**. Later, this geometry will become the eye's cornea.

5. Select the same geometry you selected in step 3 from the sphere and extrude it into the eye by pressing **E** on your keyboard.

6. Scale the selected geometry to invert its curvature by pressing **S**, then pressing **Y** to scale on the Y-axis, and then typing **–1**. Press **Enter** to confirm. Then, adjust the position of this geometry on the Y-axis so it fits into the eye in case the geometry moved out of alignment when you inverted it.

7. Select the outer edge loop of that inverted circular area and bevel it (**Ctrl + B**) so it will have a little more detail when you add the Subdivision Surface modifier later.

8. Press **Alt + H** to unhide everything and see the cornea you previously detached. Move it back to its place and even scale it up a little bit if it's needed to cover the gaps that you made when beveling the borders.

9. Apply a Subdivision Surface modifier with two divisions. Go to Object Mode and, in the Tools Region, click the Smooth option so the eyeball doesn't show the edges of all the flat faces.

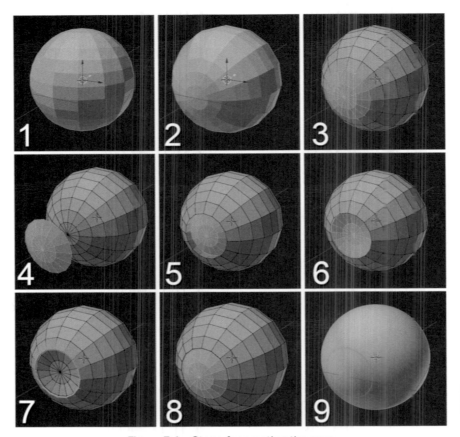

Figure 7.4   Steps for creating the eyes

> **Note**
>
> For this exercise, the lamp and the camera are in a different layer. Press **M**, select one of the squares, and then on the 3D View header you can turn those squares (layers) on and off. You'll learn more about layers in future chapters. Alternatively, you can delete the lamp and the camera to get them out of the way until you need them in the final stages of the project. If you do this, though, you'll need to create them later when you need them again.

Using Lattices to Deform the Eyeballs

Now you have one eyeball, but it's completely round and in the reference designs for Jim, the eyes are more oval. Fortunately, Blender has a tool called Lattice that lets you deform geometry and then it will maintain that deformation when you rotate the

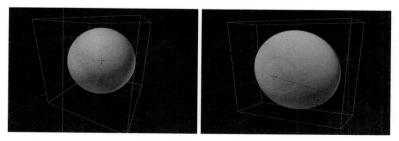

Figure 7.5   A lattice (left) and how it affects the eyeball (right)

geometry, which is exactly what you need for the eyeballs. You could just go ahead and scale the eye on the Y-axis to make it flatter, but when you rotate it to look at something, it won't fit the eye socket. Figure 7.5 shows the effects of the Lattice modifier.

Follow these steps to apply a Lattice modifier to the eyeball:

1. Press **Shift + A** and create a lattice.

2. Scale it up so it covers the whole eyeball.

3. Select the eyeball and add a Lattice modifier to it. It's better if you add it on top of the Subdivision Surface modifier; that way, the lattice will deform the low-resolution mesh and the deformed mesh will be subdivided afterward, so it will work more smoothly.

4. From the Lattice modifier options, select the name of the lattice you created in step 1 of this list in the Object field.

5. Now, you can select the lattice, press **Tab** to enter Edit Mode, and see how, as you move its vertices, the eyeball deforms accordingly.

6. Select all of the vertices (press **A**) and scale them down on the Y-axis.

7. Pick the outer side's edges to better align the eye with the side view.

8. Exit from Edit Mode and rotate the eyeball. It should rotate while keeping the lattice deformation in place, which is exactly what you need.

Mirroring and Adjusting the Eyes

We've made one eyeball, but Jim needs two of them! First, you need to align the existing eyeball to one of the eyes in the background image. Keep in mind that as the lattice is now deforming the eyeball, you'll need to select both eyeball and lattice to move them together. To create the second eyeball, you'll duplicate and mirror the first one (see Figure 7.6).

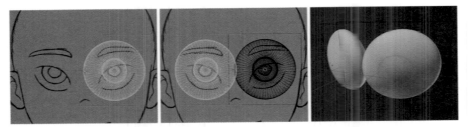

Figure 7.6   Aligning the eyeball (left),
mirroring a second eyeball (center), and the result in 3D (right)

Here are the steps to adjust and mirror the eye:

1. Select the eyeball and the lattice.
2. Move and scale them to adjust them to the shape and size of the drawn eye in the front view. Adjust their position in the side view as well. Don't worry if they don't fit perfectly.
3. Once the first eye is aligned, make sure you place the 3D cursor in the center of the scene. You can press **Shift + S** and select the option of Cursor to Center, or you can press **Shift + C**.
4. Press **Shift + D** to duplicate the eyeball and its lattice. Right click to cancel the movement and this will leave the new eyeball and lattice in the same exact location as the originals.
5. Press **.** (period) on your keyboard to set the pivot point in the 3D cursor.
6. Press **Ctrl + M** to enter Mirror Mode. This will make the current pivot point the mirror plane (that's why you should use the 3D cursor for mirroring; otherwise, you'd be mirroring from the selection's origin). Remember to set the pivot point to Median Point (**Ctrl + ,**) or to Bounding Box Center (**,**) before you continue working.
7. Once in Mirror Mode, you can press **X, Y,** or **Z** to select the axis of the mirror. In this case, press **X** and the new eyeball and its lattice should move right into place (see Figure 7.6). Press **Enter** to confirm this action.

Caution

When using this mirroring method (**Ctrl + M**), you may find that sometimes it can give you unwanted, weird results such as the object doesn't mirror in the expected way. What usually happens is that you've rotated or negatively scaled that object and its axes are not correctly aligned with the world space. If you find yourself in this situation, select the object before mirroring, press **Ctrl + A** to apply the Rotation and Scale, and try again. This should solve the problem.

Modeling the Face

Now that Jim has a good pair of eyes, it's time to start modeling a cool face for him to support those eyes! Throughout this stage, box modeling will be the method you'll use for creating the face, so you can get a good idea of how this method works.

Studying the Face's Topology

Remember how important the preproduction phase was for a project? Well, it's also important for any modeling task, and the face is one of the trickiest parts of the body to model. It's useful to look at the reference drawings you created and quickly study the topology that could work for the face so you'll have an idea of how to model before you begin, which is a much better approach than modeling blindly! Figure 7.7 shows a topology study for Jim's face, with quick sketches over the reference drawings.

Blocking the Face's Basic Shape

In this section, you'll start by blocking the face. *Blocking* is what we call the first stages of creating a model, animation, painting, or any other artistic endeavor. It is the stage in which you define, quickly and roughly, how something will look; you're not paying a lot of attention to detail, but just defining the base. In this case, for example, the blocking consists of creating the very basic shape and geometry of the face to which we'll add definition in later steps.

Blocking is very useful because it's the part of the process in which making substantial changes is easier and faster, so during this stage you can experiment with different modeling ideas.

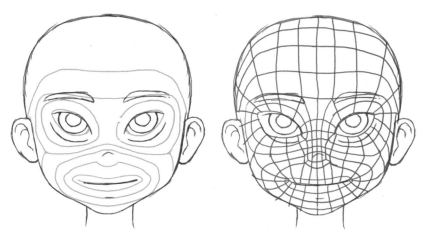

Figure 7.7   A representation of the edge flow around the main areas of the face such as the eyes, nose, and mouth (left), and a drawing of a possible topology (right)

Remember that keeping your scene organized is important, so now that you'll start creating a lot of new objects, it's a good choice to name them intuitively.

In Figure 7.8, you'll see the first steps for modeling the face, which we'll use to create the basic shape. Explanations of each step immediately follow the figure.

1. Create a cube, go to Edit Mode, and divide the cube as shown in the first image: three vertical divisions for the front of the face, one horizontal division through the front and sides of the face, and one vertical division for the sides of the face. These edge loops will help you set the basic shape of the face in the first stages. The reason for three vertical lines in the front is that you'll need additional details for the mouth and the eyes. You can perform these divisions using Loop Cut and Slide (**Ctrl + R**).

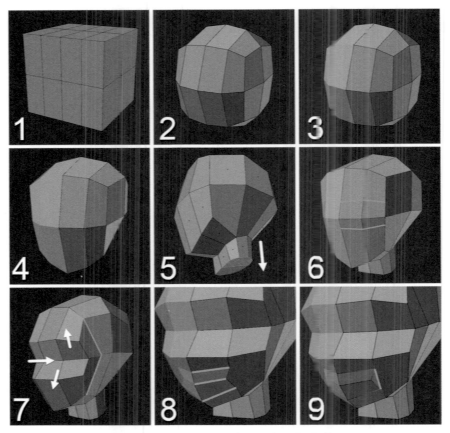

Figure 7.8   First steps of modeling Jim's face

2. Select all vertices with **A** and use the Smooth Vertices tool from the Tools Region or from the Vertices menu (**Ctrl + V**). Once smoothing is applied, increase its iterations in the Operator panel. The idea is to get a more spherical shape. Now, scale the whole shape to make it approximately fit the size of the head in the reference images.

3. From the front view, select the vertices of the left section of the mesh (negative X) and delete them, so you're left with only one-half of the face model. Now, add a Mirror modifier and the default settings should be enough to make the mirroring work. Just activate the Clipping option in the modifier so the vertices in the middle are prevented from jumping to the opposite half of the mirror center. At this point, you can work on half of the face and those changes will automatically be reflected on the other side.

4. Using Proportional Editing (press **O** to enable/disable it), adjust the shape of the geometry to fit the reference images of the head. The eyes should be placed on the horizontal line in the front. At the bottom of the head, the faces in the back will be the base for the neck.

5. Select the faces in that area and extrude them to create the neck. To form the neck, adjust the vertices so they look round. At this stage, you'll be defining the basic shape, so avoid cubic shapes; otherwise, as you start adding details, those cubic shapes will be more noticeable and it will be more difficult to arrange them properly at that later stage.

6. With the Knife tool (**K**), make a couple of cuts in the front as highlighted in the corresponding image in Figure 7.8.

7. From the previous step, you're left with three edge loops. Move them accordingly to fit Jim's face: the top one will define the eyebrows, the middle one will determine the center of the eyes, and the bottom one will establish the nose and cheeks. After that, using the Knife tool again, make the cuts highlighted in the image to end up with a round face loop that surrounds the face.

8. Perform three cuts in the mouth area and move them as needed. The middle one will establish the mouth, the bottom one can help define the chin, and the top one will mark the area of the mouth near the nose.

9. Join the side vertices of the edges above and below the mouth to form a triangle in the corner of the mouth.

Defining the Face's Shapes

After the blocking stage, in which we've already created the face's basic shape, we'll now go ahead and add some definition to the geometry.

Figure 7.9 shows the next steps of the face's modeling process, with step-by-step explanations.

> **Tip**
>
> When you're adjusting your mesh to the reference images, it's better to overestimate the shapes' sizes and make them a little bigger. The reason is that as you add more and more details, some of those vertices will be divided and this will cause the shapes to shrink. This can also happen when applying a Subdivision Surface modifier: when you smooth shapes, they'll shrink.

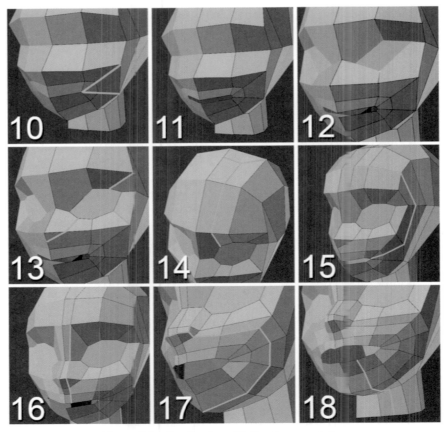

Figure 7.9   Continuing with the face modeling

10. Using the Knife tool, cut the triangle generated in the mouth's corner in step 9 above and create two new edge loops to connect the mouth with the cheek and the jaw. Now, the loop around the mouth is completely composed of quads (four-sided faces).

11. Select the mouth's edge, bevel it just a little, and delete the new geometry so you can make the mouth's opening and the area surrounding it with circular loops formed of quads.

12. Select the vertex in the middle of the eye and bevel it (you can use the Bevel Vertices tool: **Shift + Ctrl + B**). Then, move the resulting vertices to make a shape similar to the eye in your reference images.

13. Perform several cuts around the eye with the Knife tool, as highlighted in the corresponding image. This will give you more vertices to define the eye's shape, as well as some additional cuts to start defining the nose's geometry.

14. There was a side of the eye that was not cut in step 13. Cut it now but keep the cut going to the top of the head and convert the two edge loops into one as shown in the image. You only need the loop in the front of the head, so this way you can end the loop where it's no longer needed.

15. Using **Ctrl + R,** add a new loop from the mouth corner all around the face and adjust its shape and the surrounding vertices.

> **Tip**
>
> When you add a new loop to an organic shape with the Loop Cut and Slide tool (**Ctrl + R**), you can take advantage of the Smooth option in the Operator panel to make the new loop less rigid and flat between the two existing loops. Also, when you have an area with quite a few vertices, you can select all of them and use the Smooth Vertices tool to smooth them.

16. Cut a line from the eyebrow to the mouth and define the nose a little more.

17. Make a new cut from the eye down to the nose, and join it with a new loop around the mouth area. Adjust the shapes and you'll now have the geometry necessary to create the nostrils.

18. Create some new edges from the bottom of the neck to the lower lip, and then from the upper lip to the nose. Move things around a little to adapt the new vertices to the reference images and you're ready to add some more details and create the lips.

Defining the Eyes, Mouth, and Nose

Little by little, Jim's face is starting to take shape! The next steps, shown in Figure 7.10, add definition to the eyes, mouth, and nose.

19. Select the mouth's loop, extrude it, and adjust the vertices to get the lips' shapes, according to the reference images.

20. Using **Ctrl + R,** add a new loop to the lips to add a little more detail to that area. You can probably inflate the lips by just adjusting the Loop Cut and Slide Smooth options in the Operator panel. At this point, you can add a Subdivision Surface modifier to the mesh and enable it from time to time to make sure the geometry is behaving correctly when it's smoothed.

21. Select the outer loop of the lips and press **Ctrl + B** to add a bevel to it. Then, slide the loops near the mouth's corners to separate them a little more than the

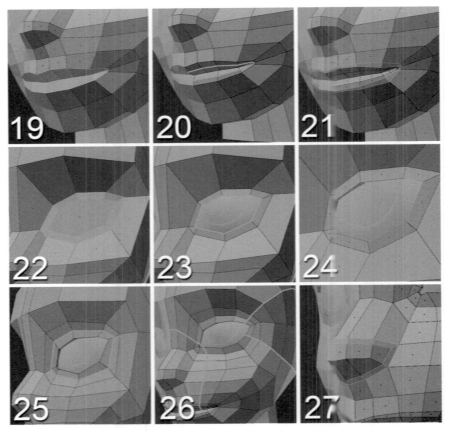

Figure 7.10   Adding more definition to the eyes and the mouth

other loops. This will define the shape of the lips when you add a Subdivision Surface modifier. Separating the vertices near the mouth corners will make those areas smoother, while the central area of the lips will have more definition, as its loops are closer together.

22. Select the n-gon of the eye and press **I** to inset and create the base of the eyelids.

23. Unhide the eyes and adjust the eyelids' geometry to the eyeball's surface. Proportional Editing can help with this. Leave a space between the eyelids and the eyeball.

24. Select the inner loop of the eyelids and extrude it to fill in the space between the eyelid and the eyeball.

25. Select the outer loop of the eye and slide the vertex out to make some space for a new loop to help define the eyelids a little more.

26. In the eye area, add some more loops with **Ctrl + R** to define the section between the nose and the forehead; then, adjust the vertices to the reference images and make sure the vertices are smooth between the rest of the geometry.

27. Select the nose's bottom and nostril faces. Inset them and turn the Boundary option off (you'll find it in the Operator panel) so the nose's front faces don't inset in the center.

> **Tip**
>
> While you model, try to think ahead to plan how you'll perform the next steps. If you have in mind what the final topology will look like, you can add loops and vertices to achieve that specific goal. Modeling blindly is also possible, but you'll probably lose some time figuring it out, and sometimes you'll have to delete certain parts and rebuild them to create a better topology.

Adding Ears

The face is almost done! Figure 7.11 shows additional steps that add more details to Jim's face. At this stage, you'll add the ears and define the neck and head a little more.

28. Move the nose vertices you just created to define the shape of the nose. Turn on the Subdivision Surface modifier to see how the model looks when subdivisions are enabled. You may want to play with the nose geometry; in this case, as the design presents a pretty stylized character, we're not going to model the nostrils.

> **Note**
>
> While you are working on the model, it's useful to enable the Subdivision Surface modifier from time to time to see if the geometry behaves correctly when subdivided. Also, this modifier provides several display modes (the four buttons located at the top of the modifier panel), and the last two are really helpful for this stage. One of them allows you to see the subdivided model in Edit mode, while you keep working

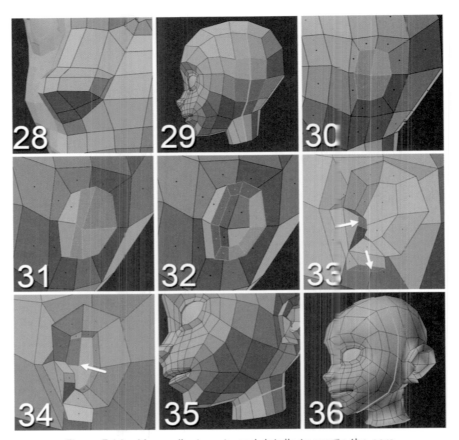

Figure 7.11   More adjustments and details to create the ears

on the original mesh as if it were a cage for the subdivided model. The last button modifies the option previously described, letting you work directly on the subdivided model without displaying the original mesh cage (an option that, in some situations, can be more useful and intuitive).

29. Go to the side of the head and create a new loop from the neck to the top of the head. The highlighted faces are going to serve as a base from which to extrude the ear. Ears are quite tricky, but in this case, we're making an anime design, so let's create a simple ear, not very realistic but one that will fit the overall look of the character.

30. Inset the selection to create the base for the ear.

31. Extrude it and adjust the shape to resemble an ear.

32. Make an inset within the ear.

33. Extrude and shape the highlighted areas to define those parts of the ear.

34. Add a new extrusion to create the ear canal and arrange those vertices a little. Don't worry if the geometry looks weird; just keep an eye on the subdivided mesh because when it's smoothed it will look quite different.

> **Tip**
>
> In the images that accompany the modeling steps, you're seeing the low-resolution mesh, so you can get a clear idea of how the polygons and vertices work; however, at this point in the process, you could have been working with the subdivided mesh from the beginning.

35. Cut a new loop in the neck to define the articulation between it and the base of the head.

36. Keep adding more and more loops in the areas where you think you'd like to have more detail. In the image for this step, two loops that were added to the mesh are highlighted: one is at the bottom of the neck so later on you won't have an empty space under Jim's jacket. Also, there is now a clean loop surrounding the whole face, which you can think of as a division you could use to extract a mask from the face.

Building the Inside of the Mouth

In this section, you'll add the final details to Jim's head. The face is looking good, but you need to create the interior of the mouth, so when Jim opens his mouth, you won't see empty space or the back of his head! Look at Figure 7.12 to see the last steps.

37. Select the inner lips' loop and extrude it into the head. In these images, the rest of the head has been hidden so you can clearly see what's going on.

> **Tip**
>
> Sometimes it's easier to select what you don't want to hide, then press **Ctrl + I** to invert the selection and finally press **H** to hide it.

38. Add some loops to better define a rounded area inside the mouth. Most importantly, add a loop near the inner lips; otherwise, they'll lose some shape when subdivided. Don't worry if the geometry overlaps in the inner lips area.

39. Close the back of the hole and refine the shapes a little. You can also add another loop near the inner lips so the inside of the mouth in that area is more vertical: this will create some space for the teeth later on.

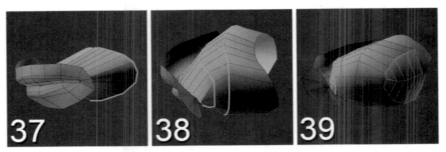

Figure 7.12   Creating the inside of the mouth,
so it isn't empty space and Jim can open it

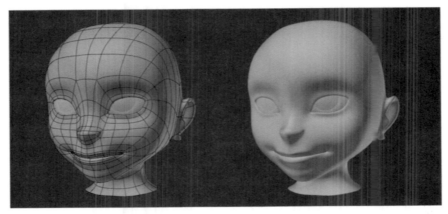

Figure 7.13   The topology for Jim's face (left) and the final subdivided result (right)

You're done modeling Jim's face! In Figure 7.13, you can see the result. The face is often one of the trickiest parts when modeling a character. You get used to seeing faces and it will immediately look wrong if something is out of place, so it can be difficult to achieve a pleasing result.

Modeling the Torso and Arms

Up to this point, you've been working on the face, but now you'll switch to the body. That means the face's reference images in the background are not useful anymore. You can just go to the Background Images panel in the 3D View Properties Region, delete the images, and load the full-body references; alternatively, you can replace the head references with the full-body references, but this time, you'll do something different: in the side view, you'll modify the reference image so the feet are touching the floor (increase the Y position value) and copy that Y value to the front and back reference images (see Figure 7.14).

The first thing you'll notice is that now the face is really big and out of proportion, so select everything you created so far (face, eyes, and lattices), move them, and scale them to make them fit the new references. The head should now be in place and you should have space to start working on Jim's body!

There is another problem you'll have to work out, which was created on purpose so you'd have an opportunity to play with your imagination a little and confront a situation you might encounter at some point in your own projects: Jim's designs show the character's arms in a pose slightly different to what you're actually going to model. Sometimes, arms are modeled in what is often called a T pose: completely extended and parallel to the floor. While the T pose is appropriate for modeling purposes (if everything is aligned to one of the 3D world's axes, it's easier to manipulate), it may not be the best thing for the model in future stages. For example, if you create the arms completely extended and parallel to the floor, when they are deformed you could find issues with the shoulders due to their large rotation range.

In Jim's case, the shoulder area has some details in the jacket, so you should create the arms slightly flexed at about 45 degrees or so; whether you rotate them up or down, the deformation won't be really big and Blender will keep those details. So in this situation, the reference images that were provided to you show something a little different. As a result, you'll have to create your model in a slightly different pose, but don't worry because during the process you'll learn a couple of tricks that will be very useful.

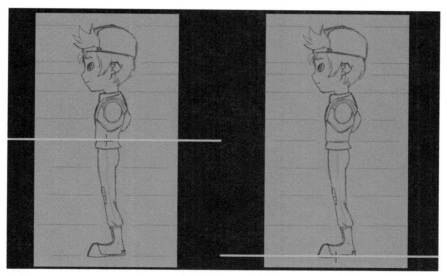

Figure 7.14   Jim's side reference floor position right after you import it (left) and after you slide it up until the feet are "touching" the floor (right)

Modeling the Basic Shapes for the Torso and Arms

Let's start blocking the shapes for Jim's torso and arms. In Figure 7.15, you'll see the first steps in the process for creating them. Because the face was modeled using box modeling, you'll have a chance to see how poly to poly works at this stage, even though it will be combined with box modeling.

1. Create a circle with 12 vertices, delete the left half, add a Mirror modifier to it (similar to what you did when you started working on the face) and place it in the base of the neck area. Enabling the Clipping option of the Mirror modifier will help with the central vertices of the torso.

2. Perform three extrusions (**E**), each one using two edges of the circle (two edges at the front, two at the back and two at the side). The two frontal edges will define the front of the torso, the two side edges will draw the trapezoids that go

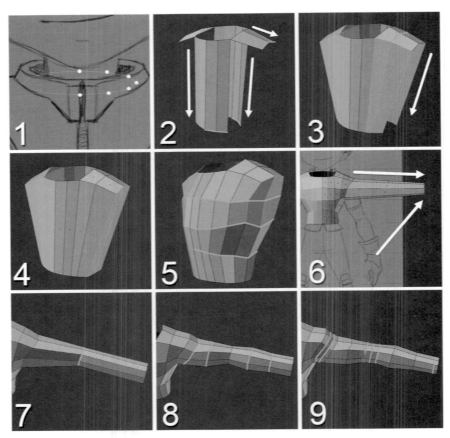

Figure 7.15   First steps in modeling Jim's torso and arms

to the shoulders, and the two edges in the back will extend to the hips and define the back.

3. Use the Loop Cut and Slide (**Ctrl + R**) tool to divide the trapezoid, then select the front and back outer edges and extrude them down. Now, select the four vertices that have an empty space between them and press **F** to create a face in that space (do the same with the empty spaces in the front and the back).

4. Select the side middle vertex of the shoulder, extrude it down to the hips, and then select the vertices and use **F** to fill them with faces. At this point, you have the envelope of the torso.

5. Make three horizontal loop cuts through the torso and adjust the shapes to the reference images. Keep an eye on the highlighted faces: you should be giving them the shape from which the arm will be extruded.

6. Select the faces highlighted in step 5 and extrude them horizontally to create the whole arm down to the wrist.

> **Tip**
> Even if you extrude it completely horizontally (on the X-axis), take the reference's arm as a guide. Imagine where the wrist would be if the arm were extended in a T pose. Later, you'll pose it better, but right now it's easier to work with it aligned to one axis (X, in this case). Also, the shape of the wrist will be a little irregular, so after the extrusion you can scale its vertices to 0 on the Y-axis, and from the front view it will now look flat.

7. Cut a new loop in the middle of the arm and adjust it a little to define the elbow. From the top view, move the loop back just a bit as if the arm were slightly flexed. This will help achieve the arm's shape. Keep in mind that you should rarely have the arms extended at 90 degrees, as that would look unnatural.

8. To continue defining the arm's shape, add some new loops with **Ctrl + R** in the biceps and forearm areas. Each time you add a loop, move the vertices around a little: if you add a lot of loops and try to modify the shape later, it will be more difficult.

> **Tip**
> There are a lot of ways to model things like arms or legs. One good way is to extrude (in the case of an arm) from the shoulder to the wrist, then cut the elbow, then divide the biceps and forearm, and keep dividing until you're happy with the result. This way, first you'll have the general shape of the arm, then you'll define the main articulation and it will have two divisions, then four, then eight. For me, it's easier to model this way, and better for developing details little by little than just extruding the shape piece by piece.

9. Add more loops in the articulation areas such as the shoulders and the elbow; it's important that you have enough geometry in those areas so they can deform correctly later on. You should also add another loop near the wrist to define the shape better when it's subdivided. As with the face, this is a good time to add a Subdivision Surface modifier and start checking on how the subdivided model will look.

Defining the Arms and Torso

In this section, we'll add more definition to the arms and torso, and we'll begin to add Jim's backpack. Continue with the next steps shown in Figure 7.16.

10. Add some more loops and definition to the arms.

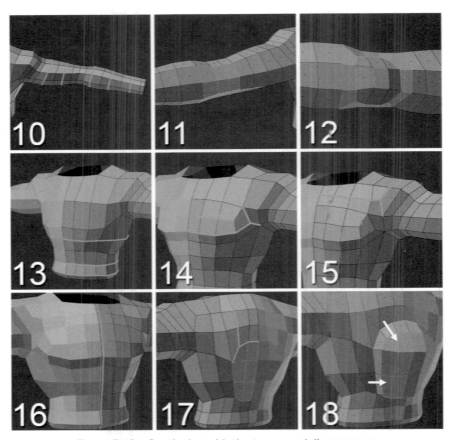

Figure 7.16   Continuing with the torso modeling process

> **Tip**
>
> If you really want a character's model to be awesome, work on the topology for the muscles in the arms and torso as you did for the face. In this specific model, the muscles are not very defined and the jacket deformations will be pretty simple, so we can go with topologies that are less complex.

11. Select the faces surrounding the elbow area. You'll want to add some definition to the elbow to make sure that when Jim flexes his arm, the elbow responds accordingly.

12. Make an Inset (**I**) in those faces and, using the sliding tools (select a vertex or edge and press **G** twice), make the loops around the elbow rounded. Also, select the face in the middle of the elbow loops (the one highlighted in the image) and move it out a little bit: this will give the outside of the elbow a little bulge.

13. Go back to the torso and add some loops to define the waist area.

14. Using the Knife tool (**K**), make a few cuts similar to those shown in the image and adjust the new geometry to define the pectoral area.

15. With the Knife tool, cut some new edges around the neck and near the shoulder to add a new loop in that area. (In the image, you can only see the front part of the torso, but the cut is exactly the same when modeling the back of the torso.)

16. Make two cuts vertically near the frontal mirror plane to create the zipper for the jacket.

17. Now, jump to the back side of the model. If you haven't done anything to it yet, adjust the shape of the vertices there according to the reference images. Create the cut indicated in the image and adjust the highlighted faces; they'll serve as a base for the backpack.

18. Extrude the selected faces for the backpack and adjust the shapes.

Detailing the Backpack and Jacket

Next, we'll add detail to Jim's jacket and backpack. Continue with the steps shown in Figure 7.17.

19. Select the edges that comprise the corners of the backpack and bevel them (**Ctrl + B**). Some triangles may appear (they're marked with red circles in the image); you'll have to get rid of them.

20. Two of the triangles are easily solved: they are triangles with an adjacent n-gon, generated because there were more than four faces sharing the same vertex. Select the edge between one of the triangles and the n-gon and simply collapse it, so the resulting geometry will be just an edge instead of a triangle (marked with light green circles in the image).

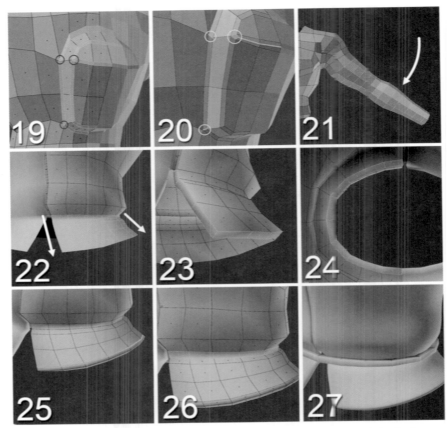

Figure 7.17   Adding some details to the back and the bottom of the jacket

The third triangle is a little trickier, because if you take it out, you'll also take out some of the detail added by the bevel. In this case, just add a new loop to the side of the triangle that is facing the beveled faces and slightly move the fourth vertex created with the new loop. This way, adding a few more faces to the model, you'll end up with a quad instead of a triangle.

21. Select all the arm's vertices except those near the shoulder. Place the 3D cursor in the shoulder and, using the Proportional Editing tool, rotate the arm to relax it a bit. Also, select the four faces at the end of the arm (the wrist) and delete them. They won't be visible at all and won't be useful later on, so it's a good idea to get them out of the way now.

> **Note**
>
> This step used a very nice utility of the 3D cursor that allows you to pose characters that don't yet have a skeleton! Just place the cursor in the articulation, select the part of the body you want to move, and, with the help of the Proportional Editing tool, you'll be able to pose your character pretty well (keep in mind, though, that you might need to adjust the vertices along the articulations after these operations).

22. Create a few extrusions to make up the shape of the flap at the bottom of the jacket.

23. With all the faces of the flap selected, press **Ctrl + F** to access the Face menu and use the Solidify tool to add some thickness to the flap. In the image, the thickness has been highlighted.

24. The thickness you added using Solidify in the previous step also created faces at the top of the flap that are not very useful there and can even cause some problems when subdividing the mesh, as they're welded onto the back side of other polygons. Delete those faces now. In the image, the faces are highlighted in a view from the jacket's interior. Also, Solidify didn't recognize the mirror's clipping in the back part of the jacket's flap and it generated a few faces in its inside. Get rid of them as well.

25. Add a new loop at the bottom of the flap so that when the model is subdivided, it's more defined there. You can merge (**Alt + M**) the bottom vertex of the zipper with the top vertex in the same area that the Solidify tool created, so you don't have an empty area there.

26. Select the faces all around the waist to create a new object for the belt. Press **Shift + D** to duplicate, and right click to leave the duplicated faces at their original position. Now press **P** and pick the Selected option: this will send those duplicated faces to a new object that you'll be able to modify.

27. Select the new object and, in Edit Mode (**Tab**), select the edge in the middle at the front and move it to the left until it attaches to the other side of the belt. Select all the object's faces, extrude them (**E**), and right click to cancel the movement and leave the new geometry in its original position. Now, make sure the Proportional Editing tool is disabled, press **Alt + S** (to scale along the normals) and scale the object's faces outward just a little to adjust the belt's thickness.

> **Note**
>
> When you duplicate an object or use the Separate tool to move a set of polygons from one object to a different one, the new object will keep the original object's modifiers.

Finishing the Belt and Adding a Neck to the Jacket

The jacket is almost finished, but we have to add a little more detail to the belt and the jacket needs a neck, so let's see how to model these features using the steps shown in Figure 7.18.

If you want to focus only on these details, you can hide the jacket itself so it's not in the way while you work. Just select it and press **H** to hide it. Press **Alt + H** to unhide everything again.

28. Select the top and bottom edges of the belt and bevel them so they'll look sharper when you subdivide them.

29. Place the 3D cursor in the neck area and create a circle (even though you could create the circle inside the jacket itself, for now it may be better to create a new object so you can treat the jacket and its neck separately). Similar to what you did when you started modeling the jacket, make it with 12 vertices, delete the left-side vertices, and add a Mirror modifier to the object with the Clipping option enabled. Then, just move the vertices to form the shape of the jacket's neck. Select all the edges of that circle and extrude them in.

30. Select all the faces and extrude them up. Now you'll have the base shape of the jacket's neck.

31. Temporarily unhide the jacket and the head to adjust the shape of the neck to them, and also perform the two extrusions shown in the image to add details to the neck.

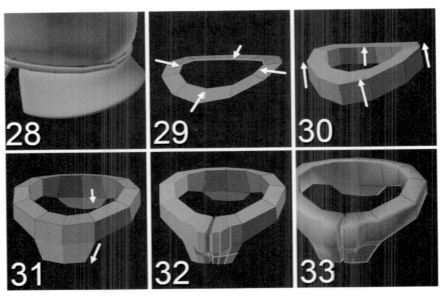

Figure 7.18   Modeling the jacket's neck details

32. Add a few loops to create the neck's front shape and the zipper.

33. Once you add the Subdivision Surface modifier (which you can always apply at any time to start checking the shapes), bevel the borders of the shape so they are more defined. Also, watch the subdivided model and adjust the shapes to make them fit Jim's head and body.

Modeling the Legs

Modeling the legs will be pretty easy compared to everything you've done so far. The process will be similar to the one you used for the arms, but you'll need to create the hips first with a base from which you can extrude the legs. Figure 7.19 shows the steps you need to follow to model Jim's legs.

1. Create another circle with 12 sides, delete the left half of the circle, and add a Mirror modifier with the Clipping option enabled. Make two extrusions and shape the model to look like hips.

2. Select the middle edges in the bottom of the model at the front and back side of the hips, and create a face between them with **F**. From this face, you'll create the crotch.

3. Divide the face you created in step 2 using the Loop Cut and Slide tool (**Ctrl + L**) and add three divisions. Move them down and adjust them to shape the crotch. At this point, the model should resemble underwear.

4. Select the loop around the hole that should be the top of the thigh and extrude it down to the top of the ankles, where the boots will start. The same adjustments you made to the arms will apply here: instead of exactly following the legs' current orientation, you can make them a little more perpendicular to the floor (more vertical).

5. As you did to define the elbow, cut a loop for the knee and adjust its vertices according to the reference images.

6. Now add some more loops to the leg and keep adjusting their shapes. Remember to add at least three loops for the hip and knee articulations so you can deform them properly later on when flexing the legs.

7. With the Knife tool (**K**), cut a shape similar to the one displayed in the image, both to add some more definition to the crotch area and to add some geometry there to make sure it will deform properly, as that area is very close to the articulations of the legs.

8. Do something similar for the back of the trousers, but give this area a slightly different shape to resemble the buttocks.

9. Create a new loop in the center of the pants to make up the seam in the cloth. This can be a little tricky and there are two different methods you could use: The

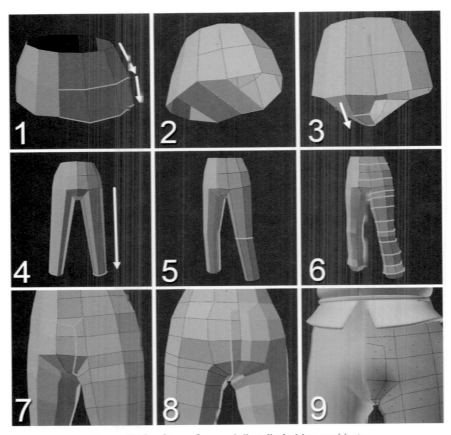

Figure 7.19   Steps for modeling Jim's hips and legs

first method is to use **Ctrl + R** to cut a new loop, and then slide the vertices near the mirror plane. At the bottom of the crotch near the legs, the new loop will be very close to the others surrounding it, while at the front, it will be further from them as there is more space.

The second method is to disable the clipping option for the Mirror modifier, move the central vertices apart, activate the mirror clipping again, and extrude those vertices to the middle. This way, both loops will be completely vertical and will become welded into a single loop at the center. Then, pick the central loop and scale it with **Alt + S** slightly to the inside, but very subtly. At this point, unhide the rest of the objects and make sure the trousers fit well inside the jacket's bottom flaps.

> **Tip**
>
> Sometimes, when you model using the poly to poly method, the normals of consecutive faces might be looking in opposite directions. When you see some faces that are darkened or have edges with strange dark and light colors, it may indicate this problem. A face's normal determines the direction in which the face is oriented, so if you join two faces that are looking in different directions, those weird effects may arise. If this happens, you have two options at your disposal to solve the issue: First, in the Face menu (**Ctrl + F**), select Flip Normals to invert the normal of the selected faces. Second, if you select several faces, you can press **Ctrl + N** to let Blender automatically calculate in what direction all the normals should be looking and it will conform all of them at once.

Modeling the Boots

Jim needs some feet to stand on, of course. In this section, we'll model the boots. Figure 7.20 shows the steps for doing so. At this point, you should be getting up to speed and you're probably becoming more proficient with modeling and using Blender's tools, so the boots should be an easy task!

1. Create an eight-sided circle at the top of the boots, as shown in the reference images. Keep in mind that you'll need two boots: you can add a Mirror modifier to get the second boot (place the origin of the boot in the center so they'll be aligned), or you can just manually duplicate and mirror the boot afterward.

   > **Tip**
   >
   > In situations like this one, you can use a little trick to save some time: select the bottom loop (**Alt + RMB**) of the trousers where they meet the boots, duplicate it (**Shift + D**), and separate it (**P**) into a different object that will become the boots. This way, you'll already have the Subdivided Surface and Mirror modifiers added to the new object.

2. Extrude (**E**) all the edges down to the ankle. Perform a couple of loop cuts to define the shape.

3. Select all the edges from the circle at the bottom except the two in front and extrude them down to the heel. Then select the two in front and make two extrusions to create the toe shape.

4. Create a face in the empty space at both sides of the boot.

5. Fill the sole of the boot with quads.

   > **Tip**
   >
   > One of the reasons why you should work with even numbers (like eight sides for the initial circle, for example) is that usually you'll be able to fill empty spaces with quads quite easily.

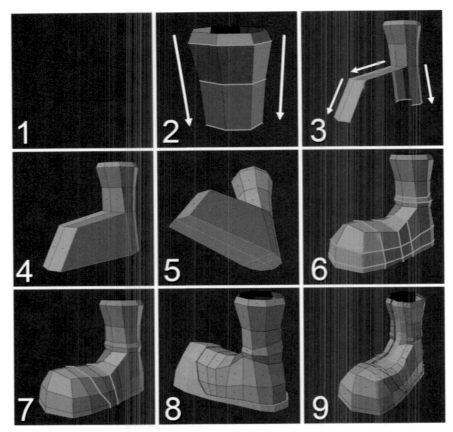

Figure 7.20   Steps for modeling Jim's boots

6. Add some loops to start defining the boot's shape.

7. Perform a couple of loop cuts (**Ctrl + R**) to add definition in the articulation of the foot (also remember how several loops were added previously at the knee and ankle articulations), so deformations will work well later on. One of these loops will also help you create the shape of some of the details in the next step.

8. Select the area highlighted in the image (leave the sole of the boot unselected), extrude it (**E**), right click to cancel the movement, and scale in the normal with **Alt + S**. This will "draw" the boot's details.

9. Finish the details with a few minor operations: Select the two central face loops that go from the top almost to the toe and create an inset (**I**) there, then extrude it in to define the area where the shoelaces would be (see Chapter 9 to learn how

to paint textures). Also, when you extrude, two faces will be generated at the top of the boot with the same thickness as the extrusion and you can delete them. As a finishing touch, you can add some loops to the thickness of the seams and small features to make them much more defined when subdivided. Last but not least, adjust the shapes of the boots where they meet the trousers: some deforming may be needed and don't hesitate to use the Proportional Editing tools for that purpose.

Modeling the Hands

Hands are quite difficult to model, but in this example we'll keep it simple so you learn an easy way of doing it. (If something goes wrong, don't worry—just start again. Sooner or later, you'll get it right!)

Building the Basic Hand Shape

Figure 7.21 shows the modeling process for a hand. You can model it wherever you want and move and scale it later according to the rest of the model.

1. Start by creating a cube.
2. Make it narrower and move one of the edges to the middle of what will be the palm of the hand. The diagonal face left there will serve as the base for the thumb.
3. Add two loop cuts, one near the wrist, another one near the fingers. The fingers will be in the upper part of the shape.

> **Tip**
> Remember to keep adjusting the vertices as you add them; the sooner you make adjustments, the easier the modeling process will be later when you keep adding new vertices.

4. Select the base face and extrude it to create the preliminary shape for the thumb.
5. Select everything and, in the Specials menu (**W**), use the Subdivide Smooth tool to add geometry to work with. Notice how the vertices have been distributed in a way that forms the four finger bases at the top of the palm.

> **Caution**
> There are two major errors people commit when modeling hands at this stage: they model so the thumb grows from the side of the hand instead of partly from the front, and they make the other four fingers all the same height. Both of these errors can make your hand look very unnatural.

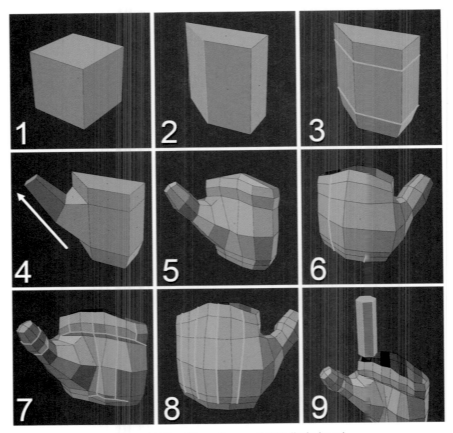

Figure 7.21   Steps for modeling Jim's hand

6. Delete the top faces (the base for the fingers) and, on the back of the hand, add two cuts to end up with the same four bases for the fingers.

7. Make some cuts as shown in the image. The purpose of these cuts is to create two edges on each side of the hand to prepare the geometry for connecting the fingers later. You can see how the outer cuts are made in such a way that they stay at the top of the hand, while the central cuts go almost to the wrist to help define the shapes of the palm. Also, add a couple of loops to the thumb to give it some detail.

8. Make some similar cuts on the back of the hand that will help define the tendons and knuckles. Look at how the cuts end before reaching the wrist. This allows you to extrude the flap of the glove with fewer edges later on and then arrange the topology with the Knife tool.

9. On top of the hand, create a cylinder with six vertices (and fill the top with an n-gon). This will serve as a preliminary shape for the fingers. You'll model one of the fingers and then duplicate and modify those duplicates to create the other fingers.

Adding the Fingers and Wrist

As you've realized by now, modeling hands is quite challenging and it's difficult to get them right. Follow the steps shown in the Figure 7.22 to add the fingers and wrist, and finish the hand modeling. From time to time, it's a good idea to add a Subdivision Surface modifier to take a look at the smooth shape that results.

10. Make a few cuts in the finger to define the articulations. Join two vertices at the top to convert the n-gon into two quads. You can also delete the n-gon at the bottom, as you won't need it.

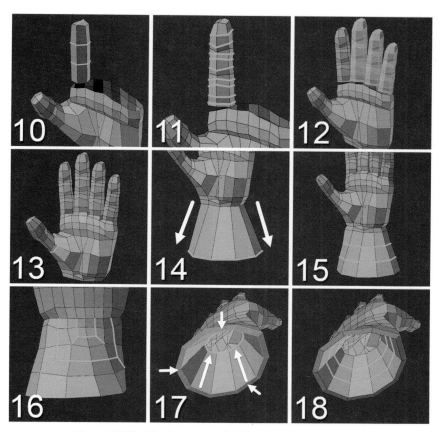

Figure 7.22   Final steps to finish modeling Jim's hand

11. Add some more loops to the finger and define its shape.

12. Select the whole finger (you can select groups of connected faces with **L**) and duplicate it three times. Move, scale, and adjust the duplicates to fit on the hand.

13. Activate AutoMerge (on the 3D View header near the Snapping options or in the Mesh menu), and use the vertex snapping tools to drag the vertices at the bottom of the fingers to the corresponding vertices at the top of the hand. Then, adjust the vertices to make the fingers look natural. You could also add another loop at the base of the thumb.

14. Extrude the base of the hand down to create the shape for the glove's wrist flap.

> **Tip**
>
> The extruded edges may not be as circular as they should be. If you activate the LoopTools add-on, you can use the Circle tool to select that loop and it will be converted into a perfect circle. Then, you can scale it and adjust it to become an oval that is more typical of the wrist shape.

15. Add two loop cuts to the flap to define the shapes a little more.

16. Remember those unfinished cuts from step 8? Go ahead and use the Knife tool (**K**) to arrange them, making some cuts similar to the ones shown in this step's image. Then, if the shape gets a little messy, you can select the whole area and use the Smooth Vertices option.

17. Select the bottom loop of the flap, extrude it slightly to add some thickness to the glove, and extrude it up again to the interior of the wrist. This is just to prevent an empty space between the arm mesh and the glove.

18. Add a couple of divisions to the interior of the flap so in case you need to deform it, you'll have enough geometry.

At this point, you may want to adjust the overall shape of the hand. Unhide the rest of the models (if you hid them previously) and scale, rotate, and move the hand to place it where it needs to be according to the arm, and make sure it has the right scale. Once it's in place, you may want to mirror it on the other side. You can do this with the same procedure you used for the eyes: select the hand (in Object Mode; you can also use **Ctrl + A** to apply the rotation and scale to assure that the hand will mirror as expected), place the 3D cursor in the center of the model (press **Shift + C**), press **.** (period) on the keyboard to set the pivot point to the 3D cursor, press **Ctrl + M** to mirror, and then press **X** to select the mirror axis. Finally, press **Enter** to confirm. Figure 7.23 shows the results up to this point.

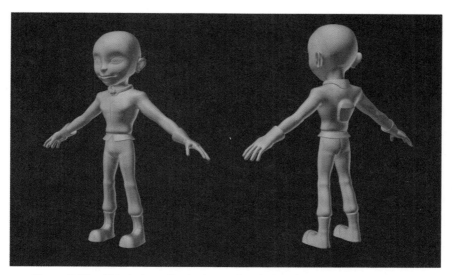

Figure 7.23 This is how Jim looks so far. Only a few details are missing.

Modeling the Cap

Next, we're going to create the cap and later we'll model some hair to poke out around the cap. Modeling the cap should be easy, but it involves a few tricky steps.

Creating the Base of the Cap

The first steps for building Jim's cap are shown in Figure 7.24.

1. Create a UV Sphere with eight vertices and six rings. Delete the bottom and left section of the sphere and add a Mirror modifier to it. Scale it on the Z-axis so it's no longer perfectly spherical.

2. Convert the selected faces from triangles to quads using the Dissolve Faces tool (**X**). Repeatedly select two adjacent triangles and invoke the Dissolve Faces tool until all the triangles are converted to quads. You can add a Subdivision Surface modifier now.

3. With the Knife tool (**K**), make two cuts through the cap similar to those in the image. The two cuts should be very close to each other so that when the model is subdivided, the seam will be sharp. At the top of the cap, the inner line touches the center of the mirror and the other line continues through the cap's center to its other side.

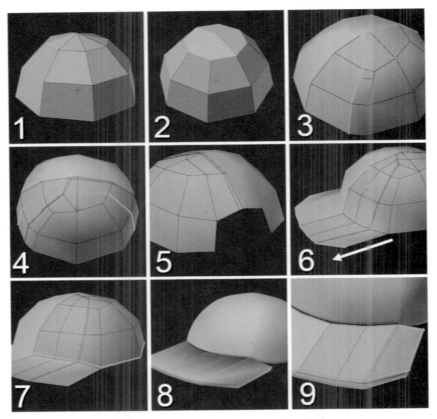

Figure 7.24 The first steps in modeling Jim's cap

4. Perform a loop cut and adjust the resulting vertices to smooth the cap's shape.

5. On the back side of the cap, delete the two central faces at the bottom.

6. Go back to the front side and extrude the front edges at the bottom to create the cap's visor.

7. Move the central faces of the cap up a little to make the visor bend up in the middle. Also, add a new loop near the bottom all around the cap's body. Add a Solidify modifier before the Subdivision Surface modifier in the stack and adjust its thickness until it looks right to you.

8. Now, select the visor's faces and press **P** to separate them from the cap's body. Doing this after adding the modifiers to the original model gives you the modifiers in this new model as well.

9. Add some new loops near all of the visor's borders to help define its shapes.

Adding Details to the Cap

Now that we have the cap's base and visor, let's keep going and add some details to them! The steps for this are shown in Figure 7.25.

10. Move the sides of the cap's visor back until there is no empty space between them and the cap's body.

11. Create a little sphere, scale it on the Z-axis, and place it at the top of the cap.

12. Go back to the cap's body and use the Knife tool (**K**) to create a new loop around the hole at the back of the cap. If you have to create some triangles to perform that cut, do so and merge the vertices afterward to leave only quads. Also, create a new loop at the bottom of the cap.

13. Make an extrusion to create the strap on the back of the hat and divide it once to give it more definition.

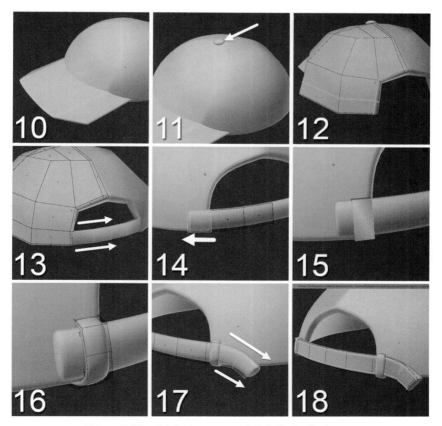

Figure 7.25   Adding some cool details to Jim's cap

14. Select the two strap faces and separate them to a different object with **P** (pick the Selection option). Make one extrusion to the left, adjust it to the cap, and cut a loop very close to the outer edge so that shape becomes more defined when you subdivide it.

15. Select one of those outer faces of the strap, duplicate it (**Shift + D**), and separate it to a different object (**P**). You'll use this as the support for the strap.

16. Make some extrusions and cuts to create something similar to what you can see in the image. You may also need to adjust the Solidify thickness.

> **Tip**
>
> Keep in mind that in the modifiers' options, you can activate the Subdivision Surface and the Solidify modifiers in order to see their effects while in Edit Mode and this will give you instant feedback while you're modeling.

17. Make one side of the strap a little loose. If you're in Edit Mode, go to Object Mode by pressing **Tab** and apply the Mirror modifier. (You can only apply modifiers when you're not in Edit Mode; once a modifier is applied, its effect will then be part of the object's original mesh.) After you apply the Mirror modifier, return to Edit Mode and perform some extrusions on one side of the strap. Move them and rotate them so one hangs down a bit.

18. At the top and bottom of the strap, add two loop cuts with **Ctrl + R** so the shape is much more defined. Another thing you can do at this point is to select every object that will be part of the cap and then finally select the cap's body. Press **Ctrl + P** and choose Object from the list: this will connect all the objects to the cap's body, so now you only need to select and move the cap's body and the rest of the pieces will follow.

The cap is finished, so you just have to move it, scale it, and place it on top of Jim's head. Follow the reference images to do that, or at this advanced point of the modeling process, you can probably ignore the references and just place the cap where you think it fits best!

Modeling the Hair

Modeling hair is very complex and there are a lot of ways to create it, each one of them producing different results. For example, you can model it with flat surfaces, each one of them representing a lock of hair, perhaps with a hair texture applied to them. Another option, which is the most realistic, is to use hair particles: you select the areas of the head that you want to have hair, and Blender will generate hair that you'll be able to comb, cut, and style. After that, you can even simulate the effects of gravity or wind on it. That's a pretty complex operation, though (and it requires a powerful computer as well). In this case, you'll be creating a mesh hair, which is basically modeling the hair shapes manually and adapting the meshes to the character's hair style.

> **Tip**
>
> In 3D, there is a situation that almost represents a rule: if it won't be seen, don't create it! For example, if Jim is always going to wear a cap, why should you create the hair under the cap if it can't be seen? We'll be creating Jim's hair in this section, but we'll only be focusing on the parts of it that will be seen.

Shaping Locks of Hair

In Figure 7.26, you can see the basic steps to follow to start creating locks of hair.

1. Select the top faces of the head; the hair will be created from them. Duplicate them (**Shift + D**) and separate them into a new object (**P**). Also, once the object is separated, apply the Mirror modifier (press the Apply button in the modifier's options), as from this point on you will be doing different things on each side of the head so the hair looks more realistic.

2. Delete some of the faces from the sides of the head to prevent every lock of hair from extruding from the same height on the scalp. (In the image, the Subdivide Surface modifier has been disabled so you can better see what's going on, but it will be enabled again for the next steps.)

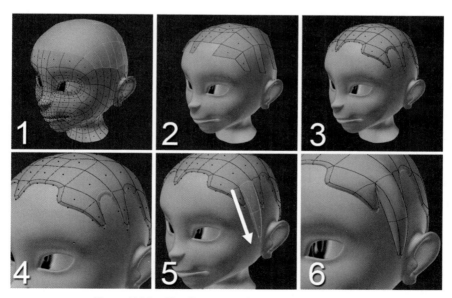

Figure 7.26   The first steps for creating Jim's hair

> **Tip**
>
> At this point, to make things a little easier, you can send all the objects you've created in the scene to one layer (press **M** and select one of the squares), the cap to a second layer, and the hair to a third layer. This will allow you to work on the hair and be able to show or hide the components of the cap very quickly (by pressing **Shift** to add or subtract a layer from those that are visible on the 3D View header). Keep in mind that you have to be in Object Mode to enable or disable layers, and that you can also use the numbers on your keyboard, not those on the NumPad, to show or hide layers.

3. Select all the faces of the scalp, go to the Faces menu (**Ctrl + F**), and choose Solidify. Adjust its options; you may want to select everything again (**A**) to scale the new model up or down as needed to give it just enough thickness to stay on the head's surface.

4. Select some of the faces created by the thickness of the Solidify tool. You'll be extruding the locks of hair from them.

5. Make a couple of extrusions and make sure to scale the final face down a lot so it looks like a spike when subdivided. Adjust the vertices to how you want the lock of hair to look. The lock in the image is adjusted to the face's surface.

6. Add some thickness to the lock by moving the edges that are on the lock's front side.

Now, continue to do the same thing all around the head. Turn on the visibility of the cap layer now and then to see how the hair fits with it.

Adding Natural Details to the Hair

To make the hair look even more natural, take those locks of hair and, by adjusting their vertices and edges, make them overlap other locks of hair (see Figure 7.27).

Once you've created and overlapped locks of hair all around the head (it may take a while), you'll probably have some empty areas. Something you can do to fill those areas is to select a whole lock of hair, duplicate it several times, and adjust its vertices to layer it over other locks of hair, placing it above or below them (see Figure 7.28). Figure 7.29 shows you how the geometry of the hair looks so far.

Recall from the reference images that the cap is on backwards and the hair at the front of Jim's head that protrudes from the cap's hole will be a little tricky to model. You can select a lock of hair, similar to the one you duplicated before, and place it on the cap's hole. Add some loops to it, adjust it to fit the shape you want it to have, and make the lock large enough for its base to cover a good portion of the hole. After that, you can duplicate it, scale it, and rotate it to adjust it and cover some of the remaining parts of the hole, this time making the lock much smaller. Try to cover the hole completely with the big lock of hair and two or three of the smaller locks. In Figure 7.30, you can see the steps to create that aspect of the hair.

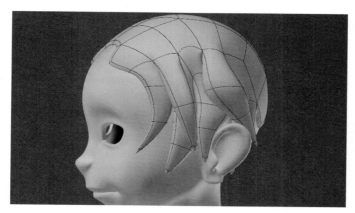

Figure 7.27   Overlapping locks make the hair look a lot more natural.

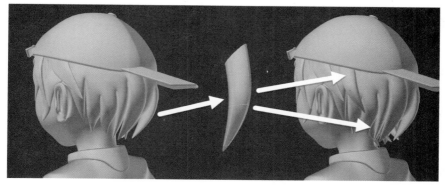

Figure 7.28   Duplicating locks of hair and placing them to cover empty spaces

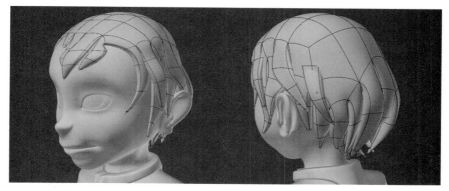

Figure 7.29   The result so far gives you an idea of how the vertices look.

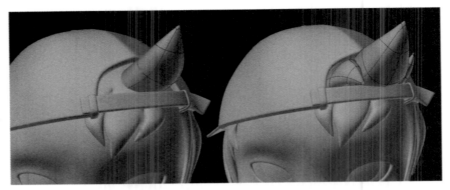

Figure 7.30   Adding the hair that will protrude from the hole in the cap

As you can see, modeling hair is not an easy task, especially since it needs a lot of adjustments in order to make it fit the head and the cap, but now it looks quite natural, so let's move on to adding the final details!

Modeling the Final Details

After all you have done throughout this chapter, you should already know how to use the modeling tools and be able to interact pretty well with meshes (tools may not be user friendly the whole time, but meshes are generally easy to use, once you get used to them). In this last section, I ll briefly explain how I modeled some of these final details and added them to the previous models, but there aren't any step-by-step instructions in this section. The images show the results so you can check them out and get ideas for other ways to work. Consider this section an exercise: study the results, try to use your acquired knowledge about Blender modeling tools, and figure out how to model these final details on your own.

The details that are modeled here (and of course you can create some more if you want to) are the eyebrows, the badges for the chest and the cap, the communicator in Jim's ear, his teeth and tongue, and a couple of details in the clothing.

Eyebrows

Creating the eyebrows was pretty simple. I selected three edges on top of the eye that had the eyebrow shape. I duplicated and separated them in a new mesh. I extruded them up to have some shape and thickness, and moved the vertices around a little to create the eyebrow's shape. Then, I applied a Solidify modifier with a little thickness before adding the Subdivide Surface modifier. It's important that you keep an eye on the modifiers' order: if you apply Solidify after the Subdivide Surface modifier, the result will be completely different. In Figure 7.31, you can see what the eyebrows look like.

Figure 7.31 Jim's eyebrows added

> **Tip**
>
> For this and some of the other details that follow, you'll see how mixing several modifiers is quite helpful for achieving the results you need easily and very quickly.

Communicator

The communicator earpiece was modeled from a part of the ear. When you need to make one object fit another one, as in this case, it's a good idea to create the second object from a part of the first one: doing this will make sure the geometries fit together. Just select the faces of the ear that can be useful for the communicator and then duplicate and separate them, as you've already done a number of times before. From the new object, just start modeling and giving shape to the communicator, extruding, beveling, and using every kind of tool you need. The antenna (see Figure 7.32) was created with two cylinders—pretty simple!

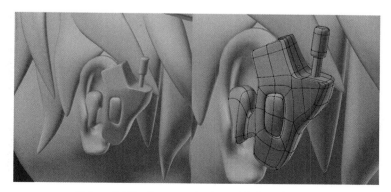

Figure 7.32 Communicator added to the ear

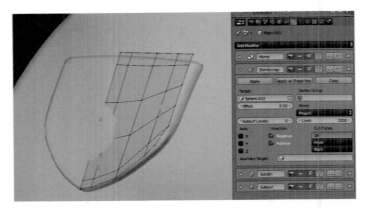

Figure 7.33   For modeling the badge,
several modifiers were used to simplify the process.

Badges

The badges take advantage of another modifier, Shrink Wrap, which lets you "project" an object over the surface of another object. Just add the modifier and, in the object's name field, select the one over which you want to project the Shrink Wrap modifier. Before doing that, you can move the badge, which is a very simple and flat object, to the surface on which you want to project it, such as over the chest. Play with the options for the Shrink Wrap modifier until you're happy with the projection and then you can apply a Solidify modifier. What's cool about this is that if you applied thickness to the model, it would be lost in the projection with Shrink Wrap, but because the Solidify modifier adds thickness after the projection, it works just perfectly! Finally, just add a Subdivide Surface modifier. Mixing different modifiers to achieve a particular effect is, as you can see, a very powerful technique (see Figure 7.33).

Teeth and Tongue

The teeth and the tongue are really simple objects to model. Just two curved surfaces with thickness will do for the teeth, and the tongue is also a very basic shape. In Figure 7.34, you can see these features and their basic topology (in the figure, the teeth are apart so you can see the tongue, but they're really touching each other inside Jim's mouth). You should be able to do something similar with the skills you've learned so far. These features are not very complex, but are stylized similar to the rest of the character, so when Jim opens his mouth, you will see something inside. When you are working on these models, you may want to adjust the shape of the inner mouth so it doesn't cover the teeth or create other problems of intersecting geometry.

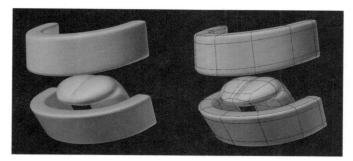

Figure 7.34   The teeth and the tongue ready to go into Jim's mouth

Other Clothing Details

In the reference images, some details were added to the clothing and the technique used was basically similar to the one used for the eyebrows: duplicating and separating parts of the clothes, and then adjusting them and applying modifiers such as Solidify to add some thickness.

In Figure 7.35, you can see Jim up to this point, looking cool!

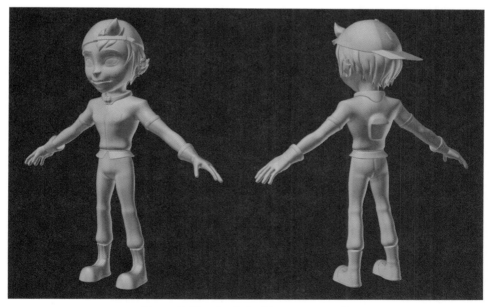

Figure 7.35   Jim is looking pretty cool!

Summary

Wow! I know this was a tough chapter, but if you've come through it, you've learned a lot for sure and you should now have your finished model. You know how to model the different parts of a character step by step and, hopefully, you've developed some insights about how to use Blender's modeling tools. Also, if you've followed the instructions and tried to use the keyboard shortcuts, you might already be more efficient and will be able to remember a lot of the keystrokes for using the basic tools. Modeling with polygons is not very artistic when it comes to topology, but if you find it interesting, it can be a very enjoyable experience and, of course, when you're done and can see the finished model, it will be quite rewarding.

Exercises

1. Take the model further by adding some more details, such as the lines in the cap or some of the details on the clothes.
2. Explain why having a good topology is essential for an animated model. List some rules to follow that will ensure you have a good topology.

IV

Unwrapping, Painting, and Shading

8

Unwrapping and UVs in Blender

Unwrapping is a fundamental step in animation that comes before adding textures to a 3D model. Without it, the textures would be randomly projected on the model's surface. UVs (the 2D counterpart to XYZs in 3D space) are the internal 2D positions of the vertices of a three-dimensional mesh; they define how a 2D texture will be projected on the mesh's surface. Unwrapping may look a little odd and it's a task a lot of people dislike, but that's usually due to their lack of understanding of how it works. Sometimes, it can indeed be a little tedious, but if you learn to like it, unwrapping can be a fun part of the process! Watching how everything starts to make sense and work properly can be a very rewarding experience, but be aware: you'll need some patience.

Fortunately, Blender provides some helpful tools to unwrap your models and people who come from other software usually love the way the unwrapping process works in Blender (there are even glowing reports from professionals working on Hollywood films who use Blender for UVs). But as with almost everything else in Blender, unwrapping is done quite differently, so if you come from other software, forget the way you worked before and just open your mind for a little while!

How Unwrapping and UVs Work

There's something tricky that happens with textures, which define the colors of your models' surfaces: You have a 3D model, but the image texture is 2D, so how do you "paint" a 3D model with a 2D texture? The answer is UVs. The 3D model has its vertices located on the X, Y, and Z axes, but for Blender, internally, they're on the U and V axes as well, and the U and V axes are 2D positions, made to be used for texture projection. In the UV/Image Editor, you can access those UVs and adjust them to define how a texture is projected onto a 3D model.

Unwrapping (also called UV mapping) is the process of adjusting an object's UVs so the texture projection works properly. It's probably easier to understand if you see how this process works.

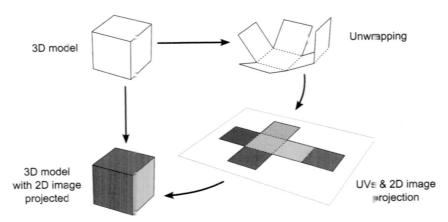

Figure 8.1   The unwrapping procedure

Do you remember those exercises when you were a kid in which you took a two-dimensional piece of paper and, by cutting and folding it in a certain way, you ended up with a three-dimensional shape like a cube? Unwrapping can be explained with that example, only in reverse order: you have a 3D model, you unfold it into a 2D shape using the UV/Image Editor, and then convert it into a plane. (It won't affect the shapes in your 3D model at all; this only happens "under the hood.") Figure 8.1 illustrates this procedure.

As you can see, unwrapping is like unfolding the 3D model and converting it to a 2D mesh. You can project an image onto that mesh and that projection will have effects on the 3D model itself.

Unwrapping in Blender

Now that you understand how unwrapping works, let's explore the tools that Blender provides to use unwrapping in the basic workflow.

To begin unwrapping in Blender, you first select the part of the model you want to unwrap and access the unwrapping options (you'll see them in a moment). Once you unwrap the selection, it will appear unfolded in the UV/Image Editor, where you can adjust the UVs, weld them to other parts of the model you've unwrapped before, or just place them where you want them to be in the image.

Keep in mind that after unwrapping a model, you will usually create textures tailored to that specific UVs; however, sometimes you're in a hurry, and you just need to display a part of an image in a specific position of the 3D model. In that case, you can adapt the UVs to the given image and not the other way around.

Now, let's take a look at the different tools and how to use them, and then you'll see how to unwrap a very basic model in order to understand the unwrapping procedures.

The UV/Image Editor

The UV/Image Editor is the part of the Blender interface where you can see and adjust the UVs. It's also useful when you want to load an image and use it for reference. Figure 8.2 shows an overview of the UV/Image Editor.

> **Tip**
>
> Loading an image into the UV/Image Editor can be as easy as dragging it from a folder on your hard drive. Click and drag the image file over the UV/Image Editor and just drop it. Blender should load it immediately.

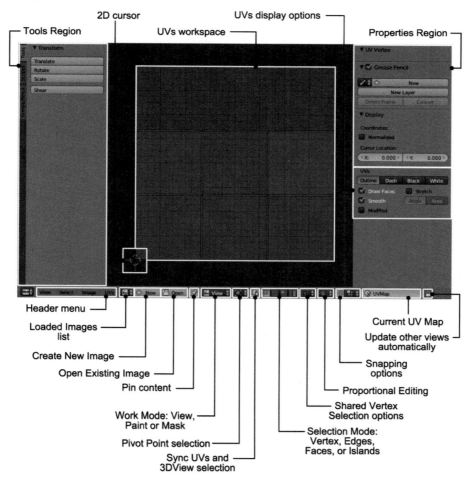

Figure 8.2   The UV/Image Editor and its options

The list that follows explains some of the main options available in the UV/Image Editor.

- **Interface:** This is basically a normal Blender editor. It has its own Tools and Properties regions at the left and right sides, the workspace is in the center, and there is also a header on which you can find buttons for most of the options.

- **2D cursor:** The 2D Editor has a cursor that is similar to the 3D cursor; you can use it to align vertices or other UV elements. Place it with a left click and, with **Shift + S,** you'll see the snap options you can use with the 2D cursor.

- **Display panel:** In the Properties Region, you can see the Display panel that lets you customize how you see the UVs; it even has a Stretch option, which shows the distortion based on the angle or area of faces in the UV map compared to the 3D model. It's quite useful for identifying complicated areas. If the faces are very stretched (a blue face is good and a turquoise face is not bad, but you should avoid green and yellow faces), the texture will probably look distorted or it will be of poor quality when you project on that surface.

The header provides quite a few options.

- **Header menu:** View, Select, Image, and UVs menus are available; the UVs menu is especially important, as it provides most of the unwrapping tools.

- **Loaded Images List, Create New Image, and Open Existing Image:** You can load images, choose some from the drop-down list that have been already loaded, or even create new ones right inside Blender (like a solid-color image or a UV Test Grid, which you'll see later).

- **Pin content:** If you click on the Pin icon, the current image will be pinned and always shown independently of other objects you have selected. However, this tool doesn't work with UV editing, only with the image you display in the UV/Image editor because the editor shows only the UV layout from the object you're working on in Edit Mode. This option comes in handy when you want to display a reference image in the UV/Image Editor.

- **Work Mode:** In the Work Mode menu, you can choose between View, Paint, or Mask modes. View is the usual mode you'll use to adjust UVs and view images. Paint Mode allows you to paint directly in the 2D image when you're in Texture Painting Interaction Mode in 3D View as well (see Chapter 9). Mask is a special mode in which you can create masks that you can use later in the Node Compositor to isolate parts of an image.

- **Pivot Point selection:** The Pivot Point works exactly the same as in the 3D View; you can select the pivot point from which to rotate or scale objects and, for example, that's how you can use the 2D cursor as a pivot point. As with 3D View, you can press . (period) and , (comma) on your keyboard to switch between the 2D cursor and the center of the selection for the pivot point.

- **Sync UVs and 3D View selection:** The tool that synchronizes the UVs selection with the 3D model can be useful in complex modeling to find out where a specific vertex or face in the model is located on the UVs. Keep in mind that using this mode all the time may not be a good idea, as it limits some options for unwrapping.

- **Selection Mode:** In the UV/Image Editor, you can switch between Vertices, Edges, Faces, and Islands selection modes. (An island is a group of connected faces.) You can also select an island, similarly to the 3D View, by pressing **L**.

- **Shared Vertex selection options:** Shared Vertex options are interesting. Let's say that on the UVs, Blender treats each one of the faces separately, but it allows you to select vertices depending on certain conditions, such as if the vertices share their X, Y, and Z position, in the actual 3D model. When this option is disabled and you select a vertex or a face, it will move alone and the connected vertices or faces will stay in their current places. If they are overlapped in the UV/Image Editor, the Shared Location option will treat them as if they were welded on the UVs, but only if they share the same location in the 3D model. The Shared Vertex option will select the vertices that share the position in the 3D model, even if they're separated on the UVs. The best way to understand this is to try it out.

> **Note**
>
> To better understand the Shared Vertex options, you have to know how Blender treats UVs. Vertices in a 3D mesh are positioned on X, Y, and Z axes, while vertices in a UV layout are positioned on the U and V axes. The difference is that while one face in a 3D mesh is typically connected to another, faces in the UV space can be freed from their neighboring faces. This allows you to apply a different texture to a different part of the model, even though the parts might be adjacent in the 3D model.

- **Proportional Editing and Snapping options:** You also have Proportional Editing and Snapping tools in the UV/Image Editor to help you manipulate UVs.

- **Current UV Map:** The UV Map name is pretty important because in Blender, a single object can have different UV maps that can be used independently when building complex materials, so you can use two textures that are differently distributed depending on the UV map they use. UVMap is the default name and, most of the time, you'll only be using a single map. If at some point you want to create other UV maps, you can go to the Properties Editor and look for the UV Maps panel on the Mesh tab.

- **Update other views automatically:** The last icon you'll see on the header is a lock. This option, when enabled, will make other views in Blender show real-time updates while you adjust UVs. If you're using an old or slow computer, you may prefer to turn this feature off and save resources.

> **Tip**
>
> Constantly switching between UVs and reference images doesn't sound like a good time, and for sure it's not efficient. Remember that you don't need to decide between adjusting your UVs and loading an image for reference; in Blender, you can have both! Divide your interface and use two UV/Image Editors at the same time. In the editor you're using for a reference image, make sure to click the Pin icon on the header; this way, it doesn't matter what you select or what you're doing, that editor will keep showing that image.

Navigating the UV/Image Editor

Navigation in the UV/Image Editor is pretty simple: **MMB** drag to pan, and use the scroll wheel or **Ctrl + MMB** drag to zoom in and out. A left click positions the 2D cursor. Apart from that, controls are exactly the same as in 3D View: right click to select, **RMB** drag to move, and **G, R,** and **S** to move, rotate, or scale the selections.

Also, there are certain features from other editors that will work in the UV/Image Editor as well, such as the Hide and Unhide feature (**H** and **Alt + H**) or switching between selection modes with **Ctrl + Tab**.

Accessing the Unwrapping Menus

Blender provides some tools for unwrapping that you can find within the interface.

- Select some faces in Edit Mode (usually, when unwrapping you'll work with faces) and press **U** to display the UV Mapping pop-up menu.
- Marking Seams is one of the key tools to use when unwrapping and you can access it from the Edge menu (**Ctrl + E**) after selecting one or more edges (you'll learn about seams in a moment).
- In the Tools Region of the 3D View, go to the Shading / UVs tab. There, you'll find the UV Mapping options and the Seams options as well.
- From the 3D View header, in the Mesh menu, you can access the UV Unwrap menu too.

UV Mapping Tools

In Figure 8.3, you can see the UV Mapping menu (press **U** in the 3D View) and the Edges menu (**Ctrl + E**) with the Mark Seam and Clear Seam options that are essential for unwrapping in Blender.

Let's cover very briefly how the UV Mapping tools work so you have an idea of what they do when you start using them later in this chapter.

- **Mark and Clear Seam:** From the Edges menu, select one or more edges, press **Ctrl + E** to access the Edge menu and choose Mark Seam. This will show those edges in the 3D View with a red outline. To clear the seam mark, just select the edges you want to clear, press **Ctrl + E,** and choose Clear Seam.

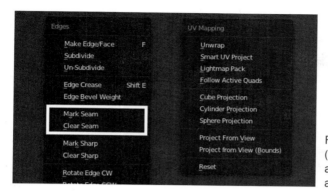

Figure 8.3   Edges menu (**Ctrl + E**) with the Mark and Clear Seam options, and UV Mapping menu (**U**)

- **Unwrap:** This is the main unwrapping tool in Blender. Press **U** to access the UV Mapping menu and select Unwrap. This option basically unfolds the model, taking into account the mesh's borders and seams. It usually gives good results if the seams are correctly placed.

- **Smart UV Project:** With this option, you don't need to mark seams and it can work nicely for simple objects. It unwraps your object, separating parts of it depending on parameters you'll define in a pop-up menu, such as the angle between faces.

- **Lightmap Pack:** This option is not recommended, unless you want to create UVs in a completely automatic way, which can be useful for complex objects you don't need to be very accurate or for objects you'll texture using automatic methods (such as texture baking, which projects details from one model onto another using textures). It separates every single face and arranges them all in order to use the most space possible in the image.

- **Follow Active Quads:** This option provides a very technical result (everything is aligned in vertical and horizontal lines), but it works well only with small selections. As the name implies, it doesn't work with faces that are not four sided, so triangles, for example, will be excluded when using this tool.

- **Cube, Cylinder, and Sphere projections:** These are really basic tools, but can sometimes be useful. These types of projections use the pivot point of the object and the view angle to work, so keep that in mind. After using them, you can find some options in the Operator panel that may be useful for adjusting the results.

- **Project from View:** This option is quite interesting, as it takes the selection and unwraps it in the UV/Image Editor while you see it in the 3D View. Of course, your point of view is key here, and perspective will be maintained as well. If you pick the option of Project from View (Bounds), it will scale the resulting UVs to the borders of the UV workspace.

- **Reset:** This option takes every selected face and returns it to its original state, occupying the whole UV map.

> **Tip**
>
> To better understand what these unwrapping tools do, try them and see the results for yourself. Some of them may seem more efficient or easy to use than others, and it's very difficult to clearly understand their effects just by reading an explanation. This is true for every part of the learning process, not only unwrapping: trial and error are the best teachers!

Seams

Seams are the "borders" of an unwrapping operation. Remember the cube in Figure 8.1? When it's unwrapped, the normal black continuous lines would be the seams. You can also think of seams in clothing; before a shirt is made, it's just a series of flat pieces that are later joined into a three-dimensional garment by stitching them together at their seams. In 3D, the most popular unwrapping method is to use seams; first, you define the seams in the 3D model, and then the UVs are unfolded according to those seams.

What's important to keep in mind with seams is that they're not desirable. Seams are usually placed in areas where they're less visible, and the reason is that when you apply a texture, in the seam area you'll notice a "cut" in the texture. That happens because where you have a seam, it appears as a border on the UVs, which means that even though you make the texture continuous without any cuts, the size of the seams on one side or the other may not be exactly the same, causing the resolution of the image to change across that seam.

In UVs, the bigger a polygon is, the more resolution it requires in the image; thus, the texture displayed in the 3D model will be sharper. What's important here is to know which parts of your model need more detail in the textures and will therefore need more space on the UVs.

In Figure 8.4, you can see the effects of seams and how the size of the UVs affects the projected texture.

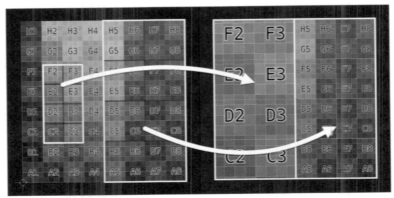

Figure 8.4   While the two halves of the 3D plane (on the right side of the image) have the same size, the texture on the left side of the 3D plane has less resolution, which is an effect of that part of the UVs (on the left side of the image) being smaller.

In Figure 8.4, you can see how the size of the faces on the UVs (left side of the image) and in the actual 3D model (right side of the image) are independent, but the size on the UVs defines the resolution of the texture in the 3D model.

Things to Consider before Unwrapping

It's important to note that not all the objects you've created for Jim's character have the same properties, and you need to make some decisions before jumping into UV mapping. The list that follows describes some things you need to keep in mind.

- **Meshes that don't need UVs:** If an object is only supposed to look like a plane material with no changes in its surface (which is not usual in realistic models, but can happen in simple models for animations), you won't need to unwrap it. Unwrapping defines how an image will be projected onto the surface of a model, but if you just need a color, a material with no texture will do. For example, this will be the case for Jim's hair.
- **Meshes with modifiers:** Some of the meshes that comprise your character may have modifiers applied. When a mesh is using modifiers that change its geometry, they will affect the UVs as well. Let's take Jim's badges as an example. They are made with a Solidify modifier that adds thickness to the model: the UVs will only be available for the original geometry, so the polygons generated by the modifier won't be able to display a texture you might want. In the case of the Solidify modifier, the "thickness" polygons will display the color of the texture's borders in the front, and the back side will display the same as the front side (which shouldn't matter to you in this case, because the back side is hidden). In these situations, you must decide if you'll get the correct result unwrapping without applying the modifiers, or if you need to apply the modifiers and then unwrap all the geometry. It depends on the amount of detail you're looking for or where you need to display the textures accurately.
- **Mirrored meshes:** Mirror is a modifier, but it's especially important when it's used with UVs. If you do the UVs and you're using a Mirror modifier, the mirrored geometry will use the same UVs as the side you've unwrapped. Sometimes, you may want to have asymmetric textures for an object, and in those cases, you should apply the Mirror modifier before unwrapping. In other cases, though, a mirrored texture could work nicely and that means two things: you only need to unwrap one half of the object and you'll also need less space in the image to texture that object. In yet another case, you might need an asymmetric shape, but the texture could be symmetric; in this situation, you could work with a symmetric shape, perform the unwrap operation, and finally apply the Mirror modifier, making any adjustments to the shape afterward. This way, you'd have mirrored UVs but an asymmetric shape (only the shape would be able to change; the topology should be the same on both sides of the mesh). The following examples in the next sections, using Jim's face and jacket, will help you to understand this option better.

> **Note**
>
> Basically, you need to determine if it's more efficient to do the UVs and then keep adjust-
> ing your model, or if it's better to apply modifiers and do the UVs afterward. This will de-
> pend on your model, what you need to do to it, and what's more comfortable and efficient
> for you.

Working with UVs in Blender

In this section, you'll go through the process of unwrapping Jim's head step by step, and
you'll learn how to use the basic unwrapping tools. After that, with some basic instructions, you'll be ready to unwrap the rest of the objects for your character. In this case,
you won't use a mirrored texture for the face, so you'll need to unwrap the full face at
once. To do this, select the face and apply the Mirror modifier while in Object Mode.

Marking the Seams

The first step to unwrap will be to mark the seams to tell Blender from where you want
your UVs to be unfolded. In Edit Mode (**Tab**), select the edges shown in Figure 8.5.
You don't need to mark them all at once; you can mark some of them now and then
mark seams in other areas as you proceed. To mark edges as seams, press **Ctrl + E** to
access the Edge menu and click Mark Seam.

Pay attention to how the edges selected to be the seams of the UVs are placed in
areas that won't be very visible; they appear on the back and sides of the head, and over
the forehead, where they'll be almost completely hidden by the hair. The closed seam

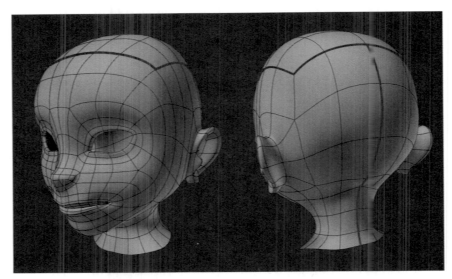

Figure 8.5   Seams marked to unwrap Jim's head (edges shown in red)

that has been selected at the top of the head is there so that part becomes an isolated UV island; after all, that part will always be hidden under Jim's cap, so you don't need a lot of definition there. This way, more space in the UVs can be used for the areas that matter and need more resolution in the texture.

Also, while you can't see it in this image, there is a loop marked as a seam in the inner part of the lips, so that on the UVs, the geometry of the mouth's interior is separated from the face's exterior. Remember, you can use **Alt + RMB** to select edge loops.

> **Tip**
>
> For marking seams, a very useful selection method is the Shortest Path option. When you need to select edges in line, select one and press **Ctrl + RMB** in another edge, and the edges between the two you've selected will also be selected, allowing you to select long lines of edges very quickly. You can press **Ctrl + RMB** again and again until you have the entire desired edge loop selected.

Creating and Displaying a UV Test Grid

At this point, you could start unwrapping, but instead you're going to create a UV Test Grid so you can see how applying a texture to the face will look before unwrapping. With the test grid, you'll see how an image is projected on the 3D model using the UVs more easily.

A UV Test Grid is a basic image made exclusively to test how the UVs of a mesh work. It's an image with a grid; when it's projected on the 3D model, it provides you with a lot of information. The size of the grid will show you which parts of your object are using more space from the texture (the smaller the grid, the more resolution the texture will have in that area). Using the test grid, you can adjust the size of every part of the object to be more or less consistent, and you can apply a smaller grid to those parts where you need more details. It's also useful to see the grid's distortion; if you notice that at some point the grid is becoming distorted, you can try to solve this by adjusting the UVs. Using a UV Test Grid, you can also see where the seams are and how well they work, or if they're barely visible.

The UV Test Grid can also have colors as well as letters or numbers. This will tell you which part of the UVs is being shown in a specific part of the model by the color, number, or letter it displays on its surface.

Creating a New Image for a UV Test Grid

Fortunately, Blender has two different types of UV Test Grids that you can generate and use in your models. To create them, just go to the UV/Image Editor header and click New Image. You can also go to the Image menu and click New Image or use the keyboard shortcut: **Alt + N**.

In Figure 8.6, you can see the New Image menu that pops up, where you can create images to paint on or UV Test Grids. You can set the image's name (Untitled by default), its resolution, and its color. The color will only apply when you select Blank as

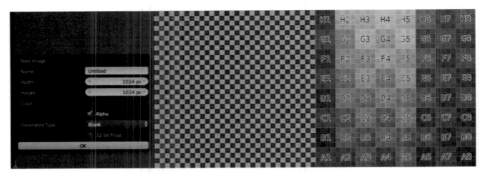

Figure 8.6   Generating a new image in Blender, with the
New Image menu (left), a UV grid (center), and a Color grid (right)

the Generated Type of image. If you select one of the UV Test Grids as the Generated
Type, the color setting will be ignored.

Once you've made your selections, click OK to generate the image. You can change
the image's name from the header and save it from the Image menu. If you open the
Properties Region (**N**), in the Image panel you can also rename the image and access
its parameters. Because the image is generated by Blender, you can change its type even
after it is created, and also change between a UV grid or a color grid (or a blank image,
or course).

Displaying the UV Test Grid in Your Model

How you show the image you're using in a 3D model in the 3D View depends on
which render engine you're using. Let's see how to display an image in both Blender
Render and Cycles.

Both render engines let you display a texture by applying it to a material and switching the display mode of the 3D View to Textured. But with Blender Render, there is
another method that doesn't require you to create a material, but you need to have UVs
in your mesh in order to use it.

Go to the UV/Image Editor and load the image while the UVs are displayed.
This is called a Texture Face, the texture that is "applied" to a UV Map. Now, in
the 3D View, you can display that Texture Face even in the Solid display mode;
open the Properties Region (**N**), and in the Shading panel, activate the Textured
Solid option.

In Cycles, there is a better way to do this that uses a material. Create a new material
from the Material tab in the Properties Editor and call it something like "uv_test_mat";
this way, you'll always have a UV Test material in your scene ready to be applied to the
object with which you're working. Inside the Material options, in the Color parameter, click the button with a little dot at the right of the color selector and select Image
Texture from the list. From the drop-down list, select the UV Test Grid you've just

created. Now go to the 3D View and use the Textured or Material display modes to see how the UV Test Grid looks.

Unwrapping Jim's Face

Unwrapping Jim's face will be fairly simple. Select Jim's face and, in Edit Mode (**Tab**), select all the faces (**A**). Press **U** and select the first option, Unwrap. What you'll see should be something similar to what's shown in Figure 8.7.

After unwrapping the model, you can see how the UVs have been unfolded, the face is completely flat, and you can see the other two islands: the top of the head and the mouth's interior, as you defined them previously with the seams. Also, the face has been unfolded using the seam from the back of the head.

When you have a UV Grid or an image in the background of the UV/Image Editor, it may be difficult for you to see the UVs accurately. When an image is loaded in the UV/Image Editor, on the right side of the header you'll see three little buttons; two provide options to display the image, and the third one will show the current UV Texture Alpha channel (image transparency), or a white background when there is no Alpha to display, letting you see the UVs better. Another option is to change how the UVs are displayed from the Properties Region.

> **Note**
>
> Something important to remember is that the UV/Image Editor only shows the UVs of the parts of your model that are selected in the 3D View, and only while you're in Edit Mode. At first, this can be confusing for people who come from other software and are used to always seeing all the UVs. If you activate the sync between the 3D and UVs selection, you'll be able to see all the UVs; however, if you want to see all of them without the sync option, just go to the 3D View and select all with **A**.

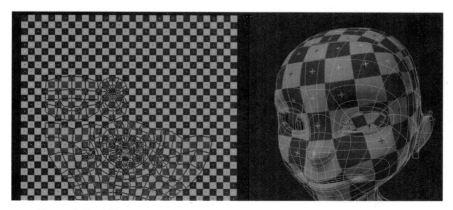

Figure 8.7   After unwrapping Jim's face, you can see the UV map in the UV/Image Editor (left) and the UV Test Grid looks much more uniform (right).

Live Unwrap

Live Unwrap is a really cool tool. It lets you pin vertices and move them to unwrap the mesh in real time. This way, you can adjust all the UVs very quickly without having to unwrap again and again or move them vertex by vertex.

In the UV/Image Editor, go to the UVs menu on the header and activate the Live Unwrap option. To pin the vertices you want to place in fixed positions, just press **P**. Keep in mind that you have to pin at least two vertices. After pinning those vertices, which can be the reference points or the corners of the mesh, just move some of them (pinned vertices will be marked in red) and you'll see how all the UVs adjust to fit your moves. In this mode, move only the pinned vertices. If you move any other vertex, when you move a pinned one, the unpinned vertices will be reset; only pinned vertices will be fixed during the live unwrap.

When you're done, you can unpin the pinned vertices by selecting them and pressing **Alt + P**. Then, make sure you deactivate Live Unwrap before further adjusting the UVs.

Adjusting UVs

You can, of course, adjust vertices on the UVs to make sure they look right in the 3D model, and you'll see real-time feedback in the UV Test Grid of the 3D model as you make those adjustments.

Remember, you also have Proportional Editing tools to move groups of vertices subtly, and you can also move, rotate, and scale them. Try to adjust the grid for the face so you have smaller squares in the face than in the back of the head; this will help you optimize the texture size and have more detail in the face, which is where you need it, instead of the back of the head where you don't need it.

You also have alignment tools for the UVs. Look at the options on the UVs menu on the header and try them out—maybe you'll find something interesting (press **W** to get the Align and Weld options). Also, when you use a tool, you may need to make an adjustment to its effect before you confirm it: in those cases, the header will show information with instructions you need to follow to use that specific tool as well as its current parameters, so keep an eye on that header!

Something else to note is that you can use the Snap tools as well, which are very useful when, for example, you want to align one vertex on top of another.

Separating and Connecting UVs

Blender offers an unusual way to separate and connect parts of the UVs, but once you get used to it, it's quite useful.

Separating UVs

The quickest method for separating UVs is to use the Select Split tool. Select the faces you want to separate, press **Y**, and they'll be separated so you can now move them independently of one another. You can also access this option from the Select menu on the header.

You've already learned that on the UVs, Blender only shows the faces you've selected in the 3D View. But here's an interesting fact to keep in mind: When you select only a face (or a group of faces) in the 3D View and move it on the UVs, it moves independently and becomes separated from the rest of the UVs. You can only manipulate the visible UVs, and when you do so, they are separated from the UVs that are currently hidden.

Another way of separating UVs is just to unwrap the faces you want to separate again. Select them from the 3D Model, unwrap them, and they'll be separated.

One other method for separating UVs is to use the Hide and Unhide features of Blender (**H** and **Alt + H**), which are also available in the UV/Image Editor. Select the faces you want to separate, press **Ctrl + I** to invert the selection, press **H** to hide the selection, and then move the remaining faces. Press **Alt + H** to reveal all the UVs and you'll see that those faces have been separated.

Connecting UVs

Sometimes, a complex mesh can be more easily unwrapped by its parts and then joined as needed to create the least distortion possible.

Blender has a rule: only vertices that are welded in the 3D mesh can be welded on the UVs. This means that you can snap or even weld (with the welding tool from the **W** menu) two vertices and they'll be in exactly the same place, but they won't actually be merged together. Thus, when you move them, you'll actually move only one of them.

That said, to merge vertices on the UVs that are also welded in the 3D model, you just have to put them in the same place by welding them or snapping them to another vertex.

One way to find out exactly which vertices are adjacent to each other is to use the Sync selection mode between the UVs and the 3D mesh; with this method, if you select a vertex in the mesh or on the UVs, it will show the shared vertices that should go with it in other UV islands as well. Another option is to temporarily activate the Shared Vertex selection to see which vertices are in the same place in the 3D model.

Stitch is a tool that can be very helpful when connecting UVs. You can find it on the UVs menu in the header and its shortcut is **V**. Select some vertices in a border of a UV island and press **V**; a preview will show you where those vertices should go in order to be joined to other vertices on the UVs. If you like what you see, left click to apply and if you don't, right click to cancel the stitching.

The Finished Face's UVs

In Figure 8.8, you can see how the UVs for the head would look after some adjustments. The UVs are nicely aligned, the top of the head and the mouth's interior now take less space in the texture, and the face portion has been enlarged so it has more

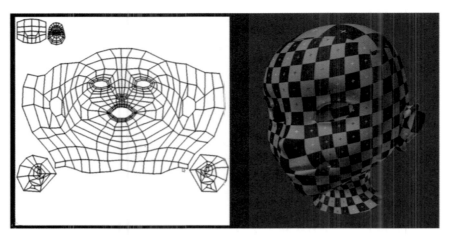

Figure 8.8   The UVs for Jim's face are finished!

detail. The ears were separated to have some more space outside of the head's UVs, but this is optional as the ears don't need that much detail in the texture.

Unwrapping the Rest of the Character

Unwrapping the rest of the character is pretty straightforward. Let's go over a brief explanation of the most important parts of the process so you can understand what to expect. Figure 8.9 will give you an idea of what we'll be doing in this section and the objects that will be unwrapped: the glove, the boots, the pants, the jacket, the cap, and the neck detail.

Unwrapping most of the parts was fairly quick and easy. The whole process took roughly 20 minutes. The pants, for example, needed only a simple seam along the inner leg, just like a pair of real trousers, and the unwrap worked nicely. Keep in mind that the Mirror modifier did its part as well.

For the hand, a seam was marked all along the palm, passing through the bottom part of the fingers. The resulting UVs were adjusted with the Live Unwrap tool, especially the island that represents the top part of the hand; it had the sides of the fingers in it, so its shape was somewhat spherical.

> **Note**
>
> As you can see, there's only one hand: the reason is that we only modeled one in the previous chapter and didn't apply a Mirror modifier to it; instead, we duplicated and mirrored it. It would have been helpful to show you a result with two hands, but it's better to unwrap the hand and duplicate it afterward so that we don't need to unwrap both hands separately.

Figure 8.9   The meshes that needed to be unwrapped, with their seams marked in red

The elements of the cap were basically unwrapped just as they were. No seams were used at all—just select everything and unwrap!

The piece at the neck was simple, too. It just needed a loop all around the interior bottom section so Blender could unfold it properly.

The jacket was a little trickier: it was first unwrapped in three pieces—the body, the arms, and the flaps. Later, after adjusting the UVs a little using the Live Unwrap and Proportional Editing tools, the arm was joined to the side of the jacket, first using the Stitch tool and then snapping and moving some vertices around. The purpose of that was to have no seam in the shoulder, as the jacket will have the shoulder pads painted in the texture for that area, and having a seam in the middle would not be a good idea.

If you want to see how the UV Maps look, you can go to the next section on packing the UVs. Right now, each one of the UV islands takes the whole space and showing them together would be rather abstract. That's why packing is important!

Packing UVs

After the objects are unwrapped, you have to "pack" them, which is the process in which you put together all the UVs in a single workspace so that they don't overlap each other. The purpose is that instead of having a different texture for each object, you can have the whole character textured with a single image, so each part of it will occupy a part of the UV Map.

Figure 8.10 shows what the finished UVs will look like all together, which you'll learn how to do in this section.

With all these objects in one place, a single texture will be used for the whole character. As you can see in Figure 8.10, the face takes most of the texture space. There are also some spaces between objects: you can spend more time to fill the whole texture space and have a more efficient texture, but you should always leave a little space between UV islands, so when you paint they can have a little bleeding, otherwise you may see areas adjacent to the seams that weren't painted.

There are several ways to pack UVs; let's discuss a few of the most popular methods. The easiest way to pack UVs is to have everything inside the same mesh, so you can take islands, move them, rotate them, and scale them very easily in order to make them all fit together in the same texture space. This can be done, for example, with models that are made of numerous objects with no modifiers (such as Mirror or Solidify) applied; otherwise, you'll lose the modifiers' effects in the process. If there

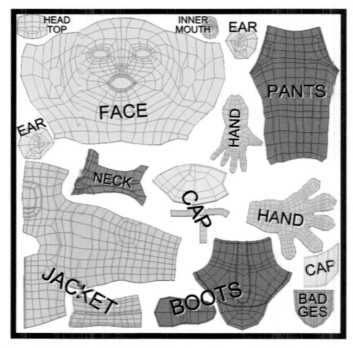

Figure 8.10   The packed UVs for Jim, shown with different colors for each object so you can see how they are distributed

are no modifiers, you can select all the objects, press **Ctrl + J** to join them all in the same mesh, and then start packing their UVs. After the packing is done, you can export the UVs (you'll learn how to do this in the next chapter) and separate them again if necessary.

A downside of this method is that when you join meshes and separate them again, you'll lose their origins (pivot points) and they'll all be in the position of the active mesh's origin when you join them. In Chapter 11, Character Rigging, you'll learn how to change the origin of an object.

> **Tip**
>
> Blender even provides tools for packing UVs when they're all together in a single object: *Average Islands Scale* and *Pack Islands*. Average Islands (**Ctrl + A**) will scale the selected islands so they have a size that is relative to the size the faces have in the 3D model. Pack Islands (**Ctrl + P**) will scale and place the selected islands automatically so they take the largest space possible inside the UVs space.

Another packing method is to use a feature in Blender that allows you to see the UVs of other meshes in the UV/Image Editor, even though you can only adjust the UVs of the currently active object in Edit Mode. Here's how it works: You select several objects with **Shift + RMB**. The last object selected is the active one. In Edit Mode, adjust the UVs and, in the UV/Image Editor, go to the header and activate the Draw Other Objects option in the View menu. Even though you will only be able to adjust the UVs for the active object, the rest of the selected objects' UVs will also be shown.

The quick way to switch between objects is to press **Tab** to exit from Edit Mode and press **Shift** and right click the next object you want to adjust. Enter Edit Mode again, and the last selected object will be the active object while keeping all of the objects selected. This is probably the most popular method of packing when you have objects with modifiers that you can't join together, and this is how I did the packing for Jim's UVs.

Summary

You now have Jim unwrapped with proper UVs and he's ready to be textured! As you might have noticed, unwrapping can be tricky and you need patience for it. However, it's a mandatory step in building quality characters because you have to properly define how the textures will be projected on the model in the most efficient way. This is especially important if you're working on video games, where everything needs to be more optimized (including textures) in order to work smoothly in real time. There are some software and tools that make the unwrapping process almost completely automated, and that's cool for some specific situations, but usually you'll want to have control over how UVs are projected, so later on it will be easier to paint your character's textures.

Exercises

1. Unwrap a cube and add a texture to it; this will help you understand how UVs work.

2. Add a photo to any model (even Jim's face) and try to unwrap it in such a way that the seams are hidden as much as possible, while making sure the texture is not distorted.

3. Unwrap an object and pack its UVs to use all the space you can from the texture.

9

Painting Textures

Textures are simply images that give color (or define other parameters such as the amount of reflection or shininess an object has) to your models when projected onto their surfaces. You've already unwrapped those parts of Jim that need textures, so now it's time to use those UVs to paint a texture and start giving your character a layer of paint to move your project closer to the final result. Textures are usually created with 2D software such as Photoshop, Gimp, Krita, and others, and they are outside the scope of this book, so this chapter will briefly explain the workflow and texture-painting process in Blender.

Main Workflow

There are two alternative workflows for painting textures on 3D models. The second one described below was discussed in the previous chapter, but it's worth noting here as well so it will be fresh in your mind.

- **Texturing before unwrapping:** Sometimes, depending on your needs, it's easier to create a texture and then adapt the UVs to fit that texture. In this case, of course, you need to create the texture before you start unwrapping. A good example of this method is a wooden floor; you may have a photo of wood and to apply it to the surface, you just load that photo and adapt the UVs so the wood in the photo has the right size and position on your surface.
- **Texturing after unwrapping:** This is the usual texturing method for characters or complex objects because it specifically tailors textures for that model. First you unwrap the model and then you export the UVs as an image to use for a reference when painting and adjusting your textures to make sure they fit the faces in your model. This is the method you'll be using to texture Jim.

Painting in Blender

Yes, you can paint textures right inside Blender and directly on the 3D model! In the Mode selector of the 3D View's header, pick the *Texture Paint* Mode and, in the Tools

Region (press **T** if it's hidden), you'll see a lot of options to control how you paint and select the brush you'll use.

Texture Paint Mode

Before actually painting (several more steps are needed before you begin), let's very briefly see how the Texture Paint Mode works. In Figure 9.1, you can see how the main interface in the 3D View and the Tools Region changes substantially. Now the cursor is circular and resembles a "brush" and the Tools Region options are completely different from those in other modes.

You can select from a variety of tools (while they're referred to as tools, they are indeed brushes), such as Brush, Clone, Smear, Soften (similar to a blur), etc. With the number of options available to you, you'll be able to adjust settings for a brush/tool at the bottom of the Tools Region. You can adjust its radius and strength (its opacity), its texture, the profile curve it will have, or you can even use the Smooth Stroke feature. You can also create your own tool presets for fast access to them. Of course, you can also select the color with which you'll paint.

For the radius and strength of the brush, it's worth noting that you can quickly change those two values with shortcuts from the 3D View: press **F**, move the mouse to define the radius (you'll see a preview of the resulting brush radius as you move your mouse), and confirm with a left click to change the radius; press **Shift + F**, move the mouse, and confirm with a left click to change the strength of your brush.

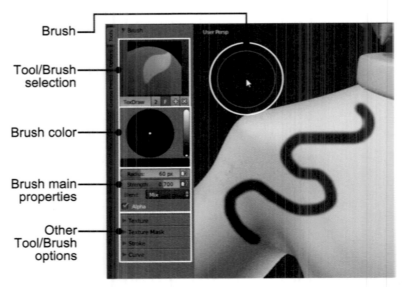

Figure 9.1   Texture Paint Mode and its options in the Tools Region

In the previous chapter, you learned a lot about the UV/Image Editor. Do you remember that there is a button on the header that lets you change between View, Paint, and Mask modes? Well, when you're working in Texture Paint Mode in the 3D View, if you switch to the Paint Mode in the UV/Image Editor, then you'll also be able to paint over the 2D image.

It's very important to know that in the 3D View, you can only paint on the object you have selected, and if more than one object is selected, you'll only paint on the active one. To paint on a different object, you'll have to switch back to Object Mode, select another object, and go back into Texture Paint Mode.

Preparing to Paint

Before you begin painting, you must make sure of a couple of things:

- The object you're painting on has to be unwrapped; otherwise, you won't be able to paint on it or, in the best case scenario, it will look weird.
- The texture must be showing in the 3D View. Apply a material to the object, load the texture on it, and make sure you're displaying it in the 3D View (change the display mode to Textured or Material). In the Blender Render engine, you can show the texture with the Textured Solid option discussed in Chapter 8.

In this case, if you've followed along with the previous chapters, Jim's textured parts have a material already applied and they're showing in the UV Test Grid. After you're done unwrapping, you might go to the Texture properties and change from a UV Test Grid to a Blank Image; you can even change the texture's name to something like "texture_base." Also, for the resolution, use a minimum of 2048 x 2048 pixels. This way, you'll have a black texture to start with.

> **Tip**
>
> Unfortunately, there is no Blender tool that will fill the whole image with a color. You may prefer to create a new image instead so you'll have the option to select any other color as its base color.

Once you're set up, you can start painting! Move the camera as you normally would, but if you left click and drag over the object you selected before entering Texture Paint Mode, a stroke will be placed in that part of the texture. If you go to the UV/Image Editor and set its mode to Paint, you'll be able to paint there as well.

> **Tip**
>
> Texture resolution should be squared with a "power of two" number (i.e., 8 x 8, 16 x 16, 32 x 32, 64 x 64, 128 x 128, 256 x 256, 512 x 512, 1024 x 1024, 2048 x 2048, 4096 x 4096, and so on). The reason is that these resolutions use the resources on your computer a lot better than rectangular images with random sizes, and they're called "power of

two" because to jump from one resolution to the previous or the next one, you must divide or multiply by 2. Usually, it's recommended that you work in a pretty high resolution, because you can always scale it down if needed, but scaling up means you'll lose detail and your model won't look right. The size you'll finally use depends on the amount of detail you need for your model. If it's a high-resolution model and in certain shots you'll be seeing it from a great distance, having textures with very high resolutions won't matter and you'll be consuming important resources. Once the texture is created, it's best to make different sizes of it that you can use depending on the object's distance from the camera.

Limitations of Blender's Texture Paint

While Blender's Texture Paint is very cool and has a lot of options (that you should explore further, as here you'll only see the very basics), it does have its limitations. It has no layers, for example, which is a pretty basic and very useful feature for texture painting. In fact, there is an add-on out there that tries to mimic layers, but using it is not very easy when you want to work directly with layers in your image. Also, painting over the 3D model can get a little slow sometimes, depending on how powerful your computer is.

Of course, Blender isn't a substitute for proper 2D image editing software, but it does provide you with a set of tools that allow you to do basic texture painting. (There are some people who have even taken Blender's painting options to the extreme and made impressive artworks with them!)

You can use Texture Paint to texture an entire character, but it depends on the character, of course, and if you feel comfortable texturing it in 3D. Instead, you might try working with 2D images, loading textures, using layers, making color corrections, adding effects, and applying masks—things that you have no access to inside Blender's Texture Paint Mode.

That said, there are a lot of things for which Texture Paint proves really useful. It works well for creating the base for textures. Sometimes in the UVs, when you're working only in 2D, it is difficult to see where a detail should be placed, so you have to find where it's supposed to go in the 3D model. But because you can paint in 3D inside Blender, that's a good opportunity to start your texture by just painting where the details should be on the surface of the 3D model, and then use that as a base for your final texture.

Creating the Base Texture

It's time to paint the details over Jim's model. We won't do anything fancy for the base texture, just a quick black-and white-drawing that you can use later as a base in your 2D image editor of choice.

Placing Texture Elements

Using the character's reference images to see where to place the basic texture elements, start painting over the 3D character. This time, the reference images are not the ones in

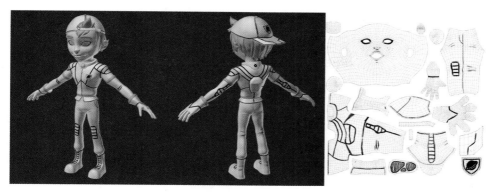

Figure 9.2   The positions of the basic texture elements
have been set into a rough painting.

the background of the 3D View (by the way, at this point you can turn them off in the Properties Region inside the Background Images panel), but you can divide your interface to have a UV/Image Editor display them. If you happen to have a second monitor, you can use it to see the references at all times without having to use up space in your main workspace. When you have all the basic texture elements in place (see Figure 9.2), you will need to save the image so you can keep working on it in 2D software.

> **Tip**
> Drawing smooth lines with a mouse can be tricky. For some elements, you may prefer to have steadier lines. To draw steady lines, go to the Tools Region and, in the Stroke panel, activate the Smooth Stroke option. Now when you paint, the brush will follow your strokes at some distance and smooth them, providing very clean and steady lines.

Saving Your Image

Blender will tell you when you have made changes to an image that you haven't yet saved. If you look at the UV/Image Editor header, the Image menu will show an asterisk (★) that indicates there are unsaved changes. Open the Image menu and you'll see the save options. Also, pressing **Alt + S** inside the UV/Image Editor will save the image. Pressing **F3** will perform a *Save as...* for the image.

Packing Your Images

In this case, packing has nothing to do with the packing in UV maps. Blender has another packing feature that allows you to include external files (such as images) in the .blend file itself. This is very useful when you work on multiple computers. Imagine you load some textures from your hard drive into your model and you want to send that model to a friend. If you send it as it is, your friend won't see the textures because he doesn't have them on his computer where Blender will look for them. In this case, you can pack them and the images will be incorporated into the .blend file, and your friend will be amazed by your textured model!

To pack an image into the .blend file, just go to the Image menu and select one of the Packing options at the top. If you want to pack every single external file into the .blend file, just go to the File menu, select *External Data,* and click *Pack All Into .blend.*

Keep in mind that saving all these files into the .blend file will increase the file's size, which will continue to multiply if you like to save your files in different versions as you progress.

Texturing in 2D Image Editing Software

Now you can take the base texture elements you just created and keep working on them in your image editing software. Photoshop was used for the examples in this chapter, but of course you can use whatever software you want.

Exporting the UVs as an Image

It's important to see the UVs while you work on the textures so you can see if the textures fit the model and make sure they will project correctly onto the model later on. Let's go through the steps you need to follow in order to export your UVs into an image file.

> **Caution**
>
> When you have UVs of different objects, as in Jim's case, the exporting procedure is a little different than if you just have a single object: you need to select all those objects first and join them (**Ctrl + J**). This will probably mess up your model, so make sure you only do this for the purpose of exporting the UVs; then, without saving your changes, reload the file to its previous state before you joined the objects. When you join all these objects, if you jump into Edit Mode and select everything (**A**), you should see all the UVs together.

Follow these steps to export Jim's UV layout into an image file:

1. Select the object.
2. In Edit Mode, select everything (**A**).
3. Open the UV/Image Editor.
4. On the UV/Image Editor header, click the UVs menu and select *Export UV Layout.*
5. In the interface for saving the image, at the bottom-left side of the screen, there are a few options you'll need to adjust. Select the *Modified* option to display the meshes with their modifiers applied, such as Subdivision Surface. (This is important because this will allow you to see just how the final mesh, in which the

textures are going to be projected, will appear.) The *All UVs* option will ensure that every UV is shown in the image, so check it as well. For the resolution, 2048 x 2048 could work, but let's increase it to 4096 x 4096 to have enough room for details. As for the format, select .png (you can also export vector images with the .svg format).

6. Select where you want to save the image and click **Export UV Layout**.

7. In this case and whenever you're working with similar characters, close your file without saving to prevent Blender from keeping a version with all the objects merged together and their modifiers messed up. Open the last saved version again.

You should end up with an image similar to the one in Figure 9.3.

Now let's see one of the typical methods with which you can create your texture using some easy-to-follow steps.

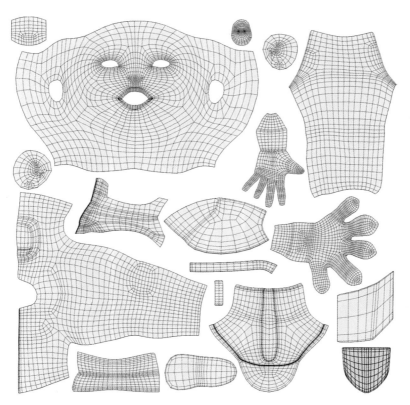

Figure 9.3   Jim's exported UV layout that you can use as a reference to paint textures

Loading the UVs and Base Elements

First, you should load the reference images: the base elements you painted inside Blender and the UVs. Place them on the top layers using the Multiply blend mode (this will make only the dark areas visible and leave the rest of the image transparent), so you can turn the UVs on and off over your texture to check that everything is in place.

Adding Base Colors

The next step is to take those lines you painted in Blender, refine them, and then clean them. After that, you can start filling the areas with colors. You can pick these colors from the color scheme images you created during the character's design process. In Figure 9.4, you can see how the texture would look at this point.

> **Tip**
>
> At this stage, it's fine if you load the texture in Blender to check that everything looks right. If you're working with Photoshop, Blender supports .psd files, so you can load them right away with no conversion. If you load the image in an UV/Image Editor, you can quickly update it by pressing **Alt + R**. Also, if you save a new version of the texture, you can go to the

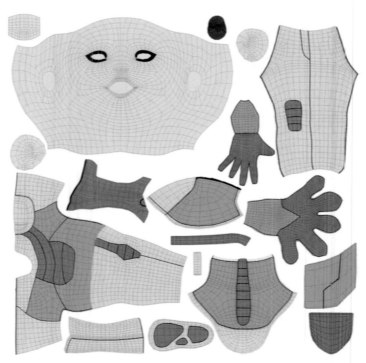

Figure 9.4   The base of the texture with the UVs on top to help you see what's going on

Image menu in the UV/Image Editor and click *Replace Image*; this will replace the old version everywhere you were using it in Blender with a new version. Sometimes, after painting the basics, you can see that in some areas of the 3D model the texture looks a bit off, so you can go to the UVs and adjust them slightly to get the desired result.

Adding Details

Once you've got the base colors, you can start painting in the details. In this case, it's been kept pretty simple with flat colors, but you can add as much detail as you want (depending on what you want to achieve in terms of the character's style).

If you look at the texture in Figure 9.5, you'll see how some details were added, such as the thick gray lines in the clothing seams, the symbol on the badge, a darker lip color, and a little blush in the cheeks. You can also add some soft shadows where you think they will fit, as well as wrinkles to the cloth and other small details.

Applying the Final Touches

Finally, let's add a little more life to the texture. You can do this by overlaying a photo of some noisy texture or perhaps painting with a brush that uses a texture. You can also

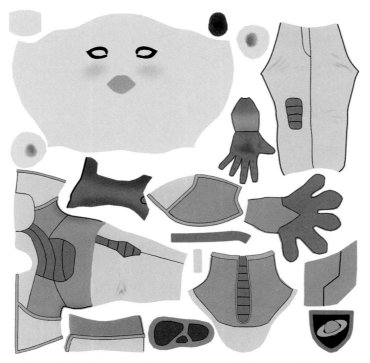

Figure 9.5   Some details have been added and the UVs and references have been turned off to help you see those objects.

Figure 9.6   The changes are very subtle, but they'll help bring Jim to life.

define certain parts a little more. In Figure 9.6, you can see how the seams of the suit have been brought to life a little more just by adding some lines with darker and lighter colors around them, giving the impression that the clothing has a little volume. This is the stage in which you finish the texture.

Seeing the Painted Character in Blender

Ok, if you haven't done so yet, it's time to load the texture in Blender to see how it looks on the various parts of the character. Don't hesitate to go back and forth between your 2D editing software and Blender to refine the texture and test it on your model. In Figure 9.7, you'll see how Jim's model looks with the texture projected on it.

Figure 9.7   Jim is starting to look a lot more like the character we designed.

Some parts still have the mesh color without texture or anything else on them. Those are the parts that will pick their color from the Blender Material that will be applied to them in Chapter 10, so there's no need for texture on them.

Summary

Texturing can be a lot of fun; it's a very creative process and you can take it as far as you want. Applying the textures is the point in the process when you really have the opportunity to make a character realistic. If you want realism, it's recommended that you use photos to create your textures (skin, wood, grass, sand—virtually anything) instead of painting them manually. In Jim's case, the style is not photorealistic at all, so some basic textures defining the colors and some details are fine.

Depending on the requirements of the texture, its effects can be very different. If it's a diffuse color texture that will be mixed with other textures to define a surface's shine or reflectivity for example, it will only have color information. However, if you're working on a video game in which lighting is more technically limited, the texture will include highlights and even some shadows.

If you're interested in how to create really cool textures, you might want to learn how to use a 2D image editor like Photoshop or Gimp. They're really powerful and allow you to create awesome textures that will bring your characters to life!

Exercises

1. Use the method of unwrapping after texturing by loading the texture from this book's downloadable files on the companion website and trying to make the UVs fit that texture.

2. Use photos of skin or cloth and compose them in your image editor to make the texture look more realistic.

10

Materials and Shaders

You already have textures that define the color of your model's surfaces, but something is still missing: materials. In Blender, materials determine how a surface is going to receive and use lights when you launch a render. It can be reflective or transparent, or it can even emit light. These are examples of properties that you have to set up using materials. They're also called *shaders* because a shader is what tells the software (internally, through programming) how to draw an object on your screen (there are even shading languages to program how these shaders work). Hence, shading is the process of adding materials. In this chapter, you'll learn about the main workflow for shading and how to use materials. After you understand the basics, the chapter will describe how to use materials in both render engines, Blender Render and Cycles, as they're quite different.

Understanding Materials

Before you start shading your character, you should first understand how materials work and the differences between materials used in Blender Render and in Cycles.

Applying Materials

The process for applying materials follows these steps:

1. Select an object.
2. Go to the Materials tab in the Properties Editor.
3. Select a material from the list or create a new one; it will be applied to the active object.
4. Adjust the material to achieve the result you want. While you're adjusting the material, it's useful to add some basic lighting and make some test renders to see how the materials are behaving. Using the Rendered display mode in the 3D View is a great help at this point.

> **Tip**
> If you want to apply the material to more than one object at a time, just select all the objects, apply a material as described in the steps, and it will be applied to the active object (the one that you selected last). Then, press **Ctrl + L** to open the Links menu and select Materials. The material will be applied to the whole selection from the active object.

How Materials Work

In the real world, materials on the surface of objects have different properties that make the light that bounces off them react in specific ways. Glass, for example, lets light pass through it, metal shines by reflecting light, and wood absorbs light. Depending on the roughness of an object's surface, the light will be reflected, and the reflection may be diffused (blurred) if the surface is rough. A surface that is hot enough can even emit light (such as tungsten or other hot metals).

In 3D, you can control the material parameters that make virtual light mimic the effects of light when it hits a surface in the real world. You can define a surface's reflectivity or how much it shines, its color, its transparency, and its index of refraction. With different configurations for these values, you can imitate real-world materials inside the 3D world. Each one of these parameters of a material can be called a channel, and channels will be explained later in this chapter.

Masks and Layers

Materials can be very simple or really complex! Materials can have different properties that work together in different areas of the model. Using "masks" (black-and-white images in which white means full effect and black means no effect at all) you can tell Blender where you want the effects of each parameter of the material to appear; for example, you can use masks to set some parts of the material to be reflective. This would be useful in the case of a metal surface with areas of rust; the rusty parts would have no reflectivity, while the "good" parts of the metal would shine. You can control these effects using textures to act as masks.

Materials can also be made of several layers. You can stack different textures, shaders, and effects to create complex layered materials. For example, let's say you've modeled a car and applied a base paint to it, and you want to add some decals; you can do it using layers and adding those decal images on top of the base paint material.

Channels

Materials can have different channels (usually, textures are loaded to affect each one of those channels) and each one of them controls different properties of the material (color, reflectivity, transparency, and so forth) A lot of people find it hard to understand what channels are, so here is a brief description of the function of some of the most commonly used channels:

- **Diffuse Color:** This channel defines a surface's color.

- **Transparency:** This channel defines the parts of a surface that should be either transparent or opaque. A black-and-white image or an image with alpha (transparency) is usually used for this channel. Black areas of the image would be transparent and white areas would be opaque.

- **Emission:** Usually, this channel is a black/transparent image with some areas of color. Where the image used for this channel has color, the software will take that color as the light emission color and the alpha value of the image as the emission intensity. Emission works by adding light to the surface in those parts in which the image used has color.

- **Specular:** This channel defines the parts of a surface that are more or less shiny. Black has no shine at all, while white has full specularity. If you use colors, they will tell the software the color of the shines in those parts of the texture.

- **Reflection:** This channel's texture would make some parts of a surface reflective. Again, black has no reflection, any other color defines the color of the reflection, and the lighter the color is, the more reflection you'll get.

- **Roughness:** When used together with specularity and reflection, a black-and-white texture tells the software where a surface is more or less rough; this channel diffuses and blurs the shine and reflections in those areas with a rough surface.

- **Bump:** A black-and-white image gives the appearance of relief to the surface. The software uses this channel to determine how light reflects off a surface. It's very useful for small details that are not big enough to be modeled, such as scars or scratches.

- **Normal:** This channel is like an advanced bump. It's an RGB texture in which each color tells the software in which direction light should be reflected off a surface. This effect is widely used in video games to make the objects appear to have much more detail than provided by the model's geometry. Normal maps (also called normal bumps) are rarely hand painted. They're usually created by having two versions of your model: one with high resolution and one with low resolution. Normal maps are then generated by "baking" the details of the high-resolution model into a texture for the low-resolution model.

- **Occlusion:** With a very minimal effort from the artist, this channel can significantly improve the lighting realism of the model. It's basically like a soft shadows pass in which holes and cavities of the model are marked. This channel is also used to create realistic contact shadows between objects—the type of soft shadows that you'd see on a cloudy day. The occlusion channel is usually generated automatically by baking from the model into a texture.

Basically, in most of the channels, black and white in the textures define the values, and colors define the colors. This can apply to specularity, reflection, emission, and so on.

> **Note**
>
> Not all animation software uses the same names for these channels and, even in Blender, they're named differently (you'll see how to use them later in this chapter); this is just how animators usually refer to them. These are the "common" names that you will typically find in software and that people in the community will understand, knowing that other software may use different names. Also, in other software, these channels may not work exactly as do those explained above.

Blender Render Materials

As you learned in the first chapters, the Blender Render render engine is not a realistic renderer. Even though you can achieve realistic results, you'll have to work very hard to simulate how real-world lighting looks. But it renders a lot faster than Cycles, making it a cool alternative, if you don't need a lot of realism, for things like motion graphics.

Materials in Blender Render have a lot of parameters. Basically, every material has the same parameters, and by adjusting them carefully you can simulate the properties of real-world materials.

Emission is not actually supported, as Blender Render doesn't use bouncing light or mesh lights. Objects will be bright if they have an emissive material, but they won't cast light over the scene.

While you can create very complex materials using nodes, in Blender Render you usually work in the Properties Editor, on the Material and Texture tabs.

Cycles Materials

Cycles is a realistic render engine, meaning that light behaves in a similar way to how it appears in the real world. Materials in Cycles are set up very differently than in Blender Render. While you can access their basic properties in the Properties Editor, to create complex materials you'll have to go to the Node Editor and mix different shaders to achieve the result you need.

Cycles materials are made of shaders. There are different kinds of shaders that represent different types of surfaces: Diffuse, Glossy, Glass, Emit, and Transparent, for example. Sometimes, using one of them will do, but to create cool and realistic materials, you'll have to mix several shaders together. Shaders are pretty simple and each of them has only a few properties, but mixing them together can get very complex.

As discussed in the first chapters, you'll get a more realistic result quite easily in Cycles, but it will usually cost you more render time.

Procedural Textures

Procedural textures are widely used in computer graphics. There is even procedural modeling. When something is procedural, it means the computer can generate it in large amounts without the need for it to be done manually.

Let's use an example: Say you want to build a city. You can create a few buildings, but then you want to place them throughout your city. You can do this manually, duplicating them one by one and then placing them where you want them. It's a big city, though, with thousands of buildings, so this method wouldn't be very efficient. That's why software offers you ways to do it procedurally; using different tools and giving you some level of control, the software will randomly place the buildings in the city for you.

A procedural texture is a texture that the software generates automatically and that can fit on any surface. These textures are like patterns that repeat randomly and you have some level of control over their features.

In Blender, you have a number of options for procedural textures. On the Texture tab of the Properties Editor, under Texture Type, instead of choosing Image or Movie, you can select any other type of texture to create procedural textures (you'll see where this option is located very soon). One of these textures is Clouds, and it generates a noisy pattern, useful for giving color variations to a surface. When you select a texture type, the Image panel will be replaced with specific options for your selection that give you control of its properties.

There are a lot of textures: Clouds, Blend, Wood, and Checker to name a few, and each one of them has its own properties and uses. Make sure you check them out!

Shading Your Character with Blender Render

Let's dive into the Blender Render materials and learn about their properties! You can access the base structure for these materials from the Material tab and the Texture tab in the Properties Editor. On the Material tab, you edit the surface properties such as color, reflection, and roughness, and on the Texture tab, you load textures and tell Blender how to apply them over the material.

Caution

If you want to work with the Blender Render render engine, this is when you have to make that decision and remember to set it in the main menu at the top of the interface. In the middle of the top menu, there is a button that shows a list of the available render engines: be sure to select Blender Render. You can always change it later, but if you start creating your materials in one engine, when you switch to the other render engine, you'll have to build them again and, in the process, you'll probably lose the ones you originally created.

Blender Render Materials

First, you'll learn about how to set up materials and for that, you'll want to explore the Material tab in the Properties Editor, shown in Figure 10.1. To make Blender display these options, you'll need to create a new material or select an existing one from the list.

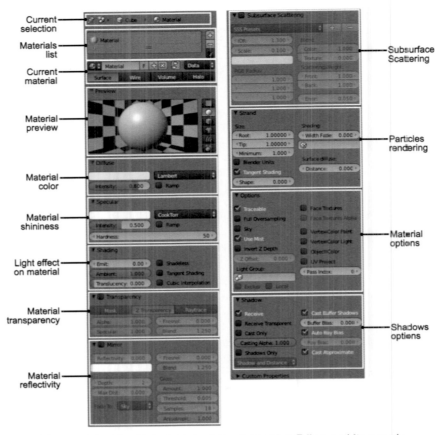

Figure 10 1   The Material tab of the Properties Editor and its panels

The following list describes what all those panels in Figure 10.1 are so you can have a better understanding of how to use them and their basic options:

- **Current selection:** At the top of the Material tab, you can see the symbols and names of the object, and the material for which the settings are being displayed. As always, if you click the pin to the left, it will "pin" those options and will keep them visible even if you select a different object with a different material. This is handy if you want to compare two materials (remember you can have two or more Properties Editors in Blender) or if you're working on a material but want to move things around without losing sight of it.

- **Materials list:** In the Materials list, you'll see the materials that are applied to the currently selected object. Yes, it is possible to apply more than one material to a single object (you'll learn how to do it later). This list has different slots and when you select a slot, you can see the material that has been used in that slot and you can replace it with another material.

- **Current material:** Under the Materials list, you'll see the current material's name. You can rename your materials in that box. If you see a number at the right side of the name, that's the number of objects using that material: click that number to duplicate the material so you can modify it as a new material for only the currently selected object. You can also duplicate it by pressing the **+** button. If you want to discard the material for that object, just select a different material from the list or click the **X** button to discard it.

  Near the material's name you have the icon to enable or disable nodes. If you want to use nodes for this material in the Node Editor, activate that option to make it available.

  Right under the material's name you'll see four buttons: these indicate the type of material with which you're working. *Surface* is the usual material type. *Wire* shows only the wireframe (edges) of the mesh. *Volume* is used to simulate objects with volume such as clouds, smoke, and mist. *Halo* makes the vertices of the object shine and produces a halo effect.

- **Preview:** The Preview panel shows a real-time preview of what the material would look like with the current settings. At the right side of the tab, you can select the shape in which you want to see the preview of the material.

- **Diffuse:** The Diffuse panel is where you set the base color of the material. If you select the *Ramp* option, you'll be able to define a gradient. In the drop-down list that appears, you can select the shader type you want to use (by default, Lambert), which will affect the algorithms Blender will use when computing the material's surface.

- **Specular:** In this panel, you can tell Blender if you want your material to be shiny and where you set the shine's color, intensity, and hardness. You can also use a gradient for the shine by enabling the Ramp option.

- **Shading:** You can set some options in this panel for how the surface of the material reacts to light. *Emit* will make the object look like it is emitting light. With the *Shadeless* option, the material will be unaffected by lights or shadows (you'll only see the original color), which is very useful when you want something to appear in the render exactly as you colored it (such as with background images and videos that you use as textures in the scene).

- **Transparency:** When transparency is enabled in this panel, your material will become transparent. *Mask* mode lets you display the background image where the material is shown. *Z Transparency* is a very basic transparency that renders fast and it's simple to use. *Raytrace* is the most realistic option and it provides an IOR (Index of Refraction) option that makes the material refract light, which is very useful for simulating glass, for example.

- **Mirror:** This panel defines the reflectivity of your material. You can increase the material's amount of reflection and its color as well as some other options to make it look better (such as *Fresnel*, which smooths the effect toward the parts of the object that are not facing the camera). If you have a lot of reflective materials in your scene, you may want to increase the *Depth* value, which defines the number of times a reflection can be reflected in another reflection; it sounds crazy, but it's very useful to prevent infinite reflections that would take a long time to render. *Max Dist* (Maximum Distance) controls over what distance the material can reflect until, after that point, it fades. *Gloss* options will make the reflections softer. The *Samples* option reduces the noise: the higher the samples number, the less noise reflections on the material will have, but more samples will also take longer to render.

- **Subsurface Scattering:** This is a very interesting option you can use to achieve some complex realistic materials such as skin or rubber. Basically, it computes the light passing through an object, so the surface color will depend on the thickness of that part of the object. Imagine an ear, for example. If you put a light behind it, you'd see the light passing through the ear and becoming reddish because of the blood vessels just below the surface of the skin.

- **Strand:** This panel has a set of options to define the material when you're rendering hair particles.

- **Options:** In the Options panel, you'll find some advanced options for defining a material and you want to check the Blender official documentation for more information on what they can do. An interesting one is the *Traceable* option, which, if disabled, will prevent a material from casting shadows or producing reflections (i.e., anything that uses raytracing methods).

- **Shadow:** This panel is very useful and you'll be using it in Chapter 14. It allows you to tell Blender how you want the shadows to act with a material. If you have transparent materials, they'll only cast transparent shadows over other materials that have the *Receive Transparent* option enabled, for example (to save render time). The *Shadows Only* option will make an object transparent, but when rendering, you'll see any shadows cast over it, making this option very useful when you want to compose objects that cast their shadows on top of a photo or another image.

As you can see, there are a lot of options you can manipulate to get the desired result for a material. And this is only the tip of the iceberg because mixing all these properties with textures gives even more options and really nice-looking materials.

> **Caution**
>
> Remember that if a material is not being used by any object when you close Blender, it will be removed and won't exist when you open the file again. If you really want to keep a material, make sure to press the **F** button next to its name (Fake User) to prevent Blender from deleting it.

Textures in Blender Render

Now let's look at the Texture tab and its main features, so you can proceed to the next part of the chapter and start using all this information to actually shade your character. Figure 10.2 shows the Texture tab and its panels.

The following list describes the basics of what you can do in each one of these panels:

- **Current selection:** Similar to the Material tab, this part of the interface shows a list of the current objects/materials/textures on which you're working. You can use the Pin exactly as you would in other editors and, at the bottom of this panel, you'll find three little icons to select the type of texture you want to work on.

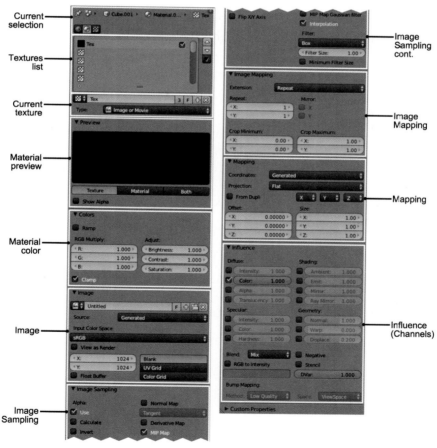

Figure 10.2   Texture tab in the Properties Editor and its panels

The first icon (the World) uses a texture, the second one lets you work on the textures for the current material, and the third one lets you create textures for things like brushes.

- **Textures list:** This panel works similar to layers. You can select one of the slots and then create or load a texture for that slot. You can load another texture in the next slot and make it transparent; then you'll see the first texture behind it. Similar to modifiers, the top layers are beneath those that appear at the bottom of the list. This panel is not only used for layers, but it can also contain different textures affecting various properties of the material.

- **Current texture:** The current texture's name and drop-down list work exactly the same as they would for any other datablock. Right below the name, you can find a list from which you have to select the type of texture you're going to be using inside this slot. In this case, *Image or Movie* is selected, as it's the one you'll need when you want to load your own images to use as textures for the materials. The rest are procedural textures. The other panels on the Texture tab can change a little depending on the type of texture you select in this panel

- **Preview:** In this panel, you can see what the current texture looks like and decide if you want to see the texture, the material, or both.

- **Colors:** This panel shows several options that will change the image's colors. Options such as Brightness, Contrast, or Saturation will change how the image looks.

- **Image:** The Image panel is specific to the Image or Movie texture type. It basically gives you some options to load an existing texture or to create a texture generated by Blender, as you've seen in Chapters 8 and 9 (such as a UV Test Grid).

- **Image Sampling:** This important panel shows options that tell Blender how to interpret the image you've loaded. Interpreting the alpha of an image, for example, is one of the things you'll determine with the Image Sampling options.

> **Tip**
>
> If you want to use Normal maps, you should activate the *Normal Map* option in the Image Sampling panel and select the type of Normal map you want (usually it's *Tangent*).

- **Image Mapping:** In this panel, you can offset, resize, and crop the image you've loaded into Blender or repeat it over and over beyond its boundaries.

- **Mapping:** Not to be confused with Image Mapping, this panel lets you define how the image is "mapped" onto the object. If you've unwrapped the model to which you're applying this material, you should pick UVs from the *Coordinates* drop-down list.

- **Influence:** Remember what you learned about channels earlier? Well, this panel is where you select which channels of the material are affected by the current texture, as well as the amount of effect the texture has. You can see that, by default, the texture is affecting the *Color* (Diffuse) channel only. If you have a Normal map loaded, for example, you should disable Color, and in the *Geometry* section, enable *Normal* to define its effect. If you have a black-and-white image, you can turn on *Ray Mirror* to define the reflectivity of the material.

  Let's say you want to mix two different images together: you can load them in different Texture slots and adjust the influences in their respective channels. Also, you can even change the blending mode (by default, Mix) just as you would change the layers blending modes in Photoshop or Gimp.

  You can also use a mask. If you enable the *Stencil* option, the current texture will be used as a mask for the next slot in this editor. Combinations of options can really expand your choices!

> **Tip**
>
> Usually, you may need to load a texture with alpha (like a .png image) and you need to use that alpha as the transparency in Blender. This can be kind of tricky if you don't know how to do it, so here are two steps to make this operation straightforward:
>
> **1.** Activate Transparency for the material (Z Transparency or Raytrace) and, in order to give the power to the texture, set the Alpha of the Transparency option in the material to 0.
>
> **2.** Load your image, including the alpha, enable its Alpha influence, and set it to the maximum. The material will now use the alpha from your image.

Shading Jim in Blender Render

So now that you know how materials work in Blender Render, let's start shading Jim!

Setting Things Up

Before you start shading your character, you first need to make sure that you have a few important options selected; otherwise, you won't see what's going on when you start adding materials:

1. In the 3D View Properties Region (**N**), find the Shading panel and select the GLSL shading method (this is the one Blender uses to display materials in the 3D View).

2. On the 3D View header, set the Display mode to Texture, so Blender shows textures and materials in the 3D preview.

3. If you have no lights in your scene, add one (**Shift + A**). You probably want to add a Sun light; it's directional and illuminates the whole scene, while an Omni light would only illuminate a single spot and you'd need to move it all the time to see what's going on.

> **Note**
>
> The reason you have to add a light is that without one, you'd see everything completely black (unless you set the materials to Shadeless, which is useful when testing your textures, but not when you are setting material properties such as the shininess or reflection).

Even though you set everything up correctly, keep in mind that in the 3D View, you won't see all of the properties of a material—its reflections, transparencies, shadows, refractions, and so forth. These properties will only work correctly in the final render, and even though you can preview things such as transparencies and shadows (only with Sun and Spotlight lights), these effects won't have good quality. In the 3D View, you'll get a basic preview of what the material will look like. That's why when you work on a complex material, you should perform test renders now and then to have a better idea of how the material behaves.

> **Tip**
>
> You can also switch to the Rendered display mode in the 3D View, which shows a preview of the final render right in the scene in real time. You can switch to this mode from the Display Mode selector on the 3D View header or by pressing **Shift + Z**.

Adding Basic Materials

Let's add a very basic material by following these steps:

1. Select Jim's face.
2. Go to the Material tab in the Properties Editor and create a new material. Name it Jim_mat (material for Jim).
3. Jump to the Texture tab in the Properties Editor. Create a new texture and instead of Clouds, set the Texture type to Image or Movie.
4. Inside the Texture properties, search the Image panel and load the texture you've created for Jim. At this point, you should be seeing the texture weirdly applied over Jim's face. Obviously, the UVs are not at work just yet!
5. To set the texture to be projected using the UVs, scroll down to the Mapping panel on the Texture tab and set the Coordinates to UV. Now you should see the texture of Jim's face properly projected.
6. Select all of the objects that will use the material that includes the textures you've made, such as the jacket, cap, boots, gloves, and pants. Finally, select the face so it becomes the active selection. Press **Ctrl + L** and select Materials from the list. This will make all those objects use the same material as the face.
7. Select the hair objects and the eyebrows. Add a new material to them and call it Hair_mat. In the Diffuse panel, use the blue color that was used in the original designs for Jim.

Figure 10.3   Jim, after the addition of a few basic materials

Tip

Keep in mind that you can load the original designs into a UV/Image editor. When you need to use a color that is present in a reference image, just click the color selector, pick the Eyedropper tool, and then click anywhere in the image to select that color.

8. For the rest of Jim's objects that still don't have materials (like the little details in the arms), add materials to them as necessary and set their colors. Later, you'll refine those materials. Leave the eyes alone for now. In Figure 10.3, you can see something similar to what you should have after following these steps.

Adding Several Materials to a Single Object

Jim's eyes require a different process. Although they are a single object, they will need different materials to define the pupil, iris, cornea, and eyeball. Figure 10.4 provides a

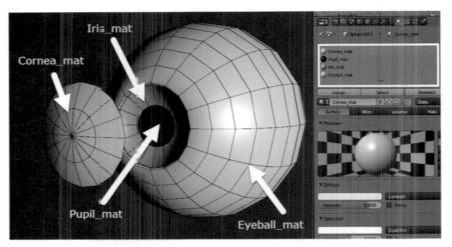

Figure 10.4   Materials for the eyes, with the cornea separated
so you can see what's going on inside the eyeball

reference for the materials you'll be using and where. Pay attention to the materials list in the Properties Editor.

Here are the steps you need to follow to add these materials:

1. Select the eyeball. Apply a material to it and call it Eyeball_mat.

2. In Edit Mode (**Tab**), add a new material slot to the list and create a new material in it. Call that material Cornea_mat. Select the cornea (you can select it by placing the cursor over it and pressing **L**). Make sure you have the Cornea_mat selected in the material list and, with the cornea selected in the model, click the *Assign* button: this will assign that material from the list to the selected faces. With the cornea selected, you can press **H** to hide it and you'll be able to work on the faces inside it (the pupil and the iris).

3. Using Figure 10.4, as a reference, repeat the process by creating two new materials called Iris_mat and Pupil_mat, and assign them to the iris and pupil faces the same way that you did for the cornea. Pupil_mat should be black and Iris_mat should use the same blue color that you used for the hair. Now you can press **Alt + H** to unhide the cornea.

4. Unfortunately, you have to repeat the process for the other eye, or delete it and duplicate the one you just worked on by mirroring it again.

For now, the materials are very basic, but in the next section you'll learn how to tweak them to make them look better and add more advanced properties to them.

> **Tip**
>
> You can quickly add the different materials to a single mesh as you did for the eyeballs using only very basic versions of the materials and naming them correctly. After they're assigned to the faces of the mesh, you can select them from the list to adjust them and make them look cooler, even in Object Mode, so you won't need to be selecting the faces for anything after you've assigned the materials to them.

Refining Materials

It's time to start tweaking the details of the materials' properties to achieve a better-looking result. First, you'll do some retouches on the objects that are using materials alone, such as the hair and the eyes. With those retouches, you'll learn the basics on how the properties of the materials work and what you can achieve.

Let's start with the hair:

1. Select any object with the hair material on it (eyebrows or the hair itself) and jump to the material properties.

2. Reduce the Specular Intensity to 0.3 to make the material less shiny.

3. Set the Specular Color to the same color as the blue you used for the Diffuse Color and give the Specular Hardness a value of around 100, to make the shine a little sharper.

> **Tip**
>
> If you hover the cursor over a parameter (even a color) on the menus and press **Ctrl + C,** you'll copy it to the Clipboard. By hovering the cursor over another color selector and pressing **Ctrl + V,** you'll paste it there. This is very useful for cases such as the one above when you want to copy the diffuse color and paste it on the specular color.

Now let's arrange the eyes' materials to make them more realistic. Usually, you could use textures for the iris and pupil, but in this case, let's keep it simple, so you'll only be playing with a few material values:

1. Select the eyeball to access the four materials that the eyes own.

2. The first stop will be the cornea, as you need to have it transparent in order to see the iris and the pupil. On the Materials tab, go to the Transparency panel and select Raytrace, set the Alpha to 0 (this will make the material completely transparent), set Specular to 1 (this will make the shine visible even though the surface of the cornea is transparent), and set IOR to 1.5. This will refract light inside the cornea, distorting the pupil and the iris in an interesting and realistic way, so they don't look like they're inside a hole.

> **Tip**
>
> At this point, you may want to have a small render preview (using the Rendered display mode in the 3D View) to check how things are looking as you tweak materials.

3. To make the shine in the cornea sharper, go to the Specular panel again and set the Specular mode to Toon. This will give a cartoon effect to the shine, making it very sharp. Set the Intensity to 0.3, the Size to 0.07 (the very small size will prevent the shine from covering the whole cornea) and set Smooth to 0 (this will make the shine spot completely sharp).

4. Now we'll work on the pupil. To make the pupil always absolutely black, select the Pupil_mat from the materials list. In the Shading panel, enable Shadeless so lights and shadows won't affect the pupil and black will always be its base color.

5. For the Iris_mat, you might want something similar, but you want to capture little shadows and some shine in the iris. Set the Specular Intensity to 0.2 so the shine is more subtle. Turn the Specular Hardness up to 100 to make the shine sharper. In the Shading panel, set the Emit value to 0.05.

6. The material for the eyeball is quite simple, so just give it some additional hardness to make the shine more defined.

Using Textures to Control Material Properties

Let's go back to the material that has the textures in it, because now you'll use textures to control the material's properties. Right now, the material shines and it has a very bright and plastic look to it. You'll solve that issue by using textures. When you have a surface that is completely made of a single material, it's very easy to add a material to it, set the new material's properties, and you're done! But when you have an object or character that is made of several different materials with different properties, controlling the materials' properties with textures is the way to go: the textures allow you to control different parts of the materials to give each one of them different property values.

Using Jim's diffuse texture as a base, I've turned it to black and white to make a specularity texture and added some layers on top of it to darken and brighten some areas to create a specular hardness texture. You can see the textures in Figure 10.5.

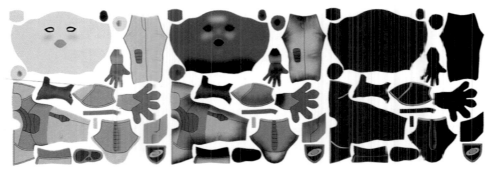

Figure 10.5   The diffuse (left), specularity (center),
and specular hardness (right) textures for Jim

Use the following steps to add textures to Jim's material:

1. Select Jim's material (the one to which you added the main color texture). On the Texture tab, select a new slot from the list, name it Specular, and switch its type to Image or Movie.

2. In the Image panel, load the texture for the specularity. Make sure that you set the coordinates to UV in the Mapping panel.

3. Look for the Influence panel on the Texture tab. Turn Color off so Jim doesn't look black and white—and weird. Turn on Specular Color and leave its value at 1. Now, Jim should look a lot better and if you rotate the camera around him, you'll see how the darker parts of the texture don't shine at all, giving it a more natural look.

> **Note**
>
> Remember to enable the Textured display mode in the 3D View to be able to preview the materials in real time and see an approximation of how they'll look in the final render while you adjust the materials' parameters.

4. Pick a new slot from the textures list, call it Hardness, and load the Hardness texture. This one usually needs to be really dark to work properly and the darker it is, the softer the shine will be; however, you don't want some areas to be that soft, so you'll leave them with light colors in that texture.

5. Set the Coordinates to UV again. In the Influence panel, disable Color and enable Specular Color and Hardness. As this texture is "on top" of the Specular one, the Specular Color setting will override the effect of the Specular texture, but if you decrease the influence of the Specular Color, the Specular channel will gain some effect underneath.

> **Tip**
>
> Another thing you can do to try to improve the result is to select the Diffuse slot (the one for the base color texture), go to the Influence panel, and enable the Normal channel. Set it to something really low, such as 0.1, so it's not very visible but it may add a little variation to the surface if you added small details to the textures. This will make the surface look bumpy. Usually, you should do a separate texture for the normal map, but if you are out of time, you can try to use the base texture as a normal map, as it usually can add some detail to the result.

Final Adjustments

Now, some small, final adjustments are needed, such as adding the materials for the little details on the clothing. Adjust their Specular value and hardness so they fit the rest of the character. Do the same with the communicator. The teeth and the tongue are hidden, but of course, you have to add materials to them as well! Just add a white material to the teeth and a reddish one with red specularity to the tongue.

Render Tests

You've probably made a few render tests during the process to see how everything was looking so far. But now, instead of just a basic, flat render, let's perform a more elaborate render with some lights and shadows to see how Jim might look in the final render (see Figure 10.6).

1. Create a couple of lights and set their type to Sun. Rotate one of them as the main lighting source, and rotate the second one so it comes from the back of the character as a "rim light" to illuminate the borders or the part of the character that are not directly hit by the main light. You can also reduce the intensity and change the color of the second light.
2. Enable the Suns' Raytrace shadows. You can also increase the Samples to around 8 and increase the Soft Size as well.
3. On the World tab of the Properties Editor, under the World panel, change the Horizon Color. There are a few other settings you can adjust to make your render look better. You can change the background color, for example.
4. Enable Ambient Occlusion (AO) and set it to multiply: this will create some soft shadow effects and multiply them over the image to give it a more realistic lighting effect. If you want to see the effect of the AO clearly, use it in a scene that only has white materials and you'll appreciate how cool it is. You may get a little

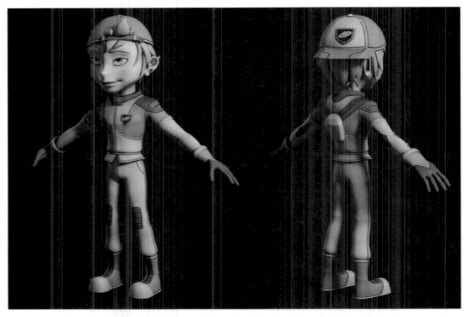

Figure 10.6   Final test render with Blender Render materials . . .
Jim is looking pretty good!

noise in the result: in the Gather panel, increase the samples to 10 or more. Keep in mind that fewer samples render faster, but more samples give a better and less noisy result.

5. Enable Environment Lighting to add light coming from everywhere. Use a low value, just to prevent the shadow areas from being completely black, which would look very unnatural.

6. Finally, create a plane on the floor. Add a material to it and, under the Shadow panel of the material properties, turn on Shadows Only. This will display the floor shadows in the final render, but will let the camera see the background color through it as well.

Shading Your Character with Cycles

Now that you have Blender Render under control, let's see how Cycles works because its features are quite different. Materials and lighting are physically based on reality and the material properties are also very different from those of Blender Render. In addition, the way in which you will build materials in Cycles has almost nothing in common with how you created materials in the previous sections with Blender Render.

> **Caution**
>
> Make sure you select Cycles from the Render Engine selector in the main menu at the top of the interface; otherwise, you won't see the options explained in this section.

Using Cycles Materials

First, you need to understand that in Cycles, a material is made up of shaders. You have different shaders from which you can pick; each one of them has different properties from real materials and you'll have to mix those properties together to create your own materials. Before you start diving into shaders and how to mix them, take a look at Figure 10.7 to see how the Material tab looks when you use the Cycles render engine. It's very different from Blender Render's Material tab!

At first sight, this menu may look simpler than Blender Render's menu, but here's the difference: in Blender Render, all the settings are visible to you from the start; with Cycles, the Material panel is very basic to begin with, but you can extend it in order to create complex materials as you add more shaders. Let's very briefly discuss the panels you'll find on this Material tab:

- **Current selection, materials List, and current material:** The first three panels on the Material tab are exactly the same as those in Blender Render. They show the current selection, a materials list that allows you to use different materials inside the same object, and a menu where you can select a material that you have previously created, rename it, or create a new one. (The menu shown in the image is the one that appears after you click the button to add a new material.)

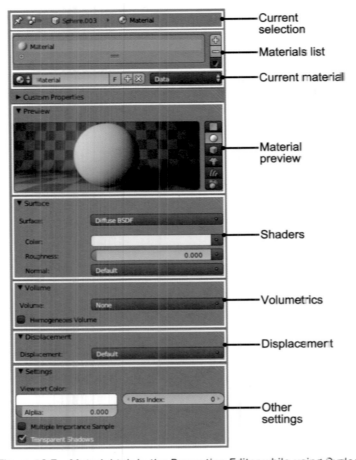

Current selection

Materials list

Current material

Material preview

Shaders

Volumetrics

Displacement

Other settings

Figure 10.7   Material tab in the Properties Editor while using Cycles

- **Preview:** In this panel, you have a material preview, almost the same as the one in Blender Render, although you'll notice this one will update little by little and, at first, you might get some noisy results. This happens because Cycles is a progressive rendering engine; when the number of samples is low, you'll get noise that will clean up slowly as more samples are added to the rendered result.
- **Surface:** This is the main panel of the Cycles Material tab where you select the type of shaders you're going to use and their properties. You'll learn about shaders in the next section.
- **Volume:** This panel was added in Blender 2.70 and it allows you to apply volumetric effects to the objects that use this material. Volumetrics is the technology

that simulates such things as fog, smoke, and gases, and it's very useful for adding ambience to a scene. This material lets light pass through it to create cool effects. Unfortunately, this is the first version and, while it does work, it's very slow and has some limitations.

- **Displacement:** This panel allows you to use a gray-scale (height map) texture to deform the surface of a mesh so that it has much more detail. When you displace a material in Cycles, you can also load normal maps and bumps. However, using this feature is kind of tricky because it's still under development and it requires advanced knowledge to edit the nodes properly. Alternatively, there is a modifier you can apply to the mesh to use displacement, but working with it is really slow because you have to subdivide the mesh a lot to make it work properly.

- **Settings:** In this panel, you'll find some more options for the material such as its color in the 3D View, the Pass Index (to separate elements in the Compositor), and enabling the material to receive transparent shadows.

Basic Shaders

As we mentioned before, Cycles materials are made of shaders. How can you add shaders to a material? When you add a new material, in the Surface panel you'll see a *Diffuse BSDF* shader option. By clicking the shader's name, you can pick a different shader option. Let's look at some of the most commonly used shaders.

- **Diffuse BSDF:** It's the basic shader—just a colored surface.
- **Transparent BSDF:** This shader makes the surface transparent.
- **Glossy BSDF:** A shader that is shiny and reflective, by controlling its roughness you'll get shine and reflections that are more blurred.
- **Hair BSDF:** This shader is specially designed for use with hair particles.
- **Refraction:** This shader adds refraction effects to the surface of an object.
- **Glass:** This shader will add effects such as transparency, refraction, reflection, and glossiness.
- **Anisotropic BSDF:** This shader is very useful for simulating metallic objects. What makes it different from the Glossy shader is that it adds an anisotropic shine to an object's surface.
- **Emission:** Probably one of the coolest shaders, it allows you to convert any mesh into light! This shader emits light and you can control the intensity and color (something not possible in Blender Render).

There are more shaders, but these are the ones that you'll probably use most often. Try some of the others, though; you may find them useful. Each one of them will show a couple of options that you can adjust to control its properties (color, roughness, intensity, etc.).

Mix and Add Shaders

Of course, the shaders mentioned before can't do much on their own. That's why inside the Shaders list there are two special shaders that are actually not shaders: Mix Shader and Add Shader.

Mix Shader lets you combine two of the other shaders and adjust the influence each one of them has on the result. Imagine that you want a simple colored surface that has some shininess: you can use a Mix Shader and, in its two slots that appear, you can add a Diffuse BSDF and a Glossy BSDF. Adjust their properties and colors, and finally define the Mix Shader Fac (Factor). A value of 0 will show only the first shader, while 1 will show only the second one, as if they were layers; values in between will blend the effects of the two shaders.

Add Shader, instead of letting you select the blending values for the two shaders, will just add the two colors together and will generally give you brighter results.

Of course, you can add Mix Shaders inside Mix Shaders to get even more complex shaders. For example, imagine a rusty metal; you can have a mixture of shaders for the parts of the surface that don't have rust and combine that mixture with another mix of different textures and materials for the rusty parts. Can you see how you can make Cycles materials as complex as you want?

Loading Textures

To add a texture in Cycles, under the Diffuse BSDF shader, for example, go to its properties and click the button to the right with the little circle to get a list of options. In that list, pick Image Texture and Blender will display the options to load and control the image.

A new parameter will appear as well: Vector. This parameter is similar to the Mapping Coordinates in Blender Render: if your object has UVs, it will pick them by default, but if you want to make sure your texture is projected correctly, you can select the option *Texture Coordinate | UV* from the Vector list.

> **Note**
>
> You won't have to use the Node Editor to create materials in Cycles right now, except for a couple of very minor adjustments. The materials you're going to create for Jim are pretty basic. Later on, in Chapter 14, you'll learn how to use the Node Editor. After that, you'll understand the basics of how nodes work and you'll know how to use them to create materials. Nodes are important, as you'll have more control over Cycles materials when you work with them from the Node Editor.

Shading Jim in Cycles

Now that you have a basic understanding of how Cycles materials work, let's jump right in and use shaders to make Jim look great!

Basic Shading

Cycles materials are more complex to render than Blender Render materials, so you may want to add one or two lights to be able to see your scene when you switch from time to time to the rendered mode display in the 3D view to preview how everything is looking.

1. Select Jim's face and add a new material called Jim_mat. Add a Mix Shader to it and, for the first slot, pick a Diffuse BSDF shader. In its color field, load Jim's textures as an image and make sure the Vector is set to Texture Coordinate | UV. The image may look a little dark, but don't worry; it's because the other half of the material is still empty and you'll make modifications later.

2. For now, select all the objects that use the textures and then select the one to which you just added the material, press **Ctrl + L,** and select Materials. This will make all those objects use the same material.

3. Add a material to the hair elements called Hair_mat and set its Surface as a Diffuse BSDF with the blue color from the designs.

4. Select an eyeball and follow the same steps you followed to add materials to its parts with Blender Render (you can find the instructions in the earlier section, Adding Several Materials to a Single Object). Create four different material slots in the list and call them Eyeball_mat, Cornea_mat, Pupil_mat, and Iris_mat. For the pupil and iris, add Diffuse BSDF shaders with black and blue colors, respectively.

5. The cornea and eyeball will be a little trickier. For the eyeball's material, add a Mix Shader. Select a white Diffuse BSDF in the first slot and a Glossy BSDF in the second slot. Adjust the roughness of the Glossy shader to 0.5, so the shine is more blurred.

6. For the cornea, add a Glass BSDF shader. Give the Glass shader's color a light-blue tone, increase the IOR (Index of Refraction) to 1.38 (similar to what you did in Blender Render), and set the roughness to something very low, such as 0.03, so that external light sources are reflected in the eyes to create a visible "highlight."

7. The cornea is really dark and this is because even though it's mostly transparent, it's casting a shadow in the eye's interior. To correct this, go to the Object tab in the Properties Editor (the one with the yellow cube) and, at the bottom under the *Ray Visibility* panel, turn off *Shadow*. This feature will prevent the eyeball from casting shadows and now the cornea will look completely transparent.

Advanced Shading

A few more steps are needed to finish the shading of Jim using Cycles. You need to adjust the material that uses the textures so it works properly. Remember the Mix Shader you added to those parts of Jim that was half empty? Let's work on it.

1. In the second slot, pick a Glossy BSDF; this will cause the material to reflect light.

2. Load a couple more textures to control the effect of the Glossy BSDF shader's properties. Take a look at Figure 10.8 to see the textures that you will load. The one that controls the Mix Shader Fac is the same one you used for the Specular Intensity in Blender Render: a grayscale image in which the white areas will be shiny and the black areas won't.

3. Finally, in the Roughness for the Glossy BSDF shader, you'll use yet another texture. This one is similar to the Hardness value in Blender Render, but this parameter controls roughness, where white in the texture is rougher and black is smoother; this means that it is the opposite of the BI Hardness. In Figure 10.8, notice that in the texture to the right, there are some darker marks; those will be areas with a sharper shine.

4. Adjust the material nodes in the Node Editor to arrange them. Unfortunately, when you load these types of textures from the Properties Editor, they automatically pick their Alpha value, but you need to use their color and there is no other way to do it than by using nodes. For that, follow the next steps to make some basic adjustments to the material nodes.

5. Select an area of the interface and switch it to a Node Editor. It should automatically show the current material nodes. If this doesn't happen, select the object with the material you're adjusting. Then, open the Node Editor and if Material nodes are not displayed by default, look in the Node Editor's header for a three-icon row that shows a sphere for Materials, a checkerboard for Textures, and a couple of layers for Compositing; click the icon for Materials.

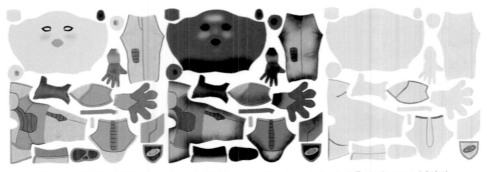

Figure 10.8　Diffuse color (left), Specularity (center), and Roughness (right)

6. In the same header, select Jim_mat in the Material list. Then, arrange the nodes because right now you'll see them all on top of each other. (This is a side effect of working in the Properties Editor with Cycles Materials: the nodes are all created in the same place.) Left click and drag them around until you can see the tree clearly (see Figure 10.9 to get an idea on how this should look).

7. Once you can see all the connections in a structure similar to the one in Figure 10.9, reconnect the marked lines as shown in the image, so the Color of those two textures is used instead of their Alpha. Left click and drag over the little dots at the sides of each node (input and output noodles) to reconnect them.

8. Finally, adjust the material for the clothing details by adding a Glossy BSDF to the second slot, setting the roughness to 0.15, and then reducing the Factor of the Mix Shader to 0.1. This will make those pieces of clothing look similar to the other details that are inside the textures.

Render Tests

Jim has been shaded and now it's time for the cool test renders again. In Blender Render, you had to activate some features to get a better result, but in Cycles, with its more

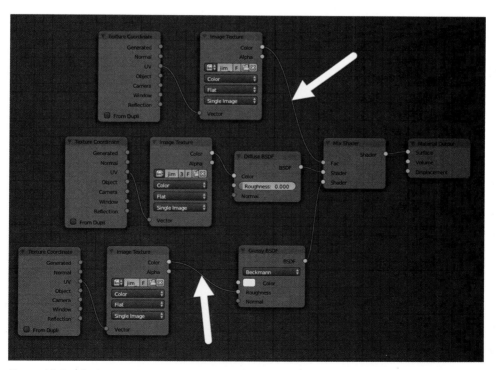

Figure 10.9   Jim's material node tree. Make sure you reconnect the marked nodes correctly.

realistic approach, the render already works well by default. Let's add a couple of details, though.

1. Create a light setup similar to the one you did for the Blender Render Scene, with two Suns, a primary one and then a secondary one as a rim light with less intensity and a warmer color.

> **Note**
>
> Unfortunately, having a material that only receives shadows is trickier in Cycles (you'd have to do it through compositing, and you'll learn how to do that in the final chapters). For that reason, we won't use shadows in these Cycles test renders.

2. Add a sky to the background. Go to the World tab in the Properties Editor and under the Surface panel, you'll see that in Cycles, the Sky option has features similar to other Materials. By default, it should have a Background shader. Click the Color to select a texture and pick Sky from the list.

3. Now arrange the settings until they look right to you. Click and drag over the sphere to change the Sun's direction.

The result so far should be something similar to the renders shown in Figure 10.10.

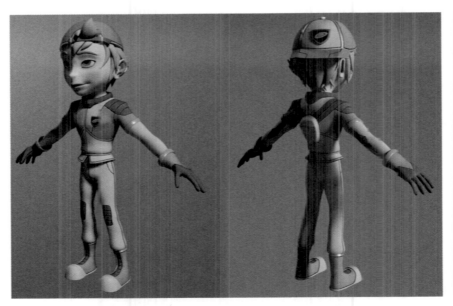

Figure 10.10   The result of rendering Jim with Cycles

Summary

As you can see, the differences between Cycles and Blender Render are quite clear, both in terms of the workflow to build the materials and the results. Now you know how to create basic materials using textures in both render engines, which should serve as a starting point for you. Also, you can now see that Cycles materials can be a lot more powerful using nodes, a subject that you'll learn more about in Chapter 14, Lighting, Compositing, and Rendering. Jim already looks quite similar to the character we initially designed.

Exercises

1. Create several spheres and add different materials to each of them. Then, add different parameters to each material and see how this results in different effects when rendered. This exercise will help you understand how materials work and what each parameter does to the final result.

2. Select Cycles as your render engine, create a floor with a white diffuse shader, and add an object with a red shader on top of it. Then, create a light that illuminates the scene. Explore how the light makes the object's red color reflect on the floor.

3. Using Cycles, add an object to any scene you want and apply an Emit shader to the object to see how it can be used to light the scene.

V

Bringing Your
Character to Life

11

Character Rigging

Rigging is probably the most technical and complex part of the character-creation process. You have a character, but it's static; it needs a skeleton that moves and deforms the mesh properly so you can animate the character and bring it to life. In this chapter, you'll learn the basics of how to create skeletons, "rig" them (which is basically setting up your skeleton so it works intuitively), and finally do the "skinning" (the process that makes the skeleton deform the mesh as if it were skin). You'll also learn how to use drivers to control your character's facial expressions.

Understanding the Rigging Process

Let's talk a little about the rigging process so you have a better understanding of how it works.

Parts of the Rig

The purpose of a good rig is to make it easier for an animator to control a character. In Blender, rigs are called *armatures*. An armature is like a container, inside of which you have the bones that comprise the rig. Here is a list of the elements that make up a rig:

- **Bones:** Everything inside a rig is made of bones and the bones can have different uses, depending on how you set them up.

- **Control bones:** When you are posing the character, it's very helpful if you have certain bones that are made specifically for controlling how the rig works. For example, the leg is made up of several bones, but with a single control bone, you can move them all. Basically, control bones are the ones that you'll animate later on.

- **Deform bones:** These are the bones that deform the character's model. Their purpose is just to deform the mesh, so they're usually hidden and are moved by the control bones.

- **Helper bones:** These bones are very important because they actually make the rig work. You could describe them as the engine of the rig because they make it function but they are hidden. They exist only to help the rig behave as you expect. You should not move them manually by any means. They're automatically transformed by control bones.

- **Constraints:** These define what bones do. You can tell a bone to follow the position of another bone, to copy its rotation, or limit its movements, or you can do other cool things like having one bone look at other bones (that's how eyes are rigged). You can think of constraints as modifiers applied to the bones that define their behavior. For example, Inverse Kinematics (IK) is one of these constraints and you'll see how to use it later on.

- **Custom Shapes:** This feature allows you to change the visual representation of the bone to a custom object. This is beneficial because it gives animators a more intuitive view of how the rig is set up and which part of the character each bone controls.

> **Note**
>
> In other software, each bone is a different object and dummies or helpers (called empties in Blender) are also objects that a rig uses. That can make it difficult to control the entire rig at the same time, or it can mess everything up when you want to scale your character up or down, or duplicate it. However, in Blender a full character's rig is a single object (making it really easy to place in the scene, scale it, or duplicate it) and, inside that object, there are the only bones, to which you can add custom shapes in order to make them look better and more intuitive.

Rigging Process

The steps below describe the usual workflow that you need to follow to rig your character. In the next sections, we'll discuss these steps in detail.

1. Create an armature.
2. Enter Edit Mode for that armature and create the main bone structure.
3. In Pose Mode, add constraints to set up the rig and jump back to Edit Mode as necessary to add helper bones.
4. Once the rig is working, add custom shapes to it.
5. Finally, "skin" the meshes to the skeleton so it deforms and, using weight painting, define the influence of each bone in the vertices of the model.
6. Now you're ready to animate your character!

Working with Armatures

In this section, you'll learn how to create and edit armatures so you'll know how to perform this critical step when you start working in the actual character rig. You'll also learn how to access the properties of an armature or a bone and add constraints to them.

> **Caution**
>
> You should know that having your character and rig correctly centered in the scene is critical for the rigging process. If you haven't yet done so, make sure your character model is looking in the direction of the positive Y-axis, in such a way that the left side of the character is on the negative X-axis and the right side of the character is on the positive X-axis.
>
> The center of the character should be exactly on the X-axis center (X position value = 0). This will help during the rigging process and some tools will use this as a requirement; they won't work properly if the character is not aligned in this way, so keep that in mind from now on.

Manipulating Bones

You can create an armature by pressing **Shift + A** in Object Mode and selecting Armature > Single Bone. If you want to create a skeleton from the default bone in the armature, you'll have to do that in Edit Mode (**Tab**) using the techniques you'll see in a moment. In Figure 11.1, you can see the elements of a bone.

When you have a series of bones connected in a line it's called a chain. A bone's direction goes from its head to its tail and that's important because it defines the bone chain's direction as well. A bone connected to the tail of another bone will follow the movements of the latter (it will be the latter bone's child). You will learn more about this later on.

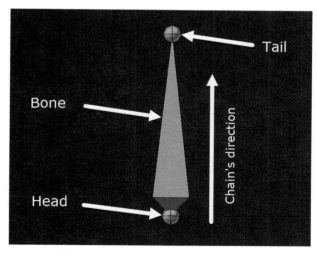

Figure 11.1   The elements of a bone

The list that follows describes shortcuts and controls that will help you work with bones in Edit Mode:

- Select bones with **RMB** and move, rotate, and scale them the same way you do with any other element in Blender (**G, R,** and **S**). Bones are made of the bone itself and "spheres" at its top and bottom, which are the bone's head and tail (these could be called joints in other software). You can transform the whole bone, or just the head or tail, to adapt it to the shape you need.

- To create a chain of bones, you can select the tail of a bone and extrude it with **E,** or use **Ctrl + LMB** in the location where you want the new bone to end, just as if you were extruding vertices. When you extrude a bone from the tail of another, the new one will be a child of the existing bone. However, if you extrude from the head, Blender will just create a new bone, with no parenting applied to it.

- In the Tools Region, you can activate the option *X-Axis Mirror* in the Armature Options panel. If you make changes to one part of the skeleton's X-axis, those changes will be mirrored to the other side of the skeleton on that axis. To use this option properly, select the tail of a bone that is situated in the middle of the X-axis (the mirror plane) and press **Shift + E** to extrude toward the sides (this will create a first mirrored extrusion). After that first extrusion, you can keep extruding and transforming the bones from that bone chain and they will be mirrored to the other side of the axis.

- You can duplicate bones by selecting them and pressing **Shift + D.**

- You can create new bones at the 3D cursor position pressing **Shift + A.**

- You can name bones in the Properties Region, in the Item panel. Keep in mind that for armatures you'll have two fields: one for the armature's name and another for the bone's name inside that armature. Alternatively, if you look at the Properties Editor, you'll notice that the tabs are now slightly different: you have the Object tab, the Constraints tab, the Armature tab, and the Bone tab. When naming the selected bone, make sure to go to the Bone tab; otherwise, you'll be renaming the armature itself (the object that contains all the bones).

- In Edit Mode, you can define the bones' hierarchy. Select the bones you want to be the children (the bones that will follow the parent), and then select the bone you want to act as the parent. Press **Ctrl + P** and you'll see two options: Connected will join the tail of the parent with the head of the children, while Keep Offset will parent all the selected bones and keep them disconnected. To remove a parenting, select the object you want to "set free," press **Alt + P,** and you'll have two options: Clear Parent will completely remove the relationship with the selected bone's parent bone, while Disconnect will separate the head of one bone from the tail of the other, but the parent relationship will still be there.

- If you select one or more bones, you can "roll" the selection with **Ctrl + R** to control its orientation. **Ctrl + N** displays a pop-up list with several predefined options for automatically orienting bones (such as aligning them to the orientation of the active bone or orienting them to look at the 3D cursor).

- If you select two bone ends (heads or tails) and press **F,** a new bone will be created to fill the gap between the two tips, similar to the operation for creating an edge to connect two vertices in a mesh. Keep in mind that only the new bone's head will be connected to its parent. The new bone's tail will be free and you'll have to parent it with the next bone in the chain if you need to connect them.

- If you select one or more bones, if you press **W,** you'll access the Specials menu. One of its options is Subdivide, which will divide longer bones into shorter ones. From the Operator panel in the Tools Region, you can set the number of divisions.

- You can select two connected bones and merge them into a single one by pressing **Alt + M.**

- If you want a chain of bones to parent in the opposite direction, you can switch the direction of a bone with **Alt + F.** This basically switches the head and tail of a bone, changing the direction of the hierarchy.

- If you have bones in your skeleton you want to remove, delete them by pressing **X.**

- As always, you can hide and unhide bones with **H** and **Alt + H** to display only the ones you're working with, or to hide any bones that are in your way.

Note

You can access all these options from the Armature menu on the header of the 3D view when in Edit Mode, but here the keyboard shortcuts are shown so you can start getting used to them.

Object, Edit, and Pose Modes

The modes for working with armatures are different than for other objects. It's important that you understand what you can do in each one of the modes.

- **Object Mode:** The full rig is inside the armature object, so in Object Mode you can move it around, rotate it, or scale it to change the size of your character. Because the rig is inside the armature, the scale of the object won't affect or cause problems to the armature's contents (the bones).

- **Edit Mode:** In Edit Mode, you have access to the bones. You can build your character's skeleton and create parenting to define hierarchies in this mode. The position of bones in Edit Mode will become the default rest pose of the bones in Object and Pose Modes.

- **Pose Mode:** Once the hierarchy and the bones are in place in Edit Mode, you should go to Pose Mode to add constraints to the bones and, finally, to move everything around and pose your character to create its animation.

To summarize, in Object Mode you don't have access to the individual bones or controls; you can only transform the rig as a whole. In Edit Mode, you can modify the bones' positions, size, and orientation to fit your character, and you can also define the bones' hierarchy. Finally, in Pose Mode, you take the skeleton and add constraints to it so it works as you expect and then you pose it. While you're setting up the rig, you'll move frequently between Edit Mode and Pose Mode to create and adjust poses while you add and modify their constraints.

When you're in Pose Mode, selected bones will be shown in blue as a reminder that you're in that specific mode. While you're in Edit or Object Mode, the selections color scheme is consistent with other Blender object types.

> **Tip**
>
> To switch between these modes, keep in mind that you can use shortcuts: using **Tab** in Object Mode, you enter Edit Mode and then **Ctrl + Tab** will put you in Pose Mode. When you exit from Edit Mode with **Tab**, you'll switch back to the previous mode. Press **Ctrl + Tab** in Pose Mode to go back to Object Mode.

Adding Constraints

Constraints make your rig work. You could say that they make bones react to other bones; for example, if you move a bone, you will cause a certain reaction in another part of the skeleton. Throughout this chapter, you'll use a lot of constraints, but for now let's see how they work and how you can add them to bones.

First, you need to know that most of the constraints have a "target," which means that when a constraint is applied to a bone, it also targets another bone and the constraint is then created between them. For example, if you use the *Track To* constraint for an eye, you'd apply the constraint to the eye and you'd select as a target the bone that you want the eye to look at.

> **Caution**
>
> You can apply constraints to any object in your scene but there's a difference between Object Constraints and Bone Constraints. If you're in Object Mode and add a constraint, it will affect the whole armature. If you're in Pose Mode when you add a constraint, a new tab will appear in the Properties Editor: Bone Constraints. The Object Constraints tab has a chain as its icon, while the Bone Constraints tab shows an icon with a smaller chain near a bone.

With this in mind, there are two main ways to add constraints; just remember you have to be in Pose Mode:

- Select the bone to which you want to add the constraint. Go to the Bone Constraints tab in the Properties Editor, click the *Add Bone Constraint* button, and select the constraint type you want to add. You'll see that the constraint is then added to the stack similar to the way in which modifiers are added to it. Inside the Constraints panel, you'll see a field for the *Target*. Enter the name of the armature and a new field for the bone's name will appear where you should insert the name of the bone you want to have as the target for the constraint.

- Another, usually faster way to add a constraint is to first select the target bone and then select the bone to which you want to add the constraint while pressing **Shift**. Then press **Shift + Ctrl + C** to open the Constraints menu to add the constraint (or go to the Armature menu on the 3D view header and find the Constraints category). This way, when you add a constraint, it will automatically pick the first selected bone as a target and you won't have to add it manually in the Constraints panel.

> **Tip**
>
> Whenever you need to insert the name of an object in a text field, start typing the name and a list will appear with the names of objects that start with the letters you've typed. This is another reason why keeping your objects named correctly can help a lot! Also, you can select an object or bone, place the cursor over its name field, and press **Ctrl + C** to copy the name; then, select the object with the constraint, go to the desired field, place the cursor on top of it, and press **Ctrl + V** to paste the name you copied before.

Rigging Your Character

Now that you know how to manipulate bones, let's create the character rig for Jim!

Basic Skeleton

Start by creating the base skeleton. In this case, you only have to create one half of it; then, when you add all the constraints to it later, you can mirror that half to the other side. Otherwise, you would have to add the constraints manually to the other side. Figure 11.2 shows what the basic skeleton looks like.

Here are some guidelines that will help you while you create this base structure:

- On the Armature tab in the Properties Editor, find the Display panel and activate the X-Ray option. This will display the bones on top of the model, even if they are inside the mesh, which will make it easier to see what you're doing while keeping the mesh visible so you can align the bones to it.
- Don't create things like the fingers just yet—just the base structure. Later, you'll add all the necessary details piece by piece.
- Naming is essential when you're working on a rig, so that when you add constraints later, you'll know to which bones you're referring: it's a lot easier to find a bone that is called D_hand than a Bone.023. Also, pay attention to the fact that all the bones in the structure have the D_ prefix: this is a nice way to organize the bone names inside your rig.

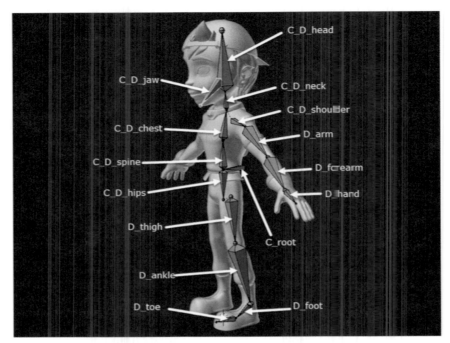

Figure 11.2   Basic skeleton, created only on the left side,
so those parts can later be mirrored to the right side

- You can use prefixes to help you recognize the type of bone: *D_name* would be a bone that is part of the main structure that will deform the mesh, *C_name* would be a controller bone, and *H_name* would be a helper bone. Also, some of the bones may be used for deforming as well as for control, such as the bones in the spine: these bones use the two prefixes *C_D_name*. Using this naming convention will help you when you search for a bone in a list, as they'll be organized by type.
- Keep an eye on the bones' hierarchy: C_D_hips and C_D_spine have to be children of C_root. D_shoulder has to be a child of C_D_chest. D_thigh has to be a child of C_D_hips, and C_D_jaw needs to be a child of C_D_head. If you made the rig correctly and go to Pose Mode to test it out, everything should follow the C_root control. If you don't parent bones correctly, when you move one part of the rig, other parts that should also move might be left in place.

> **Tip**
>
> When you're testing the bone structure in Pose Mode, it's very easy to reset a bone to its default pose (the one defined in Edit Mode). In the Armature menu of the 3D View header, you'll find the Clear Transform option, which will give you different ways to reset the pose. Otherwise, you can reset the movement with **Alt + G**, the rotations with **Alt + R**, and the scale with **Alt + S**.

- Finally, you can organize your scene. In Object Mode, select the armature and name it Jim_rig. Press **M** and, from the squares in the pop-up menu (layers) that appears, select a different layer than the model's, so you can quickly switch the layers in the 3D View header to show or hide the model whenever you need to focus on the rig.

Rigging the Eyes

Let's start with the eyes. You'll use a Track To constraint to control where Jim's eyes are looking. In Figure 11.3, you can see what the eye rig looks like. Again, you're only working on the left side of the rig for now.

The following list describes the steps for creating the eye's rig. You need to create the bone that will move the eye's model and it can be a little tricky in this case because you have an eye that is being deformed by the Lattice modifier. In normal models, the eye would be a perfect sphere, so you'd have only a single bone with its head in the center of the eye, but in this case, you'll use two different bones.

1. First, select the eye's mesh and, in Edit Mode, select the central loop and press **Shift + S** to move the 3D cursor to the loop's center. Exit Edit Mode and you'll see how the 3D cursor is not actually centered in the eye at all; don't worry, because the eye will be rotated from the 3D cursor's position before the Lattice modifier deformation takes place. Now, go to Edit Mode in the armature and create a bone at the 3D cursor's location. Duplicate the bone and move the new bone to the approximate point from which the deformed eye would rotate. You'll use this bone later to deform the eyelids slightly when you rotate the eye to create a more organic effect. That's why the first bone is a helper and is only there to rotate the eye, while the second bone is a deformer because it will deform the

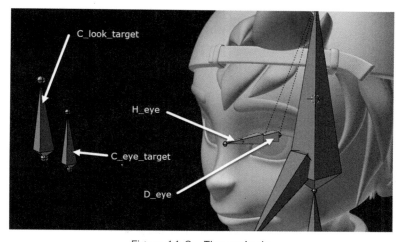

Figure 11.3   The eye's rig

eyelids. Parent these two bones to the C_D_head bone, so when you move the head, they will follow it.

2. Duplicate one of those bones and move it forward to be in front of the head. You need to end up with two new bones, one that is in the center of the two eyes, in front of the head that will control where the eyes look, and a second one that will be in front of the left eye. C_eye_target will be parented to C_lock_target, so when you move the latter, the former will follow it. This will give you the ability to make Jim's eyes look in whatever direction you want, but at the same time, you'll have independent control over each eye.

> **Tip**
>
> To make sure a bone is in the center (X = 0), you can insert the values manually in the Properties Region in the Transform panel.

3. Now add the constraints. First, select C_eye_target and with **Shift** pressed, select H_eye. Press **Ctrl + Shift + C** and select the *Track To* constraint. The bone first selected will automatically become the target of that constraint you just applied to H_eye. Now, if you move C_look_target, C_eye_target should follow and H_eye should reorient itself to look at its target. Repeat this process with D_eye.

Rigging the Legs

Let's jump into the legs, which will be a little trickier. Figure 11.4 shows the different steps of the process and the step-by-step instructions follow. You'll use Inverse Kinematics (IK) to create the legs.

Before you start following the steps, you should know what IK is. Usually, when you create a bone structure such as the leg, if you try to pose it you'll find that you have to rotate each bone and its children will follow their parent. For the leg, you should rotate the thigh, then the ankle, and then the foot. This way of working is called Forward Kinematics (FK), but for cases such as the legs or parts of the rig that need to touch surfaces (like the feet), Inverse Kinematics is a much better option.

IK works in a way that is opposite to FK and to pose the leg, you would only have to move the foot and the knee would flex accordingly to reflect that movement. This is very useful because when you move the character's torso, the legs will automatically flex and move to make the feet stand on the floor.

1. Extrude a bone from the knee joint (name it C_leg_pole) and another one from the heel joint (name it H_leg_ik). With the new bones selected, press **Alt + P** to clear their parents and disconnect them from the rest of the leg. Take C_leg_pole and move it forward a little so it's in front of the leg (it should be right in front of, and aligned with, the knee).

2. In Pose Mode, select H_leg_ik; this will be the target of the IK chain. Press **Shift**, select D_ankle. Now add a constraint with **Shift + Ctrl + C** and select

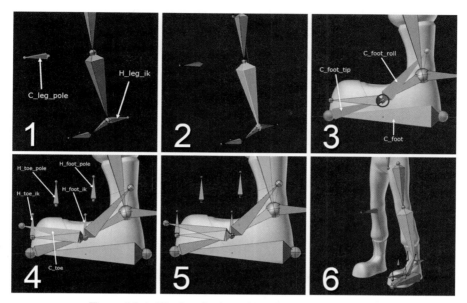

Figure 11.4 Rigging the leg with Inverse Kinematics

Inverse Kinematics; or, you can press **Shift + I**, which will apply the IK directly. Now go to the Constraints tab in the Properties Editor and, in the IK constraint, there are a couple of values you'll have to adjust.

First is the *Chain Length*. By default, the IK will go up to the root of the hierarchy (which, in this case, is the C_root bone). Set the Chain Length value to 2; this way, the IK will only work up to 2 bones in the hierarchy, which in this case are the ankle and the thigh. At this point, if you move the C_root bone or the H_leg_ik bone, you'll see the effect of the IK.

Second, let's give this IK a pole. IK makes the bones of the leg flex in a plane and the pole will define that plane, so with it you'll be able to orient the leg. In the *Pole Target* field of the Inverse Kinematics constraint on the Bone Constraints tab, insert the rig's name (in this case Jim_rig) and the bone field will appear. Insert the name of the pole bone (in this case C_leg_pole). Move C_leg_pole now and you'll see its effect.

Caution

Due to the orientation of the bones, sometimes when you apply a pole to an IK chain, you'll see that the IK becomes rotated. You can compensate for this by adjusting the Pole Angle value in the IK constraint. Usually, if bones are correctly aligned, round values like 90°, -90°, or 180° are enough to correct that rotation.

3. With the 3D cursor aligned with the foot bones, create a new bone chain. Start the first bone from the heel (use the 3D model as a reference for this, as these bones will define the pivot points to rotate the foot), the second bone from the toe tip, and the third bone from the toe articulation. The point circled in red in the image is the point to which all those joints should be aligned: that will prevent sliding later when you rotate those bones. These three bones will control the foot's movement so you can rotate the foot from the heel to the toe and roll it when it walks. The H_leg_ik bone has to be a child of C_foot_roll, so it follows its parent later.

4. Now you also need IKs in the foot so you're able to control it while you use the IK leg, otherwise it will rotate around on its own. Create a new bone from the toe articulation and name it C_toe: it will control the toe when it's not touching the ground. Now, from that toe articulation and from the tail of the C_toe bone, extrude a couple of bones and disconnect them: they'll be the targets of the IKs you'll use in the foot. Duplicate those two targets and move them up so they'll be the poles for the foot IKs.

   Don't forget to parent the extruded bones correctly: the IK target and pole of D_foot are children of C_foot_roll, the IK target and pole of D_toe are children of C_toe, and C_toe is a child of C_foot_tip. This may sound very tricky, but once you have it working, you'll understand why everything needs this hierarchy.

5. Finally, jump again to Pose Mode and add the IK constraints for D_foot and D_toe. Use the targets and poles you created in step 4 for that purpose and, in the Chain Length values, use 1.

6. In Pose Mode, move and rotate the controller bones (the ones that have been prefixed with C_) and you'll see how the deform bones move naturally as they follow the controllers. When you rotate C_foot_tip, the whole foot rotates around the tip, and when you rotate C_foot_roll, the heel lifts up while the toe stays in place, which is very useful when you have to make your character walk. With C_foot you can move the whole foot around and with C_toe you can rotate the toe alone, if necessary (usually when the foot is not touching the ground). Jim's leg is now rigged!

Rigging the Torso and Head

Let's set up the torso and head. We'll do something really simple here, but it will help you understand the power of constraints. Refer to Figure 11.2 for the bones referenced in this step.

1. Select the C_D_spine bone, press **Shift,** and select the C_D_chest bone. Add a Copy Rotation constraint to it. (Don't worry if the bone gets messed up when you apply the constraint; you still need to set up the constraint parameters.) Set the two fields in *Space* to be on the Local Space (so the constraint affects the local

spaces from the target and the current bone). Now, if you rotate C_D_spine, C_D_chest bone will rotate as well because you will usually rotate the spine as a whole, so this constraint will save you from having to rotate each spine bone individually unless some special pose is needed. In the Copy Rotation constraint parameters, enable the Offset option so it allows you to also rotate the chest manually and the rotation will be added to the rotation that the constraint will perform automatically. Also, in the constraint's Influence value slider, you can define how much of the target's rotation the chest bone will copy.

2. Select the bone C_D_head and, on the Bone tab in the Properties Editor, find the Relations panel. Disable *Inherit Rotation* so the head doesn't keep the rotation from its parent (the neck). Now, when you rotate the body, the head will remain aligned, which is usually a more natural behavior.

3. Sometimes, you may want the head to follow the neck's rotation so add a *Child Of* constraint to the head, in which the target is the neck bone. You may have to click the Set Inverse button to make it work correctly. Now, with the influence of this constraint you can control the amount of effect that the rotation of the neck carries to the head, giving you more freedom in what you want to do. Keep in mind that you can animate the influence so you can change it along an animation. You'll learn how to animate those kinds of things in the next chapter.

Rigging the Arm

While rigging the arms will be fairly easy, arms can be more complex. Usually, they're also animated using IK, but because they're not constantly touching a surface, you may prefer to use Forward Kinematics instead. For that situation, you can create what is called IK/FK Blend, which is basically a rig made of three different chains: the IK arm, the FK arm, and the deform arm, which blend using Copy Rotation constraints between the IK and the FK. As this is just an introduction to rigging, you're only going to build the IK rig, but you should look into IK/FK Blending if you like rigging. In Figure 11.5, you can see the resulting rig for the arm.

Follow these steps to create the arm's rig:

1. In Edit Mode, extrude a new bone from the elbow, clear its relationship with the arm bones (**Alt + P**), and move the new bone back (name it C_arm_pole). This bone will be the pole for the IK.

2. Duplicate the D_hand bone, disconnect it **(Alt + P),** and scale it down (name it C_hand). Now, using the 3D cursor **(Shift + S),** move the head of the new bone to the wrist joint. This bone will serve as the IK target for the arm and will also control the hand's rotation. The reason why it's scaled down is that it doesn't completely overlap the D_hand bone because these bones are in exactly the same position: making C_hand smaller or larger will let you see it in Wireframe display mode (**Z**). Add an IK Constraint using the new bone for the hand (C_hand) as its target and C_arm_pole as the IK pole.

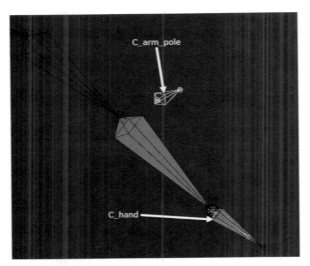

C_arm_pole

C_hand

Figure 11.5 The arm's IK rig in Wireframe display mode
so you can see the IK target in the hand

3. Select the D_hand bone and, on the Bone tab in the Properties Editor, deactivate
   the Inherit Rotation option in the Relations panel (just as you did for the head
   bone). Then, add a Copy Rotation constraint to the D_hand bone using C_hand
   as its target. Now, as you move C_hand, you'll control the arm's IK and, when
   you rotate C_hand, you'll rotate the hand's bone as well.

Rigging the Hand

It's time to create the rig for Jim's hand and fingers. The steps are shown in Figure 11.6
and the instructions follow.

1. Create the bones for a single finger and give them intuitive names such as
   D_finger_3.1 to describe the finger position and the articulation number.

2. Create a bone with its head and tail aligned to the beginning and end of the finger chain; this bone will control the whole finger. At the tip, extrude a new bone
   that will act as the IK target. Duplicate that target and move it up to be used as
   the pole for the finger IK. In Edit Mode, make the C_finger_3 bone a child of
   the hand, and the IK target and pole children of C_finger_3. Apply an IK constraint to the D_finger_3.3 bone and set H_finger_3_ik as the target and H_fin-
   ger_3_pole as the pole target. Set the IK Chain Length to 3 so it goes up through
   the finger bones only. You can try the finger rig now and you only need to use
   the C_finger_3 bone to control it. Rotate it to rotate the finger, and scale it up
   and down to flex the finger.

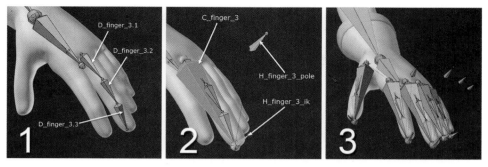

Figure 11.6 The steps for creating the hand's rig

3. Now that you have one finger set up, duplicate it (Edit Mode) and place copies of it in the rest of the fingers and make sure to align them properly. For the thumb, you may want to delete the first articulation and use only 2 bones; just keep in mind you'll need to realign the C_finger_1 bone to deform the bones.

> **Tip**
>
> Aligning the fingers may be difficult because the pole sometimes is not aligned in a single axis. What you can do in those situations is to put the pole in place in Pose Mode until the finger bones are in line with the model. Once you've done that, just select the bones you adjusted in Pose Mode, go to the 3D View header, and inside the Pose menu, look for the *Apply* option and select *Apply Pose as Rest Pose*. Alternatively, press **Ctrl + A** in the 3D View and select the same option. This will transfer the current transforms of the bones in Pose Mode to Edit Mode.

Mirroring the Rig

Now that you have rigged one side of the character, you can duplicate or mirror it to the other side.

Naming Bones

Before mirroring the complete rig, you need to know that when the rig is finished, you'll be able to copy poses and paste them mirrored and, by their names, Blender will recognize on which side of the rig those bones are located. Each bone has a name plus a suffix that tells Blender if that bone is on the left side or on the right side; for example:

- **Right side**: C_hand.R (the .R suffix tells Blender this bone is on the right side).
- **Left side**: C_hand.L (the .L suffix tells Blender this bone is on the left side).
- **Center**: C_D_spine (when there is no suffix, Blender will know that bone is in the center).

This naming convention enables Blender to translate the pose from a bone on one side of the rig to the corresponding bone on the other side and, when you're painting the weights for the skinning, Blender can mirror those weights to the other side of the rig as well.

Fortunately, Blender has tools to add those suffixes to the bones' names automatically. Select all the bones in Edit or Pose Mode, press **A,** and, in the Armature or Pose menu (depending on the interaction mode in which you're working) of the 3D View header, select the option *AutoName Left/Right*; this option will detect the bones that are on the positive or negative side of the X-axis and name them accordingly—that's why it's important that your character is centered on the X-axis.

After performing the AutoName operation, go to the bones that are in the center of the rig and check their names. Sometimes, the bones in the center of the rig are not exactly centered (X = 0) and so Blender also gives them suffixes. In this case, check their names and delete the suffixes.

Mirroring Bones

Here are the steps you need to follow to mirror the bones; they are similar to those you'd use to mirror meshes.

1. In Edit Mode, select all the bones of the rig, excluding the ones that are in the center (you can use a Box Selection by pressing **B**).
2. Press **Shift + D** to duplicate them and right click to cancel the movement.
3. Place the 3D cursor on the center of the scene (press **Shift + C**) and switch the pivot point to the 3D cursor by pressing **.** (period).
4. Press **Ctrl + M** to mirror the selected bones and press **X** to mirror them on the X-axis. Press **Enter** to accept.
5. The bones are now mirrored, but they have names like *C_hand.L.001* because Blender automatically renamed them so there wouldn't be two objects with the same name. With the right-side bones selected, go to the Armature or Pose menu on the 3D View header and select the *Flip Names* option. This will convert those duplicated names from the left side to be right-side names and it will get rid of the "001" suffixes; for example, *C_hand.L.001* would become *C_aand.R.*

Adjusting Bones

Mirroring bones can save you a lot of work by adding constraints and performing repetitive tasks for both sides of the rig; unfortunately, however, mirroring has some side effects. After mirroring, you might need to make some adjustments.

When you mirror bones, some of them may be rotated in a weird way as an effect of inverting their X-axes and you'll have to fix that manually, which can be time consuming but it's usually less work than it would be to create both sides manually.

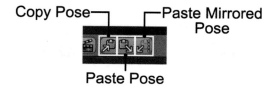

Copy Pose—⌐   ⌐—Paste Mirrored
                            Pose

Paste Pose

Figure 11.7   You can copy and paste poses using the Copy/Paste buttons
on the 3D View header when you're working in Pose Mode.

Here are some tips you can use for adjusting everything in the rig after the mirror has been done:

- On the Armature tab of the Properties Editor, in the Display panel, you can enable the Axes option, which will display the orientations of bones in the 3D View. Using this helpful feature, you can compare the bone orientations between the right and left sides of the rig to see if some of them are off. To adjust rotation, use **Ctrl + R** in Edit Mode to make any necessary adjustments.

- Some IK constraints may be off as well and you'll probably need to change their Pole Angle Value in the IK constraint properties or adjust them in Pose Mode. Then you can apply those adjustments as a Rest Pose (**Ctrl + A**) to transfer them to the bones in Edit Mode.

- A good way to determine if your rig is working properly is to test how it supports mirroring poses. If there's something wrong with a bone on one side, when you mirror a pose, the corresponding bone on the other side will rotate differently and the pose won't look the same side to side: then you'll know that bone is not OK. Figure 11.7 shows the copy/paste options for poses.

  Pose your character in Pose Mode, click the Copy Pose icon, and then click the Paste Mirrored Posed icon. If a bone doesn't work properly, go back to Edit Mode and adjust the rotation of that bone with **Ctrl + R.**

Rig Organization

Your character's rig is working, but there are a few ways in which you can organize it to increase its usability. You can use the Bone Groups and Bone Layers features to do this.

Bone Groups

The Bone Groups feature basically lets you visually organize your bones using colors and it also allows for quick group selections. Using these options, you can have different

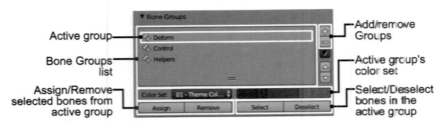

Figure 11.8   The Bone Groups panel on the Armature tab of the Properties Editor

colors for each type of bone; in this case, you'd have Deform, Control, and Helpers groups. In Figure 11.8, you can see the Bone Groups panel, which you can find on the Armature tab in the Properties Editor.

From the Bone Groups panel, you can add new groups to the list and when you click Assign, the currently selected bones will become part of the active bone group (Deform in Figure 11.8). You can select a Color Set for that active group, or you can create your own color set by clicking over the colors in that panel.

Organize your rig by assigning every single bone in the rig to its relevant group. Note that there are some objects that are part of several groups, such as the spine and the chest, which are meant to deform the mesh, but they also function as controllers. Place those objects in the Control Group so that just by looking at their color, you'll know if there's something wrong with a bone on one side. Unfortunately, a bone can't be part of more than one group. Figure 11.9 gives you an idea of how your rig should look after all the work you've done so far.

Bone Layers

Jim's rig is looking much more functional, but you still have a lot of bones that you're not supposed to move (like the helpers) and they might get in the way while you work. To hide them, you'll use Bone Layers.

Bone Layers are similar to Scene Layers, but they work only inside the Armature. On the Armature tab, in the Skeleton panel, you'll see four sets of little squares. The first two sets, under Layers, are the layers themselves. The other two sets, under Protected Layers, are layers that reset in other files when you link this rig to another .blend file to prevent changes to them (like the helpers, for example), but that's an advanced feature and won't be covered here.

When you're in Edit or Pose Mode, you can select one or more bones and, by pressing **M,** you'll access the Bone Layers. Again, this is very similar to the Scene Layers for organizing objects. When you press **M,** a pop-up menu will appear and you can select squares. Each one of the little squares is a layer. As the same bone can indeed belong to more than a single layer, select more than one layer with **Shift + LMB** to add that bone to more than one layer.

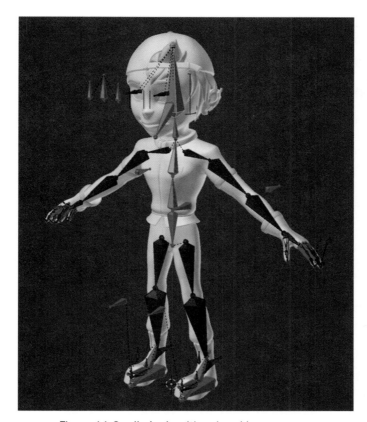

Figure 11.9   Jim's rig with colored bone groups

Once you have bones added to layers, you can show or hide layers from the Armature tab by left clicking the layers. Use the **Shift** key while you click to show or hide more than one layer.

Assign bones to layers depending on their purpose. For Jim's rig, you can add the deformer bones to one layer, the helpers to another, and the controllers to a third. Bones that are both deformers and controllers can be included in those two layers.

You can now show or hide only the layers you need. For example, when you're going to work on the skinning, you can show only the layer of deformer bones, so the rest of the layers are not in the way. When the rig is finished, you can hide the deformer and helper layers, so only the bones you should move to control the rig are visible in their layer. In other words, showing or hiding layers will make it easier to work with the rig and you'll only ever see what you need to see.

Later in this chapter, you'll create the facial rig. You can also store it in a different layer, which allows you to work first on the full character pose, and once it's done, you can show the facial rig and work on the facial expressions. Having the facial rig showing all the time can confuse you or you may accidentally move something in the face when you're working on the body pose.

Skinning

Skinning is the process with which you tell Blender how bones should deform the meshes. To do this, you'll use weights: each bone has an influence (weight) over the vertices to define how those vertices will follow the movement of the bones. Let's see how weights work with a simple example.

Take a look at Figure 11.10 to see how weights work in a mesh. In the left image, you can see that there is a simple model, a cylinder, with two bones inside it. In the center image, you see the weight of the bone at the top: red means the bone has 100% influence, while dark blue means the bone has no influence at all; all the colors in between (orange, yellow, and green) indicate intermediate amounts of influence between 0 and 100 percent. In the right image, you can see what happens with the model when you rotate the bone: the parts in red move exactly with the bone, while the parts of the model with medium influence (green and orange areas) average their movement between the bones affecting them. The parts with no influence from the bone (blue areas) don't follow the bone's movement at all.

Setting Up Models

Before you start working on the skinning, you may want to set up your model to help you navigate your scene and make the skinning process easier:

- Go through the objects in the model and apply every Mirror and Shrinkwrap modifier. Not applying them at this stage might lead to issues later when we start weight-painting.

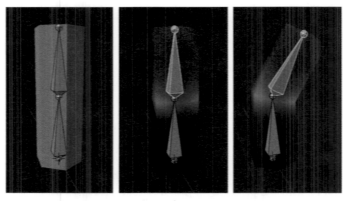

Figure 11.10   Here is how weight affects meshes when you transform bones.

- When you apply the Mirror modifier, some objects will need to be separated, such as the details in the arms and gloves or in the boots, so each side is a separate object. In Edit Mode, select the faces on one of the sides and press **P** to separate the current selection into a different object.

- Apply the location, rotation, and scale of every mesh (not the lattices of the eyes, in case you scaled them when you made the deformations) using **Ctrl + A**. This will prevent problems when you link all the objects of the character to the skeleton because if you've scaled the objects before, you may find issues later (objects jumping around or rescaling when you parent them). When you apply the transforms, keep in mind that some things might go wrong. If an object becomes darkened or looks weird, go into Edit Mode, select everything, and press **Ctrl + N** to reset the normals. Another problem that can arise is that the objects using modifiers such as Solidify might have to be revised because their thickness depends directly on their scale, so when you apply the scale, the thickness value might be affected.

- The eyebrows should be a part of the face model so they're easier to adjust later when you create facial expressions. You can move them together with the face vertices using the Proportional Editing tool. When joining them to the face (using **Ctrl + J**), you'll end up with a single mesh in which the eyebrows will have a different material applied to them.

- Name every model (if you haven't already) so you can recognize the objects in it just by their names. This will be useful at this stage and all the stages to follow.

Selecting Deformer Bones

There are a lot of bones in the rig and you need to tell Blender which ones will actually deform the meshes. By default, all of them will deform it, so let's see what you can do to define the specific deformer bones.

On the Bone tab of the Properties Editor, you can find the Deform panel. When it's enabled, you'll be able to set up the envelopes (the areas of influence that surround the bones) and some other features of the bone deformations. Now, if you don't want a particular bone to deform the mesh, then you just need to disable that option for that bone. Of course, doing it for every single bone, one by one, would be very slow, so let's look at a fast way to do it:

1. In Edit or Pose Mode, select every bone and, with all the layers enabled (all the bones visible), press **Shift + W** to display the Bone Settings options. Alternatively, you can find those options in the Armature or Pose menus (depending on whether you are in Edit Mode or Pose Mode) on the 3D View header under Bone Settings.

2. In the Bone Settings menu, click the Deform option: now all the bones have been set to not deform the mesh. Deselect everything. Select those bones that you

don't want to deform the mesh and make sure that on the Bone tab, the Deform option is disabled.

3. Now go to the Armature Layers and turn on just the layer for the deform bones. Select all those bones, press **Shift + W** again, and pick the Deform option a second time. Now those bones have been enabled as deformers, and all the rest (controller and helper bones) are not going to affect the mesh at all.

That was pretty quick, right? Can you see how layers and groups allow you to quickly select and change settings for particular types of bones?

Armature Modifier

The Armature modifier tells the mesh how it will be deformed by the bones of an armature. As with constraints, there are two ways of adding an Armature modifier to your mesh:

- Select the mesh, go to the Modifiers tab in the Properties Editor and add an Armature modifier. Then, in the Armature field, input the name of the armature you want to deform the model. In this case, it should be Jim_rig.

- Another way to add an Armature modifier is to select the mesh, then select a bone or armature while pressing **Shift**, and from there, press **Ctrl + P** to parent. When you parent a mesh to an armature, Blender will show you several options, some of which are Armature options. Pick the option for Automatic Weights; it's usually the easiest option (unless you have set up envelopes for the bones, which is another method that won't be covered in this book).

> **Caution**
>
> If you have previously added a Subdivide Surface modifier to your models, when you add an Armature modifier it will be working on top of the SubSurf, which will reduce performance and make it more difficult to weight the vertices. Move the modifier up through the modifiers stack until it's placed before the SubSurf modifier (SubSurf should be the last modifier, at the bottom of the stack).

Weight Painting

Weight painting is probably the fastest way to assign bone weights to your model. To enter Weight Paint Mode, just go to the Interaction Mode selector in the 3D View header and select Weight Paint. Now you'll see the model with blue, yellow, green, and red applied; the colors represent the weights of the currently selected bone. You can also switch to this mode by pressing **Ctrl + Tab.**

> **Tip**
>
> Before you start setting up the bone weights for the model, you may want to change the armature's display to Stick (in the Display panel, on the Armature tab) so the bones don't block your view of the mesh; also, only turn on the deformer bones layer.

Weight Paint Mode is very similar to Texture Paint Mode: on the left, you'll see painting tools and options in the Tools Region (see Figure 11.11).

When you add an Armature modifier to a mesh using the Automatic Weights option, vertex groups are created in the mesh, one for each bone, and they have the same names as the bones. Each one of those vertex groups stores the weights that define the influence of each bone in the armature.

Here are some instructions on how to work in Weight Paint Mode:

- On the left side, in the Tools Region, you'll find a series of settings to control brush options while you work in Weight Paint Mode. At the top, you'll find the different brush types such as Add, Subtract, Draw, and Blur. Each type has different effects on the weights when you paint by left clicking and dragging over the vertices.

- You can also set the size, strength, and weight of the brush. Just as you did in Texture Paint Mode, you can change the size and strength of the brush by pressing **F** and **Shift + F** in the 3D View.

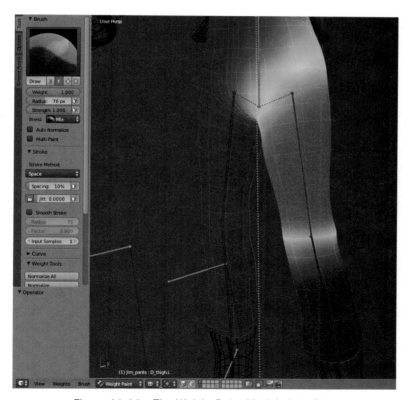

Figure 11.11   The Weight Paint Mode's interface

RMB allows you to select other meshes and paint their weights. However, they'll only be in Weight Paint Mode if you left them in that mode; otherwise, when you select them with **RMB** click, you will enter Object Mode. Press **Ctrl + Tab** with a mesh selected to switch between Object Mode and Weight Paint Mode.

To select the bone weight that you want to paint, go to the Mesh tab in the Properties Editor and, in the Vertex Groups panel, select the desired Vertex Group from the list (another place where it's useful to have the bones named correctly).

> **Tip**
>
> Selecting the vertex groups from the list is not the fastest way, though. Instead, you can select the armature and make sure you're in Pose Mode. Now select the mesh and, if you have the deform bones visible in the armature, you'll be able to select the bones with **RMB** while you paint weights! When you select a bone, you'll automatically see its influence on the vertices and the bone's vertex group will be selected. Much faster than going through the list, right?

- While painting, press **G**, **R**, or **S** to move, rotate, or scale the bone. This will allow you to move the character while you paint and test if the weights behave properly. (From time to time, you might want to reset some bones to their original positions: just press **A** to select all of them or select the ones you want to reset, and press **Alt + G**, **Alt + R**, and **Alt + S** to reset their location, rotation, and scale).

  You can even take this further and create animations that move the bones you're weighting so you can see how they behave by dragging the cursor in the timeline across the animation. You'll learn how to do this in the next chapter.

- On the Options tab in the Tools Region are some features you may find useful. One of them is the X-Mirror option: if your mesh is exactly the same on both sides of the X-axis, then X-Mirror will mirror the weights you paint on one side to the corresponding bones on the other side. Of course, that will only work properly if your bones are also correctly named with their left and right suffixes.

- The Blur brush is very handy. Paint in basic weights first and, where you need the weight borders to be soft, just pick the Blur brush to paint in those borders. Keep in mind that this brush blurs the weights of the vertices inside the brush radius, so you may need to make the brush bigger in order to use it for this purpose.

> **Tip**
>
> It's usually easier to see what you're doing with weights when you're in the Wireframe display mode (**Z**). You'll see everything in wireframes, except for the object you had selected when you jumped into Weight Paint Mode; you'll see that object in shadeless colors representing the weights.

Weight Values

Sometimes weight painting, even though it's very fast and easy, can be tricky. In complex parts of the model or in areas where you need very specific weights, it's better to add values numerically and, fortunately, Blender allows you to do this.

In the Vertex Groups panel on the Mesh tab (the tab with a little triangle and its vertices) in the Properties Editor, there are options for adding values. Just follow these instructions:

1. In Edit Mode, select the vertices you want to weight precisely.

2. Go to the Vertex Groups panel, find the group with the name of the bone to which you want to add the weight, and left click to select it. If you click the little button at the bottom of the list (you can find this button in every list in Blender), you'll be able to filter and search groups by their names, so just start typing the name of the group and press **Enter** to display only the groups with a name that matches your input (another reason why naming stuff properly is useful).

3. Under the Vertex Groups list there are a few options that are very similar to those you saw in the Bone Groups panel. Set the weight value and click **Assign**. This will set that weight on the selected vertices for the selected bone/vertex group.

There's even another way in which you can adjust vertex weights. In Edit Mode, select one or more vertices and, if they have weights assigned, a Vertex Weights panel will appear in the Properties Region. In it, you'll be able to adjust the weight values for each vertex group, as well as copy weights from one vertex and paste them to another.

Mirroring Weights

Consider Jim's gloves or his boots. They are exactly the same mesh but they're different objects on opposite sides and are affected by different bones. There are several faster ways to add weights to these objects, including only having to weight one side of them. If you weight both sides manually, it will be a slow process (especially if it's a complex model such as the hands) and you may end up with each side having different deformations. However, there are easier ways to do this by either mirroring before or after adding any weights.

Mirroring before Adding Weights

It is recommended that you mirror before you add any weights. If you're working on a mirrored mesh, you should be sure you've enabled the X-Mirror option before you start painting because after weights are painted, fixing them will be usually more tedious and slow.

If possible, join both sides of the mesh; for example, join the two gloves. Activate the X-Mirror option and paint the weights on one side, which should reflect those weights on the other side. After you're done defining weights, separate the meshe again so they become different objects while keeping their weights.

Mirroring after Adding Weights

If you've already painted the weights on one side, you can still mirror these weights. Let's use the gloves as an example to see how to do this:

1. Delete the glove you haven't weighted.

2. Select the one you have weighted. Duplicate it with **Shift + D.** Right click to cancel the transform after duplication. Set the 3D Cursor in the center of the scene with **Shift + C.** Press **Ctrl + M** to mirror the glove and **X** to mirror it on the X-axis. Finally, press **Enter** to confirm.

3. Go to the Vertex Groups panel. Delete the vertex groups from the new side and replace their names with those from the other side. Let's look at this tricky process step by step. For this example, let's use only one bone and let's pretend that the one you painted was on the left side:

   a. In the list, find the names of the vertex groups from the right side (the ones you need now), all of which end with .R (you can find them quickly by entering .R in the list filter). For this example, the one we'll mirror is the D_hand.L bone weight, so delete D_hand.R.

   b. Now find D_hand.L, double click its name, and rename it to D_hand.R. That will cause the current weights in that vertex group to be affected by the right bone instead of the left one.

   c. Repeat the process with all the bones you need to mirror.

Objects That Don't Need Weights

The objects that are not going to be deformed don't need to be weighted. You can just parent them to a bone. For example, the hair, cap, teeth, tongue (the tongue could deform, but in this case, to keep it simple, it will not), and the eyes (which should be parented to the H_eye bones, not the D_eye bones) would only need to be parented, as they won't suffer from deformations by the effects of bones.

To parent them to a bone, just make sure you're in Pose Mode in the armature. Select the object and, with **Shift** pressed, select the bone to which you want to parent them. Now press **Ctrl + P** to do the parenting, but instead of selecting the Automatic Weights option (the one you selected for the deformable options when adding an Armature modifier), pick the *Bone* option from the list.

Posing Jim

After you've weighted all the models that need deformations by following these instructions, you'll be able to pose Jim! Here are some things to keep in mind before and after weighting your character:

- The jaw bone should open the mouth and the lower lip, bottom teeth, and tongue should move with it.

- The clothing details of the arms, for example, can be deformed by bones, but you can also just parent those details to the arm bones. During the design, those details were placed where they are now because in those positions, only one bone would affect them, and that's why just parenting them should be enough.

- Enabling the arms and legs to twist can be tricky. When you twist your hand, this movement affects the forearm and, in simple rigs, simulating this is not possible. A cool way Blender has to address this problem is by using Bone Segments. On the Bone tab of the Properties Editor, in the Deform panel, there is an option for Curved Bones. You can define the number of segments, which will make the bone "flexible" and make a curve between its parent and its child. If you set the Ease to 0, the bone won't be curved but it will twist. If you want to see the segments and how they work, you'll have to change the display mode to *B-Bones* on the Armature tab. While this won't create perfect deformations, it will simulate the twisting effect in the forearms, which would otherwise require a more complex rig and more weighting time.

Creating the Facial Rig

Only the facial rig is missing at this point, which Jim will need in order to have facial expressions. For that, you'll be using shape keys. Shape keys store different shapes of the same object. For example, imagine one shape would be Jim's smile; later, you'd be able to move the vertices from their neutral position to the smile position by sliding a bar from 0 to 100 percent and you'd see the transition. After you learn how to model these shape keys, you'll create a few new bones and learn how to use them to control the shape keys. At the end of the process, you'll be able to control Jim's expressions with only a few bones!

Modeling Shape Keys

The first step in creating the facial rig is to model the necessary shape keys. You need to isolate different parts of the face and create different shape keys for each part. Here are a few examples of the shape keys you can create: smile, frown, blink, open mouth, and move eyebrows up and down.

For each one of those actions (except the ones that affect both sides of the face simultaneously) you will have to create two shape keys, one for each side of the face. For example, you'll want to be able to open and close the left and right eyelids separately. For Jim, things will be pretty simple because you don't need dramatic facial expressions; he just needs some basic things like smiling and blinking, so you can keep the shape keys to a minimum. However, if you want to create a very realistic facial rig, you might need a lot of shape keys. In Figure 11.12, you can see the Shape Keys panel, on the Mesh tab of the Properties Editor.

Creating Shape Keys

Here is how shape keys work: You start with the key called *Basis*, which is the base shape key on which all the rest of the keys are built, as this is the model itself. After that one, you can click the + button in the upper-right side of the panel to add a new shape key to the list. Double click it to name it. Let's say you're going to create the smile shape key, so you'd name it something similar to mouth_smile.L (this is the left side of the mouth that will be smiling). Now, with that shape key selected, if you enter Edit Mode, you can manually reposition the vertices to create a smiling shape on the left side of the mouth (Proportional Editing tools are really useful in this stage).

   When you exit from Edit Mode, you'll see that the model jumps back to its original shape key and you don't see the smile. This happens because the smile shape key moves back to the 0% effect. Near the shape key's name, there is the Value slider (see Figure 11.12) that you can drag left and right to increase or decrease the shape key's value. Also, you can select the shape key and drag the Value slider under the list.

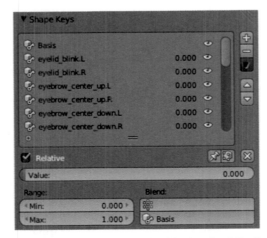

Figure 11.12   The Shape Keys panel on the Mesh tab of the Properties Editor, where you can add, remove, and adjust shape keys on the list

At the bottom of the panel, you can control the range of the current shape key's values (usually from 0 to 1). If you set the value to a maximum of 2, for example, the shape key will be able to continue the movement of the vertices until they reach double the effect that you modeled originally.

The idea is that for each part of the face, you have different shape keys that you can mix together to create facial expressions. Happiness, for example, would be a smile, maybe the lips a little opened, the eyes partially closed, with the cheeks and eyebrows lifted. So the mix of those different shape keys would help you create the expression of happiness on the face. In Figure 11.13, you can see examples of mixing some very basic shape keys to create different expressions on Jim's face.

Mirroring Shape Keys

As you saw before, you need to isolate some shape keys on one side of the face. For example, you need a right eye blink and a left eye blink. However, if your character's face is symmetrical, modeling the shape keys manually for both sides will be tedious and it may result in the shape keys producing different effects for each side. The following instructions show you how to mirror shape keys:

1. Create one side's shape key, such as the blink for the left eye.
2. Exit Edit Mode and set the value of the left eye-blink shape key to 100%.
3. Click the down-pointing triangle button just below the + and − buttons to add and remove shape keys from the list. Select the option *New Shape from Mix*: this will create a new shape key with the vertex positions that include the values of shape keys currently in use. Rename the new key for the right side.
4. Click again in the same button and select the option *Mirror Shape Key.* This will translate the vertex positions to the other side of the mesh.

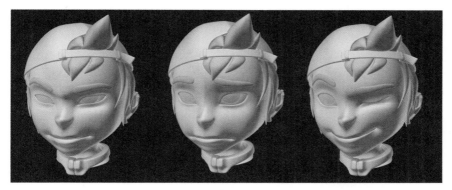

Figure 11.13   Jim's shape keys in action, with parts of the face moving together to create full face expressions

Creating the Face Rig

There are a lot of ways to create the facial rig. Controllers let you manipulate expressions right from the 3D View, so you won't have to adjust the shape keys one by one in the Shapes panel.

Depending on how you want to control your character's expressions, you'll need different types of controls. In this case, let's make a few bones in front of the face and each one of them will control a few shape keys. As an example, take the controller for the mouth: you will set it up so that when it's scaled up, the mouth opens. The controllers for the eyebrows will control how the eyebrows lift when you change their position.

You have to setup the rig in an intuitive manner (later you'll add custom shapes that will make them even more intuitive) such that it should be obvious which bone controls do what. Imagine that if you move a bone up, what it controls should move up also because, if it had a different effect that would be counterintuitive. In Figure 11.14, you can see the bones that have been created to control Jim's basic expressions; a more complex model with more shape keys (to make him talk, for example) would need more controls.

Parent those bones that control the shape keys to the head bone and make sure they're in the Control bone group. Also, you can put them into a new layer, so they are separate from the rest of the bones, allowing you to hide the facial controllers while you're working on the body. You can also name them accordingly with a different prefix such as *CF_cheek.L* (Control Facial).

Figure 11.14   These bones will responsible
for controlling Jim's facial expressions.

Using Drivers to Control the Face Shape Keys

Now you need to tell Blender how those bones and which of their properties will control the shape keys' values. For that, you'll use drivers. Using drivers is something quite technical and advanced, so here you'll only get your feet wet with the basics, but you should investigate this topic to learn how to create more complex rigs with drivers.

Creating Drivers

Divide your interface and, in one of the editors, switch to the Graph Editor. On the Graph Editor's header, you'll see an option that will let you switch between *F-Curves* and *Drivers*; select Drivers. (You'll learn about F-Curves in the next chapter; they're used for animation.)

At this point, the Drivers interface will be completely empty because you don't yet have any drivers in your scene. It's very easy to create them: just find the parameter you want to control anywhere in the interface, such as the Value parameter for one of the shapes in Jim's face, right click it, and in the menu that appears, you'll see the option *Add Driver.* Once you do this, you will be unable to control that parameter from the interface (it will be overridden by the driver) and it will turn violet so you know that it's controlled by a driver.

Setting Up a Driver

Let's set up the driver for making the eye blink when you scale down a bone, and then you'll need to use the same method for the rest of the shapes and control bones.

1. On the left side of the Graph Editor, you'll see a list of the properties that currently have drivers. You may have to expand the list items to see the different properties that they have stored inside (see Figure 11.15). Click the property and, with your cursor over the Graph Editor, press **N** to display the Properties Region. Now you'll see from top to bottom which parameters you need to adjust.

2. Find the Drivers panel in the Properties Region. The first option you have is the driver Type. Set it to Averaged Value because you won't be scripting for now. This will create an average of the variables (in this case, you'll only use one, so that's the value Blender will use, but you can add more and make this feature extremely complex).

3. In the Add Variable panel, there is already one variable, called *var* by default (there's no need to change its name, but you can in case you want to use several variables and still be able to recognize them). In the Object name fields, insert the name of the armature and another field will appear in which you will have to insert the name of the bone you want to drive this action.

4. Now you can select the type of transform you want for the bone that will drive the property. In the case of the eye-blink shape, we want to control it with the *Z scale* (actually the axis doesn't matter, as we want the transform to work when we scale the bone in the three axes simultaneously). Set the Space to

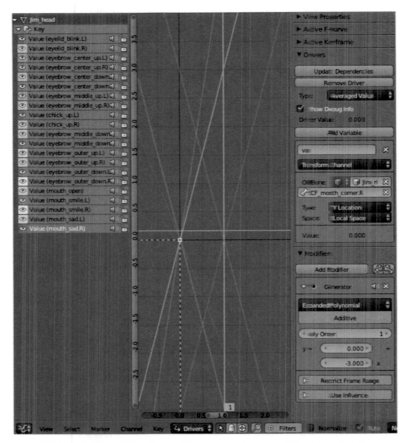

Figure 11.15   The Graph Editor showing the Drivers settings

Local Space, so the transform depends on the local position of the bones because they'll be moving around with the head, so the *World Space* option is probably not a good idea.

5. At the top of the Drivers panel there are two buttons, *Update Dependencies* and *Remove Driver*. To make sure the driver has been updated with the changes you've made, click Update Dependencies. Now go to the 3D View and try it to make sure the control works.

6. It works, but the eye is now closed and will open as you scale the object down. In order for the animation control to be intuitive, you want it to be closed when

you scale the bone down. To achieve that goal, in the Drivers panel you'll see the Modifiers panel. (Yes, drivers can have modifiers!) All those diagonal lines in Figure 11.15 represent the effect of each driver; by modifying that line's inclination, you can change a driver's effect; for example, the effect can be faster or slower.

Add a *Generator* modifier. By adjusting the Generator modifier's values, you can control the inclination of the line that defines the effect of the driver, and hence the effect the bone has on the shape. To keep it simple, with the second value you set the starting point of the line and with the third value you control the inclination of the line, which will control the speed of the effect (if you have to move the bone a lot to increase the shape's value, increasing the effect's speed will compensate for that).

> **Tip**
>
> If you want to reverse a driver's movement, you can use negative values in the Generator modifier. Remember to click Update Dependencies as you change those values to see their effects, and look at the bones in the 3D View to see if they're working properly.

7. Repeat this process with every controller and every shape.

Creating Custom Shapes

So, the rig is finished, but it's still not looking very intuitive. To fix that and to make the model easier to use, you can add custom shapes to the bones (see Figure 11.16). You can use any model or curve as a custom shape for the bones.

When you select a bone in Pose Mode, on the Bone tab of the Properties Editor, in the Display panel, there is a field for Custom Shape. Just insert the name of the shape (any object) you want to use instead of the bone. This is only an aesthetic feature; it has no influence in the functionalities of the bone. Once you set it, there is another option to enable wireframes; this will show only the edges of the object you've selected as a custom shape.

Usually, this is the procedure for creating a custom shape: you create a plane or a circle (for example) and name it (an S_ prefix will help you recognize this is a shape). You select the bone and apply the new object as a custom shape. It may look out of place, so if necessary, go back to the object, enter Edit Mode, and, keeping an eye to how the bone is displaying the custom shape, you can adjust it, scale it, and rotate it. Once you're happy with the shape, repeat the same process for every controller bone. Then, send all the shape objects to a layer and hide it.

Figure 11.16   Using custom shapes for Jim's rig

Applying Final Touches to the Rig

There are plenty of other things you can do to improve a rig like this, but for the sake
of learning, this rig is already pretty cool. One thing you can do to make it much
more usable is to lock any transforms that you don't want affecting bones. This has two
functions: it prevents transforms from occurring accidentally (like scaling a bone that
shouldn't be scaled or rotating a bone that is only meant to be translated) and it helps
you see what you can do with each bone.

To lock transforms, select a bone. As an example, let's use the foot roll: it's only supposed to rotate on a single axis because the others will make the foot look wrong, and
it's not meant to be moved or scaled. In the Properties Region of the 3D View, notice

Figure 11.17   Jim's final rig lets you pose him and make him do cool stuff!

how in the Transform panel, next to the axis, there is a lock. If you click that lock, you won't be able to transform the bone on that specific axis (locked axis will even disappear from the manipulators, helping you to see what you can do with it).

Another thing you can do to improve the rig, even though it's not absolutely mandatory, is to make sure the bones that you will have to rotate at some point have a rotation type that is easier to understand. In the same Transform panel of the Properties Region, switch the rotation type from Quaternion to XYZ Euler (this rotation type is just easier to understand when you're using animation curves).

You can see Jim posing for you with his new rig in Figure 11.17!

Summary

You've seen how rigging is the most technical and complex part of the process. It takes time and it can be frustrating when the rig doesn't behave as you expect. There are quicker ways to create rigs, such as the Rigify add-on, which automatically generates a very cool biped rig based on the proportions you set for your character. But if your character isn't a biped, premade rigs aren't going to help much. Therefore it's nice if you do the rigging manually at least a few times in different models, so you can understand the process and how it works. Sometimes you need rigs for very simple things; in those situations, knowing how to rig manually will prove really useful. Now Jim is much closer to coming to life!

Exercises

1. Create a simple rig made of just a few bones and try different constraints to see their effects.

2. Add more shape keys to Jim's face to achieve a more realistic set of facial expressions.

3. Create an FK/IK blend arm. You'll need the deforming bones, an IK chain, and an FK chain, and you'll need to set constraints that let you align the deforming bones to one of the other chains. Use drivers to control the amount of IK/FK blending.

12

Animating Your Character

Using animation, your characters will come to life. Animation is the process in which you make your character move along a timeline. To make animation realistic, you have to study the principles of motion, such as action and reaction, and you need to understand how weight affects the way a character moves. Animation is a very broad subject and there are plenty of resources, books, and courses you can take to improve your skills. In this chapter, you'll learn how to use the basics of the Blender animation system: what tools are at your disposal, how to use keyframes, and how the different animation editors can help you during this stage.

Inserting Keyframes

A keyframe is a specific saved state of a value at a given point in time. If you want to make an object move from A to B, both of those positions would be keyframes and Blender would automatically interpolate the object's movement between those keyframes. Let's see some different ways of adding keyframes in Blender.

Adding Keyframes Manually

The most basic way to add keyframes to your objects is to do it manually. Set the frame in the timeline to define the time in which you want to save that specific position, then select your object or objects and press **I**. A menu will appear in which you can choose between the different channels and transform the properties of that object, so you can record a keyframe in the desired channels. For example, you can set a keyframe just for the object's location (*Loc*) or for its rotation (*Rot*), but to keep things simple, by using *LocRotScale*, you'll set a keyframe to the three transform types, which is what you usually want.

Automatic Keyframing

In the Timeline Editor (at the bottom of the default interface, this editor allows you to define the duration of the animation, play it, scroll through it, and so forth), there is a little button on its header with a red circle in it, similar to the Record button on old ra-dio cassette players. If you press it, Auto Keyframing is enabled. With this option, every time you change something, a keyframe will automatically be saved for it. While this is really useful when you're animating, as it lets you insert keyframes just by moving ob-jects in the scene, you have to be very careful with this method because if you forget it's turned on, you may keep saving keyframes when you don't want to.

Using Keying Sets

Using keying sets may be the easiest way to add keyframes. You can select a keying set right next to the Auto Keyframing button (the options that have a key symbol on them). When you pick a keying set, you won't need to select the channels in which you want to set a keyframe each time you press **I**; Blender will automatically keyframe the channels selected in your keying set.

If you select the LocRotScale keying set, when you press **I**, a keyframe is automati-cally added to the three channels and there is no need to confirm the addition manually each time. Also, there is a keying set called Whole Character that will save a keyframe for the full rig whenever you press **I**, and you don't even need to select all the bones each time you want a new keyframe—very handy!

Animating Properties in the Menus

You can even animate the value of parameters in the menus. If you want to animate any property (almost everything in Blender can be animated), for example, the number of subdivisions in a modifier, the color of a material, or the influence of a constraint over an object, it's very simple. Just place your cursor over the property value field and press **I**. Blender will store a keyframe for that property on the current frame. That property's field will turn yellow on the frames where it has stored keyframes, and the field will be green in the rest of the frames just to let you know it owns an animation.

Animation Editors

There are several editors that help you manipulate animation. They allow you to do everything from just moving through time in the Timeline, to editing the animation curves to tell Blender how you want it to interpolate the movement between two key-frames, to mixing different animations as if you were editing video! Figure 12.1 shows the different editors.

Timeline

The Timeline is the most basic animation editor. It simply shows the time and displays keyframes in the selected objects as yellow vertical lines. You can change the current frame and scrub through the animation by pressing and dragging **LMB** and positioning the green cursor along the timeline.

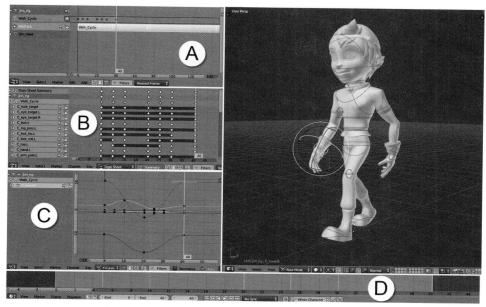

Figure 12.1   The NLA Editor (A), the Dope Sheet (B), the Graph Editor (C), and the Timeline (D)

In the Timeline, you can also set the Start and End frames of the animation: Press **S** to set the current frame as the Start and press **E** to set the current frame as the End. Also, you can enter the frame number in the Start and End fields of the Timeline's header.

The header also has controls that play the animation, go to the start and end of the animation, or jump to the next or previous keyframes. Here are some other shortcuts you can use in the 3D View (or to control time in any other editor):

- Press **Alt + A** to play the animation. Press **Alt + A** again to pause it. Press **Esc** to stop the animation and go back to the frame from which you started playing.
- Press the **Left** and **Right** arrow keys to move to the previous or next frames. Press the **Up** or **Down** arrow keys to jump to the previous or next keyframes. Press **Shift + Up** arrow key or **Shift + Down** arrow key to jump around in 10-frame increments.

Dope Sheet

This simple editor shows keyframes in objects (to the left of the Dope Sheet, you'll find a list of the objects in the scene) as yellow diamond shapes in a timeline. This editor basically lets you move keyframes in time so you can adjust the timing of your animation.

You can use basic controls such as **G** to move keyframes or **S** to scale them, or even press **Shift** while you right click more keyframes to select several at once. Press **B** to box select a group of keyframes. With **Shift + D,** you can duplicate keyframes.

Activate the Dope Sheet *Summary* option on the Dope Sheet's header to display another line at the top of the editor that shows all the keyframes in every object on the list.

The Dope Sheet Editor also has different modes. There is a mode selector on the header that, by default, is set to Dope Sheet, but there are other options, such as the Action Editor, or you can access the Masks keyframes (created in the Movie Clip Editor and used in the Compositor), Shape keys, keyframes, and more.

The Action Editor is especially important. An object can store different animations (actions) and, in the Action Editor, you'll be able to select which one is currently displayed; of course, it will also let you name them, so later you can have a list of different actions that you can mix together in the NLA Editor (explained later in this section). If you work on videogames, you probably know that a character can have different animations, such as walking, running, standing idle, picking up something, and so forth. These are different actions that you can have in the same scene and switch between them. You can create new actions or edit the ones you previously created thanks to the Action Editor.

Basically, you could say that the Dope Sheet is a more general editor that displays all the animations going on in a scene. The Action Editor works with a specific animation for a specific object and is especially useful with armatures so that you can store different animations for your characters.

> **Tip**
>
> If you come from other software in which you can manipulate the keyframes from the time-line, you can just replace the Timeline in Blender with a Dope Sheet. Activate the Summary option so you can see all the keyframes at the very top of the editor and you're all set! This is what's cool about the versatility of Blender's Interface.

Graph Editor

The Graph Editor is probably one of the scariest things you'll see in Blender. Actually, it's not that complicated, but usually the first time you see the animation curves without a proper understanding of how they work, they can look really complex.

In the Graph Editor, you'll be able to edit the animation curves, also called F-Curves in Blender. But what are animation curves? They're pretty simple.

When you create two keyframes, they are automatically interpolated by Blender. This means the value between two keyframes will smoothly transition from one to the other, as shown in the Figure 12.2. The curves define how the interpolation happens and you can control them to change that default interpolation in case you're not happy with how it works.

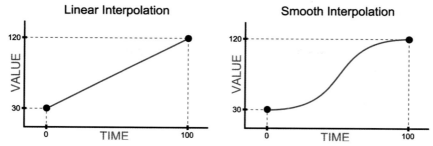

Figure 12.2 Different curves that interpolate the same two keyframes

Each transform or property on each axis has an F-Curve. For example, say you want to make an object fly from one point to another; let's see what would happen with different curve configurations (see Figure 12.2).

There are two keyframes in Figure 12.2. The horizontal position of a keyframe defines its time, while its vertical position sets its value. In this case, the first keyframe sets a value of 30 in the frame 0. The second keyframe sets a value of 120 in the frame 100.

The image to the left represents a linear interpolation, which tells Blender to increase the value from 30 to 120 between the frames 0 and 100 at a constant speed. The image to the right shows a smooth interpolation. With this type of interpolation, Blender first starts increasing the value slowly, then it accelerates, and finally it decreases its speed slowly before reaching the value of 120 at the frame 100. As you can see, these are two different movements between the exact same keyframes and they are defined by the animation curves.

In the Graph Editor, you can manipulate curves as always by moving, rotating, or scaling keyframes using **G, R,** and **S.** You can also duplicate curves with **Shift + D.**

To change the interpolation mode of a keyframe, you can select it and press **T** (you can also do this in the Dope Sheet, but the difference is more visual in the Graph Editor). A menu will appear with different options for setting the interpolation and the handle type of that keyframe. In the Graph Editor, selecting one or more keyframes and pressing **V** will let you select different positions for those keyframe's handles, which will also affect how the interpolation works.

You can adjust handles by right clicking and dragging to modify the curvature of the interpolations and control how you want the animation to accelerate or to make the animation smoother. Another way of adjusting the handles is to select a keyframe and rotate it or scale it; you will also change the orientation and size of its handles when you do this.

Tip

In the User Preferences, on the Editing tab, you have the option to set how you want your keyframe interpolation handles to be by default when you create a keyframe.

NLA (Non-Linear Animation) Editor

The NLA Editor works similar to a video editor: you can load "strips," mix them together, layer them, and make them longer or shorter. However, instead of videos, you'll
be using animations.

You can load actions you saved in the Action Editor (a mode of the Dope Sheet, as
described previously in this chapter) and mix them to build a larger animation. Later,
you'll use this editor to take the walk cycle you're going to create in a moment and
repeat it constantly. This means that instead of animating Jim taking 10 steps, you just
need a cycle of 2 steps (one for each leg) and, with the NLA Editor, you can repeat that
action as long as necessary.

Imagine that you had another action with Jim running. With **Shift + A,** you could
add it as another strip to the NLA Editor and mix it with the walk cycle animation so
Jim moves progressively from walking to running.

Another option would be to add adjustments to an animation as if they were layers:
for example, you could have an animation with Jim turning his head back and forth.
You could add it over the walking animation and Jim would be walking and moving
his head at the same time.

Common Controls and Tips

All of these editors have some common controls. Not only can you move (**G**) or duplicate (**Shift + D**) things the same way as in other Blender editors, but you can also take
advantage of some other common navigation features.

- You can pan to see other parts of the time (horizontal) and values (vertical) with
  MMB click and drag.
- Use the **Scroll Wheel** to zoom in and out.
- Press **Home** to adjust the zoom automatically to show the whole animation
  time range.
- Another way to zoom is to press **Ctrl + MMB** and drag your mouse. In some
  editors, you can only zoom horizontally, but in the Graph Editor you can zoom
  horizontally and vertically.
- Using **Alt + Scroll Wheel** takes you to the next or previous keyframes, a fast
  way to scrub through your animation (in small steps).

There are some options you might want to check out that can make working with
these editors easier:

- In the headers of most of the animation editors, there is an icon that shows a
  mouse cursor. If you enable that option, you'll only see the keyframes of currently selected objects, which can prevent you from going crazy looking at dozens (or hundreds) of curves or keyframes at the same time. It will also help you

recognize what you're currently seeing in those editors, as all of the unselected objects will be ignored and hidden.

- In the View menu on the Curve Editor header, you can enable the option *Only Selected Curves Keyframes*. This option will display only the keyframes of the curves from properties you select on the list, preventing you from selecting or accidentally moving keyframes of other curves that are overlapping the one you want to adjust.

- Also in the Curve Editor, you can find the *Normalize* option on the header. When you're working with different curves that have completely different ranges, it can be hard to navigate, as you have to zoom in and out constantly to see the part of the curves on which you need to work. When Normalize is enabled, the curves are all adjusted to fit inside a 0 to 1 range for easier adjusting. This change is only visual in the Graph Editor; it doesn't affect the real values of the curves.

Animating a Walk Cycle

In this section, you'll be guided step by step through the creation of a basic walking animation. Let's make Jim come alive!

Tip

When you animate, it's better if you have a powerful computer, but more important is that your scene is optimized to perform faster (hide objects you don't need, reduce polygon count, etc.) so you can see your animation playing smoothly while you work. On the Scene tab of the Properties Editor, Blender has an interesting option, Simplify. If you enable Simplify, you'll be able to select the maximum number of subdivisions that every object in the scene will have. In Jim's case, the model is probably using between two and three levels of subdivision, which is fine for a final render, but the impact on a computer's performance can be significant. With Simplify, you can turn subdivisions to 1 or 0 while you work on the animation. Just remember to put it back up before you launch a render!

You can also define a different number of subdivisions for the 3DView and for the render in the Subdivide Surface modifier's options. While this is better for optimizing performance, sometimes it can be tedious to define subdivisions one by one and, from time to time, you may want to be able to preview the subdivided model in the 3DView; the Simplify feature is a good one for controlling all the SubSurf modifiers at once.

Creating an Action

The walking animation will be a cycle, meaning that you'll only be animating one step (it happens in place, so the character won't move across space; that will happen later), which will then be repeated over time. As you'll be repeating it using the NLA Editor, you need to create an action that you can load later.

Each object has different actions, so make sure you have the rig selected in Pose Mode before you create an action. If you are in Object Mode, selecting the rig will create an action for the container, not for the individual bones that you need.

Open the Dope Sheet Editor and switch to the Action Editor Mode. On the header, if you haven't animated anything, there will be a field in which you'll be able to create a New Action. Press the *New* button and the new action will be called (surprise!) Action. Rename it to something intuitive such as *Walk_Cycle*.

Now, every keyframe you set for the bones in the rig will be a part of the Walk_Cycle action.

Caution

If you create more than one action, remember that any datablocks not in use when you close Blender will be deleted. Each object can only use a single action at a time, so if you want to make sure the rest of the datablocks are saved, press the **F** button next to their names so they have a "fake user"; this will prevent them from being deleted when you close Blender.

Creating the Poses for the Walk Cycle

To make Jim walk, you must define the basic poses he will make while walking. There are a lot of ways to walk, so we're going to use a basic one. There are two contact poses: the moments at which each foot touches the floor. Then there are two other poses when one foot is on the floor and the other is in the air. Those four positions of the body define the basic walking movement.

You must create a motion that can be repeated, which means that the animation needs to end in the exact same position as where it started. In Figure 12.3, you'll see the main poses and a couple of additional ones that refine the movement. Notice how after those poses, there is another one identical to the first one (pose 7): this is done just so the animation's end reflects its start.

Figure 12.3 shows several critical elements, so let's go through them:

- Poses 1, 3, 4, and 6 (marked as yellow keys) are the main ones, while 2 and 5 (marked as blue keys) are extra poses to better define the movement, and 7 is the same as 1.

- Poses 1, 2, and 3 are the only ones you actually need to create! Poses 4, 5, and 6 are nothing more than mirrored versions of 1, 2, and 3, and 7 is just a copy of 1. This will make creating the cycle a lot easier.

- Poses 1, 4, and 7 will be the Contact poses when the foot that goes forward touches the ground. Poses 3 and 6 will be the intermediate positions between two contacts; these poses set the moments at which Jim is standing on a single foot.

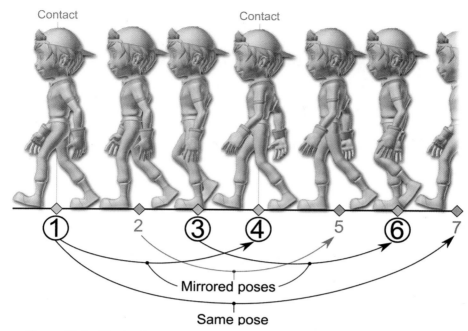

Figure 12.3   The basic poses you need to create to make your character walk

Animation Timing

Before diving into the animation process, let's take a look at the timing, which is what will define the speed of the animation (see Figure 12.4).

What Figure 12.4 represents is the frame numbers in which you should create the poses for the animation. Even though the poses are shown using this specific timing, you can create them in different frames and place them later using the animation editors (especially in the Dope Sheet). You can even use different times if you want to make Jim walk faster or slower. Basically, what you can see in the Timeline is that each main pose appears every 10 frames.

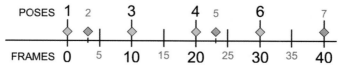

Figure 12.4   Another view of the Timeline, showing the poses
on the top row and the frame numbers on the bottom row

Let's now study the process you can follow to create the animation and add keyframes easily:

1. Set your animation to start from frame 0 and end at frame 40.

2. Pose your character in frame 0 with the first contact pose. Set a keyframe to all the bones of the rig (you can select the *Whole Character* keying set and, with any bone selected, just press **I**).

3. Select all the bones (**A**) and copy this pose by clicking the button on the header or press **Ctrl + C**. Go to frame 20, paste the mirrored pose by clicking the button on the header (or **Shift + Ctrl + V**). Set a keyframe. Move the timeline to frame 40 and paste the pose normally (**Ctrl + V**). Set another keyframe. You now have all your contact poses in place! The reason for creating those keyframes first is that now, if you go to the frame 10, you'll have an intermediate pose almost ready.

4. Pose the character so he looks better and make sure the pose for his feet is good to go (one on the floor and the other in the air). Insert a keyframe, copy this pose, and mirror and paste it into frame 30. Set another keyframe.

5. A few frames after the contacts (poses 1 and 4), adjust the poses to place the foot in front, completely on the ground, and keep elevating the back foot or its toes while you slide it back. These simple poses (also called breakdowns) will give a more natural look to your walk cycle.

6. Adjust the poses and copy them to the other moments of the animation. Also, if you want to make everything smoother, you can adjust the animation curves in the Graph Editor: if a curve is looking very rigid and not smooth at all, modify it while you play the animation to get instant feedback.

Repeating the Animation

Jim is now walking in place, taking only one step. Before you make Jim move through space, you have to repeat the animation so he takes more steps. There are several ways to do this. For example, you can just duplicate all the poses in the Dope Sheet to have another step after the first one, but in this case you're going to do it from the NLA Editor so that you'll have an introduction to this Blender feature.

First, open an NLA Editor. It will look like something similar to what you can see in Figure 12.5. The name of your current action appears (below the rig's name, which

Figure 12.5   The NLA Editor when you open it

is the object that performs the action), and next to it you'll see an icon with a snow-flake; you'll also see the action's keyframes displayed to the right of its name.

There are two ways to proceed from here. First, you can press the **X** button in the action's name inside the Action Editor (make sure to press the **F** near it first), so Jim stops performing that action and the NLA Editor can do its job. Then, you can go to the NLA Editor, press **Shift + A,** and from the list select the Walk_Cycle action you've been creating, and it will be added as a strip.

The second option, which is much easier and faster, is to click the snowflake icon in the Walk_Cycle action in the NLA Editor. This will turn the action into a strip and automatically perform the actions explained in the first option. Now you can move that strip to change the time in which the whole animation happens. You can even scale with **S** to make it faster or slower, and duplicate it to have more steps (see Figure 12.6).

Of course, you can duplicate the Walk_Cycle strip to include more steps in your animation, but you're going to learn a more elegant way to do it. Press **N** in the NLA Editor to open the Properties Region. There are two things you can adjust here. First, in the Action Clip panel, you can "cut" frames at the start or end of the animation. Set the end to 39 instead of 40 so pose 1 doesn't repeat in two frames. This will make the transition more natural when you repeat it. Then, in the same panel, you can change the scale of the strip and the number of repetitions it will have. Set the repetitions to something like 5 or 6, so you have enough steps in the animation. Then you can play with the scale of the strip to make the animation faster or slower until you're satisfied with it.

As you can see, using the NLA Editor is a very easy way of controlling actions instead of dealing with a lot of keyframes in order to achieve the same result. This is just an introduction, but you can do all sorts of cool things in this editor, such as overlapping different actions or creating transitions between two actions.

Walking along a Path

Jim is now taking a lot of steps, but he's still not moving in space! The following directions will show you how to use a constraint to make him follow a path while he walks:

1. Create a path by pressing **Shift + A** and then click Curve > Path.
2. Edit the points (in Edit Mode) of the curve to describe the path you want Jim to take. In this case, it should be a straight line. You can leave only two points of the

Figure 12.6   The NLA Editor with the Walk_Cycle
action as a strip, ready to be edited

curve, set the start point at the origin of the scene where Jim is located, and align the end point on the Y-axis. You might need to change the handles' direction to make the curve's interpolation linear; a quick way to do it is to select the vertices and press **V:** you'll see a menu where you can pick the interpolation type for the selected vertices, click Linear, and you'll be left with a straight line.

3. In Object mode, select Jim's rig and apply a constraint to it. Go to the Constraints tab in the Properties Editor and add a *Follow Path* constraint to it.

4. In the Follow Path constraint menu, select the path you just created as the path. If it doesn't work automatically when you play the animation, click the *Animate Path* button. If you want a curved path, activate the *Follow* option so the character turns with the path.

5. Select the path and, on the Curve tab of the Properties Editor, adjust the number of Frames that Jim will use to go from the start to the end of the path in the *Path Animation* panel. Adjust this parameter as well as the length of the curve and the speed of the walking cycle until you get a nice result and Jim's feet look as planted as possible without sliding over the floor (feet sliding is a common side effect of working with animation cycles, so be aware of this). You can activate the grid on the floor and add more lines to it in the Display panel of the Properties Region in the 3D View to have a reference to how Jim is moving across the floor, as shown in Figure 12.7.

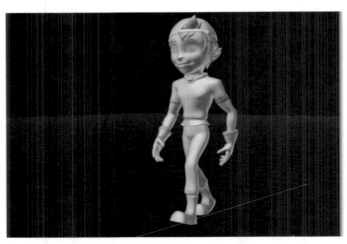

Figure 12.7   Jim is walking along the
path on the floor. He's really coming to life!

Summary

Animation is a pretty complex process and achieving characters that move realistically is very tricky and requires a lot of knowledge, experience, and dedication. Hopefully, this chapter has shown you the very basics and will encourage you to learn more!

What you have now is a finished character that walks. That's pretty cool considering you began this book with no idea of how Blender works. In the next chapter, you'll keep learning cool things.

Exercises

1. Add keyframes to an object to move it from point A to point B. Try different interpolation methods and play with the curves to see how they affect the way the object moves. Play the animation while you adjust the curves in the Graph Editor to have instant feedback.

2. Using the NLA Editor, create another animation for Jim (such as waving his hand or turning his head) and mix it with the walk animation.

VI

Getting the Final Result

13

Camera Tracking in Blender

When you want to mix your 3D objects into a real video, you need a camera in the 3D world that moves in exactly the same way as the camera that filmed the real-world footage so the 3D objects fit perfectly into the scene. Camera tracking is the process that allows you to track features in the real video to give Blender information about the perspective so it can generate a 3D camera that mimics the real one. Until very recently, you needed expensive specialized software to do this, but now Blender provides a pretty efficient alternative and the best thing about it is that you don't need to import/export scenes or use any other software; everything you need is already inside Blender! In this chapter, you'll learn the basics of camera tracking in Blender.

Understanding Camera Tracking

Before you start the process of tracking, it's important that you understand how it works.

1. First, you load a video and track features using the tracking tools in Blender. Good features are typically details in the video that are highly visible, static relative to the world, and have a high contrast. Tracking uses these features found in the video to establish which way the objects in the video are moving relative to the frame. Although this is done frame by frame, it's usually pretty automatic as Blender can track the features for you.

2. Next, when you have enough tracked markers in the video, you input the camera settings to tell Blender the type of camera and lens you used to film the video. If you don't know exactly what lens you used, Blender will be able to estimate the settings and give you something pretty close to those you used.

3. Then, you have to address the camera's movement. At this stage, Blender analyzes the points you tracked through the video and, by comparing their movements in different frames, it can reconstruct the camera's perspective and determine where the 3D camera should be to see the points in those specific positions. That way,

you'll end up with a 3D camera that moves in exactly the same way as the real camera you used.

4. Finally, it's just a matter of aligning the 3D camera and adjusting it to your scene so its orientation is correct and your 3D objects fit within the real footage.

Things to Consider before Filming

Sometimes you are just given a video that you need to track and the level of difficulty to do this directly depends on how the video was shot. If it wasn't shot with some basic considerations in mind, you'll probably have a hard time tracking it: it may not contain enough features to track or it may be very blurry or fast moving. Keep in mind that in a movie, for example, there can be a lot of these tricky shots to track, but also keep in mind that there are people with significant experience, using expensive software, and putting in a lot of effort (sometimes even performing manual "magic") to make the 3D camera fit perfectly with the camera that took the real footage. If you want to create your own videos and prevent your shots from being very difficult to track, you just need to know how the tracker works.

Camera tracking uses what is called perspective shift or parallax to detect the perspective in your footage. Imagine you are inside a train and you look out through a window: the objects closer to you appear to move really fast, and the objects further away, such as clouds, are almost stationary. This is what perspective shift is all about: an object that is closer to the camera will shift its perspective faster than one that is very far away.

Knowing this, you can understand that a video in which you move the camera to show that perspective shift will help Blender determine where the markers are. If that doesn't fit the idea you have for the shot, don't worry! You can shoot some video reference frames that capture perspective shift before shooting the actual video; then, you can use the frames of the reference footage to show Blender the correct perspective, and the rest of the video will then incorporate that perspective. This will give you better results when you're working with a video that has minimal perspective shift. When you finally edit the video, you can cut out those reference frames at the beginning, of course.

Here are some other useful tips on how to shoot a video for tracking:

- Because of perspective shift, it helps to have tracking features in both the foreground and the background; this will give Blender a better reference to analyze.

- Make sure that there are enough recognizable features that you will be able to track throughout the video (high-contrast elements with 90-degree corners offer the best results when tracking). The more often a feature appears during the video, the more stable the camera motion's solution will be. If you feel there are not a lot of features, place something in the scene that can help you: a little stone here, a piece of paper there. Just add things that will help you later and won't distract the viewer. Another alternative is to add physical markers (usually small designs that contain contrasting shapes or corners that you can print and place on your scene during filming); however, this is trickier because you'll have to remove them later in postproduction, so it's better if you place only small, unobtrusive objects in strategic positions.

- Avoid zooming if possible because changes in the lens while shooting the footage can compromise the tracking and make it much trickier.

- Try to prevent very fast moves that might blur the image. If you have blurry footage, chances are you'll have to track it almost manually and it probably won't be very precise because you won't be able to see the tracking features clearly.

- Shooting a good-quality video makes tracking a lot easier. If the video has compression artifacts or low resolution, small (and even big) features will change a lot from one frame to the next, making it very difficult for Blender's automatic tracker and you'll have to do a lot of manual work.

- To track the camera movement, you can only use features that are static. Don't use things that move as features to track because they can break Blender's perspective analysis. Keep this in mind when you are planning how to shoot the scene to make sure you have enough static features to track. Remember that the more features you track, the more stable and close to the real footage the 3D camera movement will be.

- If possible, take note of the focal length and other camera parameters you used while shooting the video footage. That information will help Blender solve the 3D camera's motion.

The Movie Clip Editor

Camera tracking happens inside the Movie Clip Editor. Turn a Blender area into the Movie Clip Editor by selecting that editor type on the area's header. Let's look at what you'll find in the editor, which is shown in Figure 13.1.

You may not understand anything about the Movie Clip Editor right now, but don't worry; here is a quick and simple explanation of what you'll see in the Movie Clip Editor:

- **Tools Region (A):** You'll find options to create new markers and to track and solve the camera's movement (press **T** to show and hide this region).

- **Movie Clip (B):** In the center of this area, you have the real footage you've shot and this is where you can track features using markers.

- **Properties Region (C):** In this section of the editor, you'll see the settings of the currently selected marker together with display and camera parameters (press **N** to show and hide this region).

You'll learn more about each part of the editor throughout this chapter.

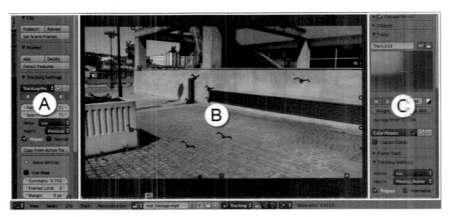

Figure 13.1   The Movie Clip Editor is where you will perform the camera tracking.

Tracking the Camera

In this section, you'll learn how to load video footage, track moving points in the image, and generate the 3D camera movement that simulates the movement of the real camera. For now, you'll only need to see the Movie Clip Editor, so you may want to make it full screen by pressing **Shift + Space** or **Ctrl + Up Arrow**.

Loading Your Footage

Of course, you can't track your footage if you have no footage, so let's load it! There are different ways in which you can load your footage. Basically, it works the same as loading images in the UV/Image Editor:

- You can press **Alt + O** and select your footage.
- You can click and drag it from your OS folder system into the Movie Clip Editor.
- In the Clip menu of the header, you can pick the *Open Clip* option.
- On the header, you can click the folder icon near the name of the clip.

Once you have loaded your footage, you can scrub through it using the Timeline at the bottom of the Clip Editor, just above the header. When you're tracking, you don't use anything else other than the Movie Clip Editor to scrub through the footage.

Left clicking and dragging the green numbered cursor in the Timeline will change the current frame and display the frame number. There are also two horizontal lines, one blue and one yellow, in the Timeline; the blue line is for the footage. As you play the video (**Alt + A**), the frames will be cached and next time they'll load a lot faster (it's recommended you play the whole video to cache it completely before you start tracking, so the process is faster). The blue line will be lighter in the parts that are cached, so with a quick look, you'll know which parts you have cached and which you haven't.

The yellow line is for the markers. When a tracker is at work (moving and following a feature), it will display a muted yellow line. In the frames where you add manual keyframes to the track, the line will have a brighter yellow color, so you'll know in which parts of the footage you added those manual keyframes and which parts were tracked automatically.

> **Tip**
>
> By default, Blender uses only 1 GB of RAM to cache your footage. If you're working with a big video or HD, 1 GB might not be enough to cache all its frames. In the User Preferences (**Ctrl + Alt + U**), inside the System tab, you'll find a section for the Sequencer/Clip Editor where you can increase that amount of memory that will be used for caching videos.

Anatomy of a Marker

Markers (also called trackers) are the main tools you'll use to track features in your footage, so before you start tracking, let's understand what a marker is and what its parts do (see Figure 13.2).

- **Pattern area:** This is the main part of the marker. The pattern is the area of the image in one frame that Blender (or you, manually) will look for in the next frame to track it. Usually, you should use some feature of the footage that is easy to recognize as the pattern's center: a high-contrast area or a specific shape that is unique in the image. You can move the marker, rotate it, and scale it as always with **G, R,** and **S.** Also, in the Properties Region, in the Track panel, you'll see an image that shows the selected marker's pattern, so you can clearly see the pattern that Blender is analyzing.

- **Search area:** This is the area in which Blender will look for the pattern defined in the pattern area in the next frame. (This area is not visible by default; you need

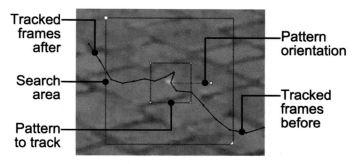

Figure 13.2   A marker and its parts

to enable it in the Marker Display panel of the Properties Region if you want to see it.) The faster the movement of the image is, the bigger the search area will need to be, because if the pattern in the next frame falls outside of the search area, Blender won't find it. However, the bigger the search area, the slower the automatic tracking will work. You can change the size of this area or its position by left clicking and dragging on its top-left and bottom-right marked corners.

- **Pattern orientation:** You can rotate the pattern (or even distort it by dragging its corners) to make tracking it easier. If you do this, you also have options to track the pattern's rotation or perspective, which can be very useful at times. In this example, though, you'll only work with the markers' locations. When you left click and drag the little square at the end of the short line, you'll be able to rotate or scale the pattern (you can also do that using **R** and **S** when you select the marker).

- **Tracked frames:** When you're tracking, the marker will show a red and a blue line, both with dots. The track is always in the current frame's position; the blue line shows the trajectory and positions of the next frames (if tracked) and the red line displays the tracked positions in the previous frames. These lines can help you compare different markers' movements to determine if one of them is clearly off.

Tracking Features in the Footage

Now that you know the basics, we can explore the marker settings.

You can modify the tracking settings for markers in two different places: in the Properties Region and in the Tools Region. The settings in the Properties Region will affect the currently selected marker's tracking settings, while the settings in the Tools Region are the parameters that will be applied by default when you create new trackers.

Tracking settings include various options and values such as what color channel the settings will be tracking, the pattern and search size, if the markers track Location only (this is the one you'll be using here), and the rotation, scale, and perspective of the features.

One of the options is the Match Type, which is very important! You can set it to match the *Keyframe* or the *Previous Frame*. Keyframe will tell Blender to look in every frame for a feature similar to the one you set in the last manual keyframe for the marker. Previous Frame will look for a feature similar to the one in the last tracked frame. Why is this important? Usually, you want to use the Previous Frame option, as a tracking feature can change slightly throughout the video (because of perspective), so it's better if the tracker adapts to that small change that happens frame by frame; otherwise, at some point in time the feature will be very different from its appearance in the last manual keyframe and the tracker will stop working.

Now it's time to start tracking! Here are the steps you need to follow to track features:

1. First, create a marker. In the Tools Region, on the Marker tab, click the Add button and then left click over the footage where you want to create the new marker.

> **Tip**
>
> A quicker way to create markers is to press **Ctrl + LMB** where you want the new marker and it will be immediately placed in that location.

2. Adjust the marker so the pattern area fits the feature you want to follow (maybe a corner or a spot). Scale it up and down with **S** to adjust it to the feature's size. In the Track panel, at the top of the Properties Region, look at the zoomed version of the pattern defined by the marker to make sure it's correct.

3. Track that feature along the footage using the Track Forward and Track Backward features. In the Track panel of the Tools Region, launch the automatic tracking or use **Ctrl + T** to track forward and **Shift + Ctrl + T** to track backward.

4. Track frame by frame using **Alt + Right Arrow** and **Alt + Left Arrow**. Press **L** to center the view in the currently selected marker and, in the Marker Display panel of the Properties Region, set the options for what you want to see on the screen (such as the Search Area of markers).

> **Tip**
>
> Sometimes, the feature won't be visible (imagine that you're tracking a window in a building in the background and it's obscured in some frames by a post in the foreground). You can just stop tracking, skip some frames, and start tracking when the feature becomes visible again. A marker will only be evaluated while it has tracking keyframes (either manual or automatic), so if you just skip some frames without tracking it, it will be treated as disabled for those frames.

5. Track the markers one at a time to make sure the tracking is progressing correctly; however, you can track multiple markers at once if you want.

6. Once a marker has been correctly tracked in all parts of the footage where the feature that the marker is following appears, lock it to prevent accidental moves or tracks. In the Track panel of the Properties Region, there are two icons: an eye and a lock. The eye enables and disables the tracker while the lock just makes it impossible to adjust the marker until you unlock it.

> **Tip**
>
> When you press **Ctrl + T** or **Shift + Ctrl + T** to automatically track with a marker, tracking will be very fast (depending on your computer and the complexity/size of the pattern Blender is searching for) and almost impossible to follow with the eye. Sometimes that's good because it will complete the tracking quickly and will stop only when the tracking fails. However, in some situations, even though the tracking doesn't fail, it's not correct because it slides little by little on the feature, meaning that the track won't be exact. What you can do to better monitor the tracking is to go to the Tracking Settings in the Properties Region and, in the *Speed option*, set it to *Realtime* or slower. This way, even though Blender can track the feature faster, it will track it at a normal speed so you can see what's going on throughout the process.

7. Repeat this process with as many features as you can (try to have a minimum of 8 to 10 in every single frame). Press **M** to mute the video (press it again to unmute) and play the video to see only the markers moving against a black background.

8. Make sure there are no markers going crazy or moving weirdly compared to others. If one or more of the markers are not right, don't worry; you can come back and adjust them at any time if the camera solution fails.

Camera Settings

Before you "solve" the camera motion, you need to tell Blender your camera parameters. Knowing the lens you used as well as other camera settings makes it easier for Blender to calculate perspective. In the Properties Region, you have the Camera and Lens panels where you can input information about the focal length you used to film the footage, as well as the camera sensor.

If you don't know this information, no problem, Blender has a tool called *Refine* that will estimate that information for those situations; you'll use it in the next section that covers solving the camera's motion.

Solving Camera Motion

In the Tools Region, jump to the Solve tab where you'll find options to solve the camera motion that will ultimately be in your 3D scene. For example, you'll see the Tripod option; if you filmed from a tripod, your footage won't have much perspective information, so Blender will only calculate the camera rotation if you enable this option.

The keyframes selection is also important. Blender needs to select two frames of the footage that will serve as a base for calculating the perspective in the rest of the frames. Those two frames should be frames that include fairly different perspectives but have a significant number of markers in common between them. This way, Blender will compare the perspective shift of those markers between the two frames and use that information as a guide. You can activate the *Keyframe* option and Blender will select those two frames for you, or you can input them yourself as the keyframes A and B

The *Refine* option is useful when you don't have the information about the camera's focal length, for example, or its distortion values (the K1, K2, and K3 parameters). So if you enable one of those options for Refine, Blender will estimate them for you.

Once you've made the appropriate selections, click the *Solve Camera Motion* button and look at the header. It will now display the error margin to the right after all of the buttons with the *Solve error field* (see Figure 13.3). Blender detects the difference between the 3D camera and the real camera's perspective information it determined from the markers. A tracking Solve error of 0 is perfect tracking, but that never happens and there is always a small amount of error. Usually, the tracking will be acceptable if it has a value of less than 3, but the camera can have a slide effect at times (when placing the 3D objects onto the real footage), and under 1 is usually pretty good, with less than 0.4 or 0.3 considered to be a very good tracking.

Figure 13.3   The solution's Solve error value, shown in the Movie Clip Editor's header

Figure 13.4   There is camera motion, but you still need to align camera
so the 3D scene is in place over the real footage.

If you go to the 3D scene, there is probably nothing going on and this is because there is still one thing you need to do to make this scene work. Here are the steps to follow:

1. Select the Camera and, on the Constraints tab of the Properties Editor, add a Camera Solver constraint.

2. Enable the Active Clip or select the clip's name from the list. Now you should see the camera and a set of little points in the scene. Each one of those points represents a marker in the Movie Clip Editor.

3. Scrub through the Timeline now and you'll see the camera moving (see Figure 13.4).

Making Adjustments

Now you just need to align the camera. The Movie Clip Editor still offers you a couple of tools to do this, but you can also do it manually. Let's use the Movie Clip Editor tool to align the camera motion:

1. Select three markers in the footage that are placed on the floor and, on the Orientation panel of the Solve tab, click the Floor button in the Movie Clip Editor. Blender will align the camera and all the markers in a way that those 3 markers are on the floor, completely horizontal.

2. To define the scale of the scene, select two markers in the 3D scene (it's better if you know the distance between them in the real scene, or you can at least make a guess). Now, on the Orientation panel of the Solve tab, in the Distance field,

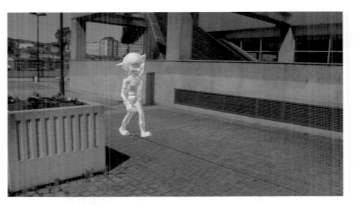

Figure 13.5   The camera is aligned and Jim is
standing on the floor of the real footage.

insert the distance between the two selected markers in the real scene. Click Set
Scale and the camera with all the markers will scale to reflect that measurement.

3. Click *Set as Background* in the *Scene Setup* panel on the Solve tab in the Tools
Region of the Movie Clip Editor. The current footage will be applied as a background to the Camera view (press **Ctrl + NumPad 0** to look at the scene from
the active camera). Make sure it fits with your scene.

4. Align the camera manually until your 3D objects fit in the background footage as
you prefer. Usually, a good way to do this is to place the 3D cursor in the origin
of the scene (or where you have a 3D object placed on the floor, such as the character), and rotate, move, and scale the camera from there until it's aligned (see
Figure 13.5).

> **Tip**
>
> At this point, you could click the *Setup Tracking Scene* button right under the button for *Set
> as Background* in the Movie Clip Editor. This option would create the nodes in the composi-
> tor, as well as the render layers and anything else you might need to make the character
> cast shadows on the floor. But you'll learn how to do this all yourself manually in the next
> chapter so you understand the process and you can adjust it as you want.

Testing Camera Tracking

Press **Alt + A** in the 3D view and see if the camera tracking works. The camera alignment may need some adjustments or perhaps you can clearly see that the camera is not
moving accurately. In that case, you'll need to go back to the Movie Clip Editor and

look for the frames in which the camera movement fails. Maybe a marker is moving strangely or it jumped from one point to another. Maybe there aren't enough markers in those frames and you need to add more to make the frames more stable.

In any case, the process is as simple as retouching those markers or adding new ones (or even deleting one that you feel is moving in a weird way compared with the others or that is following a moving feature that confuses Blender). Solve the camera motion again and realign the camera in the scene. Just keep trying until you finally get it to work and don't give up!

Summary

Camera tracking can be fast and simple or it can be tricky and frustrating. Every shot presents its own challenges, but this chapter gives you an idea of how the process works so at least you're now able to do basic camera tracking for your own projects. Also, keep in mind when you're shooting a video or developing good workflows as you're working in the Movie Clip Editor that knowing what will result in good tracking depends on your experience. Keep practicing and try to track as many videos as you can, and eventually you'll understand what makes a video easy or difficult to track.

Also, this is just the tip of the iceberg in terms of what you can do with the Movie Clip Editor. You can include lens distortions, use the tracking to stabilize footage, or even track objects in the video and translate their movements to objects in the 3D scene. (Some people even manage to use the tracking tools to capture facial expressions.) Hopefully, this chapter has shown you the very basics that will encourage you to keep learning and looking for more information on the subject. In any case, you're very close to finishing the project!

Exercises

1. Record some video and track the camera.
2. Track the camera in a video shot with a tripod to understand how it looks when the camera motion is solved.

14

Lighting, Compositing, and Rendering

Welcome to the final stage of the project! In this chapter, you'll light your scene to match the real footage, learn how to set your scene up to be able to composite it using nodes, and launch the final render. Node compositing can be a little tricky to understand when you see it for the first time, but once you do a few scene composites using nodes, you'll like it a lot. The reason why compositing is a very important and critical part of the process is that during this process, you adjust your scene and take it from merely normal render to a great-looking render by retouching colors, adding effects, mixing elements—the possibilities are nearly limitless!

Lighting Your Scene

Whether you're using Blender Render or Cycles, the first step is to add lights to your scene, so in the compositing stage you'll have shadows to work with. When you work on an animated 3D video, you can decide how you want your lights to illuminate the scene, but when you're trying to mix a 3D object into real footage, you must make your 3D lighting fit the video.

Analyzing the Real Footage

Before you add lights, you should carefully analyze the real footage into which you want to fit your 3D scene. Take a look at the shadows; they'll tell you where the light is coming from and its intensity, and pay attention to how diffused or rigid the shadows are as well. The light color is also very important.

In the footage we'll be using, the only light source is the sun, but usually on a sunny day you have more light sources such as the blue sky, which can also illuminate the scenery. For example, look at the shadows in Figure 14.1; they are not completely black, but instead they are slightly illuminated by the light bouncing off various surfaces and they also have a blue tinge due to the reflected light of the sky. In addition, notice that

Figure 14.1   The shadows in the footage provide
a lot of information about the scene's lighting.

when the shadows get further from an object that's blocking the light, they receive
more color from the light of the blue sky and they are softer and more diffuse.

Creating Lights That Match the Footage

Knowing how lights and shadows work in the real world, you can start creating lights
in your 3D scene. Again, even the light settings are slightly different between the two
render engines, but the illumination you have to achieve is similar, so let's go through
the list of things you'll need to light this scene:

1. Of course, to see how the shadows will appear on the ground, you'll need to
   create a plane for the floor to receive those shadows. For now, just create a plane
   and adjust its size so that it fits the area where the character is walking and is wide
   enough to receive Jim's shadows.

2. Next, you'll need a directional sun light that mimics the direction of the main
   light source for the original scene. Just press **Shift + A** and create a *Sun Lamp*.
   Align it by taking into account in what direction the shadows would be projected
   depending on the location of the light source.

3. Adjust the softness of the shadow to fit that from the footage. In Cycles, adjust the
   Size value on the Lamp tab of the Properties Editor. In Blender Render, enable
   Raytrace shadows and increase the samples, and adjust the *Soft Size* setting, which
   is also on the Lamp tab.

> **Tip**
>
> You can divide your screen to have a rendered preview of it on one side and the footage in the Movie Clip Editor on the other. This will allow you to compare both views and have a reference for how to move the lights until their shadows fit those in the footage.

4. Now, to prevent the areas in shadow from being completely black, add an environmental light. You could make it bluish, but because the whole scene looks slightly blue, keep it neutral (white) and later you'll have more control in the compositor to tint it with blue and integrate it better.

   - In Cycles, go to the World tab in the Properties Editor and adjust the strength (enable Nodes if they still disabled). Keep in mind this adjustment has to be very subtle and don't worry for now if it doesn't completely match the colors in the real footage, as you'll fine-tune everything later in the node compositor.

   - In Blender Render, on the World tab, enable *Environment Lighting* and use a small value in the Energy parameter (about 0.35 or so), just to prevent the areas in the shadow from being absolutely black. If you want to use another color, change the Environment Lighting from *White* to *Sky Color* and, in the World panel, change the Horizon Color to a light blue.

> **Note**
>
> At this point, lighting your scene is pretty much guess work, as you have to test and adjust by eye the light intensity, color, and direction until they match the real footage. But don't worry if you don't light it perfectly on the first try; later, when you're in the compositor, you'll see much more clearly if your lighting fits the lighting from the real footage and, if it doesn't, you can always adjust it and render again until it works nicely. Remember that making something cool is not a one-shot process; at certain points, you need to go back and try again to get a result you like.

The Node Editor

Now, before moving on to compositing, let's take a brief look at how to use the Node Editor and then you'll learn what nodes are and how they work. After this introduction, you'll be ready to carry on with the basic compositing.

Compositing Methods

While you can create a scene that is rendered exactly as you need it, it is usually faster to get something close to the desired result and then make the final modifications in the compositor. This method provides very quick feedback and making changes to the lighting and color with nodes, for example, is much faster than rendering the scene again. Sometimes, you need to render different elements in different layers and then combine them in the compositing. Maybe you just want to place a 3D object into a photo or real video, so you might need to mix your rendered 3D object with those images and adjust their colors so the lighting and contrast fit with each other. You can do such things in other software, such as Photoshop or Gimp, but you can do them in Blender as well.

There are usually two main methods for compositing: One way is to do the compositing before the rendering. You take a test render, composite it in the Node Editor, and then launch the final render (even an animation) with the effects of the compositor. For this, you use the scene render as an input.

The second way is to do the raw render of elements and then load those image sequences or videos into the compositor to adjust them. This also allows you to adjust videos, of course. Imagine that you take a video and you want to add some color correction to it: just load it into the compositor, composite it, and render it—no need to use the 3D View.

Understanding Nodes

When you take a simple render (simple means a raw render, with no compositing involved), your scene is the input and the output will be the same as the input. When you enable the use of nodes, the input and the output are connected, but you can modify the final result by adding nodes in between that will apply effects and changes to the input before it reaches the output. The modifications can be as simple as color corrections or as complex as adding visual effects or mixing several different renders into a single render.

A node structure is often called a node tree, as its connections resemble branches that ultimately connect to form a single output—the tree's trunk. In Figure 14.2, you can see a basic scheme of how a node tree can evolve as you add more nodes to the tree. The first node tree shows a basic setup, which is what you get when you enable Node

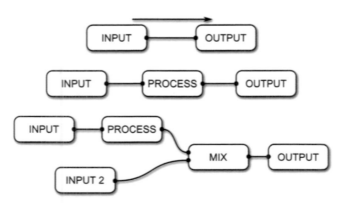

Figure 14.2   A scheme representing three different node trees that could
also represent the same tree in different stages of its evolution

Editing. The second tree adds a modification to the input before it reaches the output. The third tree mixes a second input into the result. You can see why it's called a node tree because it now has two branches and this is only a basic setup; a complex scene can have dozens of different branches that interact together.

The basic thing you need to understand about a node tree is that it is processed from left to right. You can always add more nodes between other nodes. Let's take the example shown in Figure 14.2: Each one of the inputs can be different renders of different parts of the scene. At the bottom of the figure, the first Input has a process going on before it's mixed with the second Input, which could be a color correction for example. Imagine you want to make your whole render look more reddish or have more contrast: you could just add a new color correction node between the Mix node and the Output; the color correction node will then affect all the previous nodes after the mix happens.

If you pick any node, here is what happens: the data from another node enters the current node via the Input and is processed by the node using the properties set by the user. The data is then passed along to the output node where it can be viewed, or passed into yet another node.

If you still don't get it, that's perfectly normal. Sometimes you just need to get your hands on something to really understand it. As you continue this chapter and see what nodes are all about, and then create your first node tree, you'll be able to see how your changes affect the overall result, which will answer a lot of your questions.

Anatomy of a Node

Before you start using the Node Editor, you need to know how a node works and what its parts are. In Figure 14.3, you can see the dissection of a node into its basic parts. (In this case, it's an RGB Curves node, which is used to make color corrections to the nodes you put into it).

- **Noodles:** The little colored dots at the left and right sides of a node are called noodles. They support the connections. The noodles on the left are inputs, while those to the right are outputs. Their color tells you what each of those connectors is for: gray noodles are for values (or grayscale images), yellow ones are for RGB images, and blue ones are for vectors. A yellow output noodle should usually be connected to a yellow input noodle in the next node, and there are nodes that convert one type of data into another, i.e., from an RGB image into three grayscale images.

  Next to those noodles, there is always a description that tells you what that noodle should receive (if it is an input) or what it's generating (if it is an output).

  > **Note**
  >
  > While you will usually create connections between the same types of noodles, there are some situations in which you can connect different types. For example, if you connect a yellow (RGB image) output to a gray (grayscale) input, the image will be converted from color to black and white.

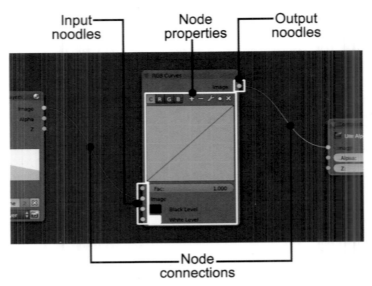

Figure 14.3   These are the main parts of a node.

- **Node properties:** Each node (and there are a lot, you'll see) has different properties and is used for different purposes. Inside the node, you'll find all those properties.

- **Node connections:** A node does nothing by itself. Every single node needs another node to work, and that's why they are connected. The way and order in which you connect them ultimately defines the final result.

There are a lot of node types, but there are three main structures: input, output, and modifiers. Input nodes only own output noodles and that's because they generate or load something, such as an image, a render, or an RGB color. Output nodes are not expected to be modified after they do their job, so they only receive input connections: these output nodes export the final result or display it. Finally, the modifiers are the nodes that are in the middle: they modify inputs and mix them together before they reach the outputs.

Using the Node Editor

In this section, you'll learn the Node Editor's basic controls: how to create and modify nodes, connect them, and so on. Figure 14.4 shows the Node Editor with a simple setup example.

Navigation in the Node Editor is pretty straightforward because it uses the same Blender navigation tools as any other editor: **MMB** to pan and **Scroll Wheel** or **Ctrl + MMB** to zoom in and out.

Getting Started with the Node Editor

When you open the Node Editor, you must keep in mind that it's also used for creating materials and textures. To use it for compositing, you need to select Compositing Mode on the header.

Once you've switched to Compositing Mode, you won't immediately see any nodes. Before you can start using nodes, you need to enable them in your scene. Click the *Use Nodes* option in the header and Blender will display a very basic node setup: the render plugged to a Composite node. This means there is nothing interesting going on for now; the final render is not being processed at all after its generation, so you get the raw result from the 3D scene.

However, now the editor is ready for you to start experimenting with nodes. If you launch a render now, it will use the basic node tree you have just created. At some point, if you need to launch a "raw" render without using the nodes, just disable the Use Nodes option.

Creating Nodes

There are three ways to create nodes in the Node Editor:

- **From the Tools Region:** The Tools Region of the Node Editor (**T**) has a panel for each type of node (categories) and, if you expand those panels, just click the node you want, move the new node until it is in the desired position, and left click to place the node in that location.

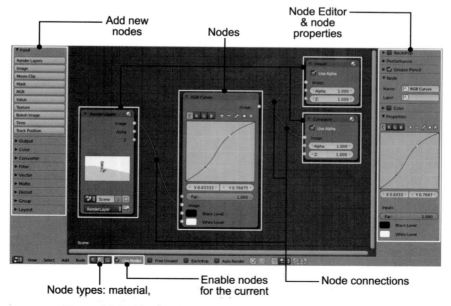

Figure 14.4   The Node Editor, featuring a simple node setup

- **From the Add menu:** On the Node Editor's header, in the Add menu, you can select the type of node you want, left click it, move the new node to the desired position, and left click again to place the node in that location.

- **Pressing Shift + A:** If you press **Shift + A** when in the Node Editor, the same Add menu from the header will appear at the cursor's position. Just as with the other methods described above, once you click to select the node type you want, drag the new node to the correct location and left click to drop the node there.

> **Tip**
>
> When you place the new node you just created, if you drag it over a connection between two other nodes, the connection will be highlighted and when you left click to drop the new node, it will be automatically connected between those other two nodes. This is a big time saver!

Connecting and Manipulating Nodes

The basic method for working with nodes is to create connections between them to make them interact with each other. It's also important to know how to move them around so your node tree is always organized. Otherwise, you can end up with a lot of nodes that overlap and that will make the tree very hard to work with.

Here is a list with the main controls for working with nodes:

- You can select nodes with both **LMB** and with **RMB**. Drag nodes with **LMB** or **RMB** to move them around.

- If you select more than one node with **B** (Box Selection) or with **Shift + LMB**, you can move them, rotate them, and scale them with **G, R,** and **S,** as always.

- Right click and drag in an empty space to perform a Box Selection at that point.

- To connect nodes, just left click and drag from one node's output noodle to the desired input noodle of another node.

- If a node has two or more input noodles and you want to switch a connection between them, just left click and drag from one noodle to the other.

- You can select two nodes and press **F** to create a connection between them.

- To remove a connection, left click the input noodle at the end of the connection, then drag it and drop it in an empty space.

- To remove one or more connections quickly, press **Ctrl + LMB** click and drag a line over the connections you want to cut. When you release **LMB**, the connections under the cutting line will be removed.

- Select one or more nodes and press **M** to mute them. Using the preview this is an easy way to see the effect a node has on the resulting image. Nodes will become red when they're muted. Press **M** again to enable them.

- You can duplicate nodes or groups of connected nodes with **Shift + D**.

- If you don't need to access a node's properties, press **H** when you select the node to collapse it so it takes less space. Press **H** again to expand it.

- Select one or more nodes and press **X** to remove them. Press **Ctrl + X** to delete them while keeping the connections between their previous and next nodes.

Result Preview

Of course, you don't need to work blindly. You can have a preview image that shows you real-time updates of what you're doing in the Node Editor. To enable a preview, you need to create a Viewer node. The Viewer node is inside the Output nodes group. Add it to your workspace and connect the output of the node you want to preview to the input of the Viewer node. The Viewer node will display a preview of the result of all the nodes in the node tree that affect the node you connected to the Viewer node.

An even faster way to enable a preview is to press **Shift + Ctrl + LMB** click the node you want to preview. This will automatically create a Viewer node and connect it to that specific node. Pressing **Shift + Ctrl + LMB** click in any other node will quickly connect that node to the Viewer, so you can see the effect of the node you want to preview really fast.

Once you have a viewer node in your node tree, you have two different options for previewing your work in the compositor.

- **Backdrop:** In the Node Editor's header, enable the Backdrop option and the preview will be shown right behind your node tree, in the background of the Node Editor workspace. Press **Alt + MMB** to pan it, **V** to zoom out, and **Alt + V** to zoom in.

- **UV/Image Editor:** Although the background preview lets you see everything in the same window, it can be very distracting at times and the nodes on top of the image can prevent you from seeing what's going on (especially if you have a complex node tree). In these cases, or if you just want to see the result on a secondary monitor, there is an easy way to do it: open the UV/Image Editor and, from the images list on the header, select the Viewer output. This way, you'll see the Viewer node preview as if it were an image in the UV/Image Editor.

> **Note**
>
> Don't forget that in order to see what you're doing in the compositor, you have to render your scene first (unless you're working with images already rendered or adjusting videos instead of a 3D scene render).

Compositing Your Scene in Blender Render

Now, let's see how you would perform the compositing in Blender Render. The compositing in the Node Editor works in an identical way for both Blender Render and

Cycles, but because the renders are different, there are a couple of things that will change in the compositing as well.

Setting Up the Scene

Before you start compositing, you need to know what to do first. In our example, there is something that obviously stands out: you need the floor to go away, but you want to keep the shadows it receives from the character so you can composite on top of the real footage.

It's really simple to do that in Blender Render because there is a setting for the materials that allows you to include an object that only receives shadows while the object itself will be transparent.

Just try it: create a new material for the floor, but in the Properties Editor on the Shadows panel of the Material tab, enable *Shadows Only*. Also, under *Shadows Only*, you'll see a drop-down list: select the option *Shadow Only* instead of *Shadow and Distance*. If you launch a render now, you'll see that the floor is not rendered, but the shadows Jim creates are there!

You can also go to the World tab in the Properties Editor and enable *Ambient Occlusion*. Set it to *Multiply* Mode and, in the *Gather* panel, increase the *Samples* to about 10, so the AO has more quality and less noise.

You could take a render now, put the footage behind Jim's figure, and the scene is done! But we're going to complicate the scene a little more. This way, you'll have more control over the individual parts of the render and, therefore, over the resulting image and you'll learn more about compositing with nodes.

Setting Up Render Layers

You now need to separate Jim from his shadow so you can control the shadows separately in the compositor. This is simple enough because the Render Layers feature allows you to separate elements in different layers and composite them later.

1. First, you need Jim and the floor to exist in different layers of the scene. If you've followed this chapter's instructions to the letter, you should have Jim in one layer and his rig in the one below (layer number 11, in the bottom row). Now, select the floor, press **M,** and select another layer. Jim's model could be in the first layer, while the floor could be in the second one.

   > **Tip**
   >
   > While in Object Mode, you can select the visible layers in the scene on the 3D View header. Press **Shift** while you left click several layers to be able to see more than one layer at a time.

2. Take the sun lamp and move it to yet another layer using the same method (for example, the last layer of the first layers group).

3. Go to the Render Layers tab in the Properties Editor (see Figure 14.5).

> **Note**
>
> In the Render Layers tab, you can create new Render Layers and define which layers of the scene are going to be rendered in that specific Render Layer. Also, in the Passes panel you can select the passes (channels) of that layer that will be rendered. For example, you can render Ambient Occlusion, Diffuse, Specular, etc., and these passes would become outputs in the Render Layer node so you can work with them in the compositor. For example, a Specular pass would give you the areas of the scene that are shiny, which can be very useful for creating the appearance of glare in the scene that could be mixed into the original render. As you can see, there are quite a few possibilities, but as this is just an introduction, you'll use only the basics for now.

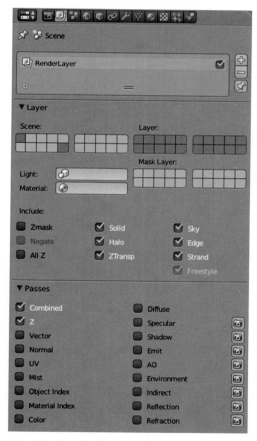

Figure 14.5   The Render Layers tab, where you can set those elements of the scene that will be rendered separately

4. Create two Render Layers and name them *Jim* and *Floor Shadows*. For both of them, in the *Layer* panel, select the layers that should be rendered for each Render Layer under the *Layer* section. Keep in mind that if you want the light to affect the elements in both Render Layers, you need to enable the sun lamp layer in both of them and that's why, a moment ago, you moved the sun lamp to the last layer in the first layers group (see Figure 14.6).

5. If you launch a render right now, you'll see the sky color behind Jim and his shadow. Go to the Render tab of the Properties Editor and, in the Shading panel, set the *Alpha* to *Transparent*. Now the background of the renders will be transparent, allowing you to insert your footage there.

Node Compositing

Node compositing can be difficult to understand, so take a look at the finished node tree in Figure 14.7. The nodes are numbered to help you understand the instructions that you'll follow in this section. Remember, you need to press **F12** and render a frame with the Render Layers set up so you can load them in the Node Editor; if they're not rendered, you won't see anything in that editor!

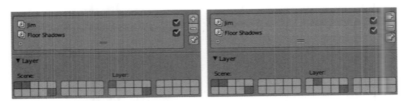

Figure 14.6   The settings for the two Render Layers

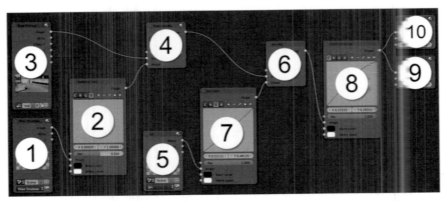

Figure 14.7   Here, the node tree is numbered so you can follow the instructions in this section. To see the full node tree with no numbers, go to the end of this section.

Now, let's go through the step-by-step process of creating this node tree.

1. Start with a Render Layers and a Composite (output) node. Move the Composite nodes all the way to the right, as the output nodes should be at the end of the tree (the Composite node is number 10 in Figure 14.7). In the Render Layers node (which is an input node, as it takes the render of the scene and inserts it in the Node Editor), at the node's bottom, there is a drop-down list from which you can select the Render Layer you want to show in that node: select the Floor Shadows Render Layer.

2. Create an *RGB Curves* Color node. Connect the Image output from the Floor Shadows Render Layer to the Image input in the RGB Curves node. The curves allow you to correct colors. Click the **B** button at the top of the RGB curves node to work with the Blue channel only. Pick the point at the lower-left corner of the curve and move it all the way up, so the curve is basically a horizontal line at the top. Create a Viewer node to see how the shadow has turned completely blue. Change the value with the Factor slider at the bottom of the RGB Curves node to decrease its effect on the image. When you have applied the factor's effect to the footage, you can come back here and adjust the factor until you're happy with the result.

> **Note**
>
> If you're not familiar with Curves from image editing software, they can be tricky to understand. You can modify the master color of an image or each one of the RGB channels. The master will control brightness and contrast, while the RGB channels will define the amount of each color in the image and the colors' contrast as well. Basically, when you click the curve, you add points to it and, by adjusting the curve, you can add or subtract color in that part of the RGB spectrum: left is dark and right is light. If you set the curve higher to the right, you'll increase the color in the bright values. If you set it lower to the left, you'll make the dark tones even darker.

3. Now it's time to mix the real footage with the shadow, so you need to take the footage into the compositor. Press **Shift + A** and, from the Input nodes, create a *Movie Clip* node. This should automatically load the clip you have been working on in the Movie Clip Editor. Otherwise, select the clip you want from the list in the Movie Clip node.

4. Let's mix the shadows over the footage. Press **Shift + A** and create a *Mix* node from the Color node type. Set the Mix mode to *Multiply* (the blending modes work the same as in any other image editing software, and Multiply places the dark areas of one image over another image, and makes the brighter areas transparent). Because the shadows have Alpha, you can click the little button to the right of the blending mode selector to enable the Alpha of the image on top.

The Mix node allows you to merge two images. Input the image you want on the background (the real footage) in the top Image input, and then place the image you want to be the foreground (the shadows) in the Image input at the bottom of the Mix node.

Play with the Mix node's factor value as well as the RGB Curves you applied to the shadows until they look similar to those in the real footage.

5. Jim should join the party now, so create a new Render Layers node from the Input group or select the Floor Shadows, duplicate that node with **Shift + D,** and switch the Render Layer selector at the node's bottom to display Jim's layer instead of the floor shadows layer.

6. You could mix Jim with the background using another Mix node; instead, create an *Alpha Over* (which is usually more efficient and gives better results when you need to just overlap a solid image with Alpha in front of another image from the Color nodes as well.

Again, the Mix node has two Image input noodles. Connect the shadows and footage Mix node to the first input, and connect Jim's Render Layer to the second input. Jim should now be a part of the image that results.

7. Jim may already be a part of the image, but it doesn't look like he belongs to the scene. This is because his lighting is different than the lighting of the real footage. Create a new RGB Curves node between Jim and the Alpha Over node so you can modify Jim's lighting until it fits better with the background.

8. Finally, you can even add another RGB Curves node after the Alpha Over node that merges Jim with the rest of the scene; this way you can apply some color correction to the whole scene. You might want to make it less bluish and increase its brightness—make whatever modifications you want until you're satisfied. The idea is that first you integrate Jim into the scene and then you fine-tune the details.

9. The Viewer node should be active all the time so you can see the effect of your efforts. Now, connect it to the node that is connected to the Composite node to preview exactly what is going to be in the final output.

10. Connect the final node of your composition to the Composite node so that when you click the Render button that will be the final image Blender outputs.

> **Warning**
>
> The Composite node is really important. While you won't need it until you're done with the compositing, you must have it there if you want the scene to be rendered when you have nodes enabled. You'll get an error if you don't have it or if you don't connect any node to it.

Figure 14.8 shows what the node tree should look like at the end of the process.

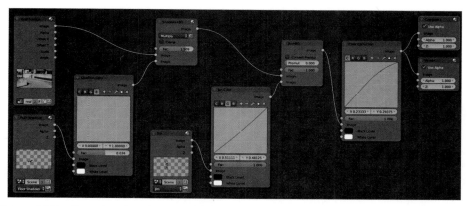

Figure 14.8   Completed node tree with Jim and his shadow composited over the footage

Compositing Your Scene in Cycles

The process to composite in Cycles is actually pretty similar to the process in Blender Render, except for the fact the there are no "Shadow Catcher" materials (these are the materials that only render the shadows they receive), so you'll need to use the Shadow pass and use a little trick to get the same effect (as in Blender Render).

Setting Up the Scene

There is not a lot to do to set up the scene for compositing. You just need to add a basic material to the floor. In Blender Render, you had to set the floor to receive only shadows, but as that can't be done in Cycles, you will set the scene up using Render Layers.

Make sure that, on the Render tab of the Properties Editor, under Film, you enable the Transarent option to avoid rendering the background. Also, if you haven't increased the Render Samples previously, you can do this now on the Render tab of the Properties Editor to improve the render quality.

Setting Up Render Layers

Now we come to the tricky part. Place Jim in one layer and the floor in another. In Cycles, it doesn't matter where the lights are; as long as they're visible in the scene, they'll affect all the Render Layers.

Just as you did in Blender Render, create two Render Layers, one for Jim and another for the ground plane (see Figure 14.9). For the floor Render Layer, go to the Passes panel on the Render Layers tab and you'll see a list of the passes you can enable. Enable the *Shadow* pass.

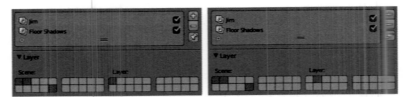

Figure 14.9   Render Layers set up in Cycles

Node Compositing

As the Cycles compositing process is almost the same as it was for Blender Render, in this section we'll focus on the different steps for setting up the shadows. In Figure 14.10, you can see another numbered node tree that shows how the shadows are composited. At the end of this section, Figure 14.11 shows the completed node tree for reference, but once you've composited the shadows, the rest of the process is exactly the same as for Blender Render.

1. Set the Render Layers node to show the Floor Shadows Render Layer.

2. Create a *Dilate/Erode* node from the Filter nodes category and connect the Alpha from the Floor Shadows Render Layer to the Dilate/Erode node's input. The Dilate/Erode node takes an image (in this case the Alpha channel of the Floor Shadows Render Layer) and either makes the lighter areas spill over the dark areas or makes the dark areas spill over the lighter areas, depending on the Distance value of the node. This is a very useful feature when you need to increase or reduce the edges of a mask. For now, keep its Distance value at 0.

3. Create a Mix node and connect the *Shadow* output of the Floor Shadows Render Layers node into the Mix node's second Image input, and then connect the *Mask* output of the Dilate/Erode node into its *Fac* input.

   The Shadow pass includes only the shadows of the floor, but the background is not transparent, it's completely black. To fix that, mix the Shadow pass with a white-colored background, but input the Alpha of the Floor Shadows Render Layer into the factor of the Mix node.

   The factor of the Mix node defines which areas of the top image will be visible, so it will make the background of the Floor Shadows Render Layer transparent and show instead the color of the first Image input of the Mix node.

   Usually, you'll get the white background, but at the edges, because they are not completely solid, you'll see a little black border. Set the Distance in the Dilate/Erode node to -1 and the floor's Alpha will shrink one pixel; then you won't see those ugly borders anymore.

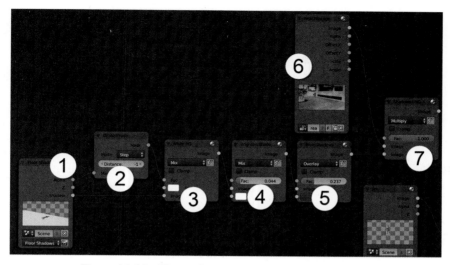

Figure 14.10   The node tree in Cycles for compositing
the shadows on top of the footage

4. To give you the chance to learn something new, let's use a different method to tint the shadows than the one you used for Blender Render. Add a new Mix node and plug the previous Mix node's output to one of the new node's Image inputs. The other Image input should have a white color. Make sure the Mix node's blending mode is Mix. Now, when you change its factor value, you'll mix a completely white image with the shadows, making them brighter. With this node, you'll be able to control the brightness of the shadows.

5. Now add another Mix node. Connect the previous Mix node's output to the new node's first Image input and, in the second image input of the new Mix node, pick a blue color in the color selector. Set the blending mode to *Overlay* to mix the blue only in the dark areas. Now play with the factor to apply the desired amount of blue to the shadows.

6. Add the Movie Clip node to load the footage in the compositing.

7. Create another Mix node and set its blending mode to Multiply. Now connect the shadows' resulting mix that was finished in step 5 to its second Image input, and the footage to its first Image input.

To add Jim to the equation, the process is exactly the same as in Blender Render. In Figure 14.11, you can see the whole node tree.

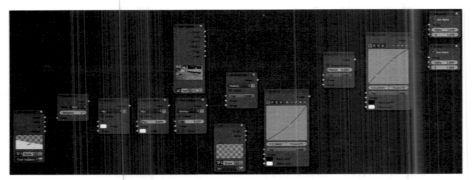

Figure 14.11   Finished node tree for Cycles

Rendering

Now we just need to adjust a couple of settings and launch the final render.

Render Settings

This is the last opportunity you'll have to change the render settings (unless you want to render again with different settings later). Make sure you're happy with your scene and that the Composite node is connected to the final node of the tree in the Node Editor. On the Render tab of the Properties Editor, set the image resolution.

> **Tip**
>
> Up to this point, you'll usually work with lower resolutions or less samples in Cycles so you can get faster renders to see if you like the result or if you need to keep adjusting things. In that case, remember to increase the resolution and the number of samples now.

Output

If you're rendering an animation, another important thing you must do is set up the output folder and format so as a frame is rendered, Blender automatically saves it. With a single image, you don't need to set up an output path and format because after it's rendered, you can save it manually from the UV/Image Editor (**F3**).

In the Output panel of the Render tab, in the Properties Editor, you can select the output folder to which the renders will be saved and the format of the exported images.

> **Tip**
>
> You can save the animation as a video, but that is only recommended for quick render tests. If you expect the render to take a few hours (or even days!), it's usually better to export the animation in an image sequence. Instead of a video, what you'll get is a series of .jpeg, .png, or .tga images—one for each frame of the animation.

This has several benefits: If the render fails at some point, you won't lose the rendered frames; while in a video, the whole video would be corrupted. Also, the videos are usually highly compressed, so with images you'll get no compression artifacts and then you can convert the image sequence to a video (you can even do it in Blender by loading it into the Video Sequencer, or as a clip in the compositor and rendering it in a video format). This is very fast because it's much easier and quicker to render images than an entire 3D scene. This way, you'll have the full quality and you can compress the image sequence into a video later.

Also, remember that it is possible to export different passes as an image sequence (OpenEXR Multilayer format is great for this because you can export different sequences for each pass) and composite the render elements in other software such as Photoshop or After Effects for greater control.

Final Rendering Results

Only one thing is left to do: click the Render button. Depending on whether you want to render a single frame or the whole animation, on the Render tab, click Render or Animation.

If you're becoming proficient with Blender, go ahead and use the keyboard shortcuts: **F12** for a still-frame render and **Ctrl + F12** to render the whole animation. In Figure 14.12, you'll see the results in both Blender Render and Cycles.

Figure 14.12   The final results with Jim integrated into the
real footage in Blender Render (left) and Cycles (right)

Summary

Compositing is a technical process, but it also leaves room for creativity. Hopefully, you've learned the basics and now at least understand how nodes work and why compositing has such a big impact on the final result of your image.

You've come a long way with Blender and your scene is done! As you can see, integrating an animated character into a real video is a lot of work and involves a lot of different skills: modeling, texturing, rigging, animation, and compositing.

Now that you have some experience with each one of those skills, keep learning about the ones you've enjoyed the most. That is the goal of this book: to show you the whole process so that you can decide which part of it you'd like to dedicate more time to and whether you want to specialize in that area. As an alternative, maybe you like the whole process so much you'll want to become a generalist!

Exercises

1. Play with Color Correction nodes (RGB Curves, for example) to see how you can change the color to give the scene completely different moods.

2. In the Render Layers, enable all the render passes and connect each one of them to a Viewer node to see the differences between them in the compositing nodes.

15

Other Blender Features

You've already seen a lot of what Blender can do, but you've just scratched the surface! Blender has a lot more to offer than what you've seen in this book. We've only touched on the basics and covered just a few of the advanced tools and features. In this chapter, you'll learn about other features that Blender provides so you know they exist in case you're interested in learning more about them.

Keep in mind this chapter is not meant to be a manual or to show you how to use these features. It will just describe what tools are at your disposal so you can decide if you want to learn more about them. You'll have to do some research to find the necessary information on how to use them in your projects.

Particles

Particles are useful when you need to create and animate a lot of objects that behave similarly. Imagine, for example, snow, rain, or leaves falling; instead of animating each snowflake or raindrop individually, you create an emitter geometry and, on the Particles tab in the Properties panel, you add a Particle System to it.

From there, you can set the amount of emitted particles, their behavior, their physics, and so forth. You can also select other objects and set them as obstacles, so particles collide with them. You can even create forces such as wind, vortex, or turbulence to make the particles behave in certain ways. You can also use particles to simulate fluid substances.

Hair Simulation

Hair is a subset of Particles, as you're actually creating hair particles. If you create a particle system and set it to be a hair emitter, instead of normal particles, the system will create a lot of hairs on the desired surface and grow strands from there.

Later, when you have a hair particle system on the selected object, in the 3D View you'll be able to switch to the Particle Mode, which will allow you to grow, cut, and comb the hair to create a hairstyle for your character.

Once your hair is in place, you can even run a simulation to make the hair follow the character's movements and automatically react to gravity and objects that touch it.

This hair simulation feature is not limited to characters, though. You can use it to "spray" a lot of objects over a surface, such as adding trees to a forest or simulating grass on a field.

Cloth Simulation

If you want to create anything from clothes for a character to banners or bedsheets, cloth simulation is the way to go. Don't worry about creating wrinkles or folds manually; on the Physics tab in the Properties Editor, just turn the cloth mesh into a Cloth object and click Play.

You can control the properties of the cloth to make it behave like a specific type of material. You also can set other objects as obstacles and the cloth will react to them.

Cloth simulation even works in real time, so if you click Play and try to grab the cloth, it will react to your touch and to the objects that collide with it.

Rigid and Soft Bodies

Similar to the cloth simulation, this feature is for rigid and soft objects. If you need to make a house fall down or destroy a wall, divide the object into pieces and, in the Physics panel, make those pieces rigid bodies. You can bind the objects to each other to define how they behave and limit the range of movements they can perform to simulate the force of gravity on them.

When you need to make an object behave as if it had weight, you can run a rigid body simulation and Blender will simulate gravity and object interactions in a realistic manner for you. Also, you can define other objects as obstacles so the rigid or soft bodies collide with them.

Soft bodies are similar to rigid ones, except they can also be deformed. For example, using soft bodies you can simulate an object behaving like jelly.

Fluids Simulation

You can also simulate fluids such as water in a glass or liquids flowing and reacting to other objects. You can let objects fall into a pool and create splashes, as well as many other simulations of a fluid's properties. Just play with the different types of fluid objects to add liquid to the simulation, subtract it, have it collide with other objects, or even use it to form shapes.

Fire and Smoke

Particles are also the base for fire and smoke, and you can create these effects and preview them in real time in the 3D View (remember that high-resolution simulations will slow down your computer a lot). You can adjust a lot of parameters for these effects, and you can control how the fire and smoke behave as well as how they are rendered.

A quick way to create a fire simulation is to select an object and, in the Object Menu of the 3D View header, look for *Quick Effects* and click *Quick Smoke*. Press **Alt + A** to play the animation and see what happens. You'll need to make additional adjustments to get the simulation to render nicely, but this is a good starting point.

Game Engine

Blender has its own game engine. While some people complain that you can't export the games you create to mobile platforms (at least for now), even more people don't really understand the power of this feature.

The Blender Game Engine is meant to create interactive content, not just games (although some people have managed to create interesting games using it). For example, 3D presentations are a surprisingly exciting option. Imagine you're an architect and you build an interactive walk-through of the building your client wants to construct; wouldn't that be useful and valuable? With the Blender Game Engine, those kinds of things are pretty easy to do.

Masking, Object Tracking, and Video Stabilization

In this book, you've learned how to use the Movie Clip Editor to track the camera motion. Although that is probably its best-known function, this editor can provide many more features. You can use the tracking data to stabilize your footage and make the video look a lot smoother.

You can also track the motion of objects in the video to apply that motion to 3D objects in your scene. Shoot a video of yourself wearing paper markers, track it, and composite futuristic weapons on top of the markers.

The Movie Clip Editor also gives you the necessary tools to create masks over your footage that you can use later in the compositor. Imagine that you want something in the real video to stay in front of the 3D stuff: you can mask it and keep it in front using the compositor.

Sculpting

Sculpting is one of the most creative ways of modeling. If you like organic modeling, this is something you really need to check out because it's very useful for sculpting characters.

In the 3D View, just switch to Sculpt Mode and use it as you would the texture brushes. However, this mode will retouch geometry; it's usually mixed with the Multiresolution modifier, which is similar to an advanced Subdivision Surface modifier because it not only subdivides an object, but also stores the different details of each subdivision level.

By combining the Multiresolution modifier with Sculpt Mode, you can create extremely detailed organic models in a very artistic way, almost as if you were sculpting with clay, which can be really entertaining.

Retopology

This is usually the next step after sculpting. It's not a specific tool or set of tools, but more like a technique where you build new geometry with a good topology on top of other geometry that doesn't have a good topology (that's why it's called retopology: it's all about recreating the same shape with a new topology). There is software designed specifically for retopologizing—and sculpting software that offers retopo tools. You can easily use this technique in Blender (even though it's just normal modeling while snapping to other surfaces). A sculpted mesh is usually very heavy (with lots of polygons) and you often start from a very basic geometry that doesn't have an optimal topology once the details are in place, so retopo tools are there to help you create the final mesh with a good topology using the high-resolution mesh as a base.

Retopology is actually very simple: just enable the Snapping tool and set it to snap to faces. Now, when you adjust geometry and create new vertices, for example, they'll be snapped to the surface of other objects, allowing you to recreate their shapes with the desired topology.

Maps Baking

This feature is really cool. For now, it only works with Blender Render, although Cycles baking is already in development and may arrive in Blender 2.72. Imagine you have lights and shadows in your scene; now you can "bake" that lighting into a texture for the selected object, so you can then load that texture in the object and it will have the lights and shadows projected on it so you can see it in real time!

This is very useful when you want to see an effect in real time while still getting the look of a final render. With this method, you'll be able to make a scene look like a final render by just displaying a simple texture that already includes light and shadows.

You can also bake details from other objects into the currently selected one. This is used to generate normal maps and displacement maps that you can later use to make the object look like it has a lot more detail than it really does.

Maps baking tools can be found on the Render tab of the Properties Editor.

Python Scripting

If the tools that Blender provides are not enough for you or you need something specific, you can develop it using Python scripts. Blender has the ability to let you create scripts and run them, and even change how the interface looks or make your own add-ons to add new functionalities.

Python scripting makes Blender quite customizable and it represents quite an attractive feature for companies or individuals who need to be able to develop their own tools to achieve very specific results in their creations.

Summary

There is a lot more than meets the eye in Blender. This book has described some of the main features and tools available to you, but there are many more!

Hopefully, you've learned a lot from this book and it has helped you to understand Blender's basic features and to get started creating animations. Now you can keep improving your skills and you're ready to learn more about its advanced features.

Keep in mind that Blender is a continually evolving software and new features are added all the time. You can see this evolution as it happens because the development process is very transparent, so you don't need to wait until the next version is released to know what will be new.

You should be very proud that you've learned how to create characters in Blender because that's no simple task. Character creation is quite challenging, but now you're on your way to expressing your creativity using the extensive features of this cutting-edge software!

Index